Counselling in Education

Counselling
in Education

Patricia Milner

J M Dent & Sons Ltd London

This book is set in 10 on 11 point Times New Roman

First published 1974

© Patricia Milner 1974

Made in Great Britain
at the
Aldine Press · Letchworth · Herts
for J. M. DENT & SONS LTD
Aldine House · Albemarle Street · London

ISBN: 0 460 07857 7

TO MY FAMILY, WITH LOVE

Preface

I hope that *Counselling in Education* will serve as an introduction to counselling as a specialist activity in our schools and colleges. It is an attempt by a practising counsellor to share the experiences of seven years of counselling at school and university level in America and England.

I have used the feminine pronoun throughout in referring to the counsellor because it comes most easily to me, but I should like to emphasize that the work of counselling is ably and sensitively undertaken by both men and women. I have often used the term 'student' to refer to the person receiving counselling help, regardless of the educational setting, because I work with students and I find the terms 'client' and 'patient' inappropriate.

It is my aim not to turn the readers of this book into counsellors, but perhaps to enable them to develop a greater awareness of the counsellor's skills and activities, as well as a deeper sensitivity to the real, as opposed to the imagined, needs of children and young people.

PATRICIA MILNER

University College,
London, 1974

Acknowledgments

I should like to thank Mr Geoghegan, Librarian of the School of Education Library, Reading University, for making available the library facilities. My gratitude goes to two secretaries, Janice Kent and Janet Carpenter, for their skill and patience. I am grateful to Dr E. M. Jones of the College Health Centre, University College, London, for her care of my physical health which enabled me to complete this book at a difficult time. To Dorothy Wade, Senior Mistress, John Hunt of Everest School, Basingstoke, for her serene hospitality and the contribution of some timely comments, my thanks and God's blessing. I offer, too, my warm appreciation for the forbearance of my family, together with that of Alison and Gregory and for the encouragement and support of many friends. Finally, an acknowledgment of my debt to both American and English colleagues who have contributed so much to this book by their teaching and example.

Contents

Contents

1
The development of guidance and counselling in education

In education our goal is guidance; our technique, among others, is counselling.[1]

Broad definitions of guidance and counselling

The Yearbook of Education for 1955 was devoted to the subject of guidance in education, defined as 'a process of helping individuals through their own efforts to discover and develop their potentialities both for personal happiness and social usefulness'.[2]

The use of the terms guidance and counselling interchangeably is confusing since although they are related, in practice the processes they describe are sometimes undifferentiated and at other times clearly dissimilar. It seems appropriate to introduce broad but separate definitions of both guidance and counselling as they relate to educational settings, whilst acknowledging the limitations of simple definitions for such complex terms.

A broad definition of guidance in education is the presentation of knowledge, information and/or advice to individuals or groups in a structured way so as to provide sufficient material upon which they may base choices or decisions.

An example of this type of guidance in education may be found in a secondary school where selection of courses is being made on the basis of a programme similar to the following outline.

1. Course descriptions made available to parents and pupils.

2. Meetings of parents and pupils with staff members to discuss courses and explain limitations of facilities, e.g. it may not be possible to study both Art and Science because these are time-tabled for the same periods.

3. Individual pupils and/or groups meet with a tutor or teacher for further information or advice before making choices.

4. Readjustment of choices to meet restrictions imposed by facilities and other exigencies of timetable.

13

Here the emphasis is on the provision both of information and of advice, from which pupils, and sometimes parents, may make choices, such as, 'Well, you didn't do very well in French in your first three years, perhaps it's not a wise choice for you now'.

Counselling in education may be described as the interaction developing through the relationship between a counsellor and a person in a temporary state of indecision, confusion, or distress, which helps that individual to make his own decisions and choices, to resolve his confusion or cope with his distress in a personally realistic and meaningful way, having consideration for his emotional and practical needs and for the likely consequences of his behaviour.

We may use the same example of course choice in school to illustrate this broad definition of counselling.

The majority of pupils make their choice of courses with varying success after receiving the sort of help outlined in the educational guidance programme. In every school there are some children who are unable to come to a decision for a variety of reasons. This inability is not always apparent because the smooth running of the school demands that all the pupils concerned make their choices at this time and parents or teachers who may be in the habit of making decisions for children are very willing to help out and make the course choice for them, often in the nicest possible way. The danger here is that when these boys and girls are faced with their next choice, perhaps that of a job, a career, or a choice of higher educational facilities, they may still be indecisive. If there were some way of helping them to choose for themselves or to look at what prevented them from doing so, they would probably have less difficulty in making future choices.

The definition of counselling proposed offers one way of helping these boys and girls, for counselling purports to help an individual to make his own decisions and choices in the light of his feelings and needs. Although this is not the only kind of problem with which school counsellors are able to offer their time and skill, it is one of the important areas in which guidance and counselling are interrelated. Some of the students whom I see as a student counsellor did not positively choose to come to university, rather they arrived almost as a result of their inability to make a positive choice not to come and it is often only afterwards that they stop to think why they are there.

Guidance, counselling and the counsellor

A broad definition of a counsellor in education is one who uses interpersonal skills and understanding in a relationship to help a student to resolve those practical and personal difficulties which arise from his particular developmental problems.

Guidance is a term which encompasses much of our educational endeavour outside, and sometimes within, the area of subject teaching. Teachers, tutors, counsellors, doctors, school secretaries, caretakers, dinner ladies, lollipop men and friends may all at some time or another offer guidance in the school setting. In higher and further education the list is equally comprehensive: tutors, lecturers, counsellors, doctors, welfare officers, lodgings officers, wardens, other students may all be concerned at some time or another in this process which we call guidance.

Counselling, at its most useful, is an integral part of guidance in the sense that it usually provides a more personal, individualized kind of help which is complementary to the other guidance activities. Counselling is usually carried out by a person who, one hopes, would have had some training for this work, although just as there are a few people who can teach well without training, there are a few who can counsel without training, for interpersonal skills are present or absent to some extent in all human relationships. However, there are probably more angels able to dance on the point of a needle than there are good untrained counsellors—and even the performance of angels might be improved with training.

Influence of American patterns of guidance and counselling on the developing English pattern

I think the most poignant feature of education in England is the general acceptance that what you term 'pastoral care' of students is a responsibility of teachers and that many of the administrative and guidance functions performed by administrators and counsellors in the United States are being handled in England by teachers, housemasters, or yearmasters. This is a term that I never encountered in the educational jargon of the United States. Although not all teachers have adequate training, or perhaps the requisite personality to ensure their ultimate effectiveness in this role, the very fact that they accept as part of their responsibility the total welfare and personal development of the student is something that distinguishes English education, and perhaps more than any other factor, accounts for some significant differences in counselling practice and trends.[3]

The development of counselling in schools owes much to American influence and experience, and the first full-time courses to train

Many heads of English schools see themselves in the role of counsellor, but there are usually basic differences in philosophy, ability and training and often, of course, differences in personality which make it difficult to equate the two roles. The head is the chief authority figure in the school, he is responsible for the school as a whole, for discipline, for school policy and rules, he has wide administrative, educational and professional responsibilities which differ from those of the counsellor; and in his dealings with pupils, parents or teachers the headmaster is usually direct, instructive and formal, regarding advice-giving on numerous problems as one of his major functions. The counsellor is specially selected in terms of personality and training to carry out a much narrower role, which is usually not authoritarian. She attempts to view the school society from the child's point of view, as well as the teacher's; she offers time to pupils to help them to explore personal problems, and the relationship she builds with a child encourages him to make his own decisions.[5]

Counsellor roles in America

I have chosen three interpretations to represent the role of the American counsellor. Wrenn distinguishes between those activities performed by the counsellor and those activities for which she assumes responsibility but which are carried out as part of a team approach. He proposes that the counsellor is directly responsible for:[6]

1. counselling with students on matters of self-understanding, decision-making and planning, using both the interview and group situations;

2. consulting with staff and parents on questions of student understanding and student management;

3. studying changes in the character of the student population and making a continuous interpretation of this information to the school administration and to curriculum development committees;

4. performing a liaison function between other school and community counselling resources and facilitating their use by teachers and students.

Patterson quotes the outline of the Committee on the role of psychology of the American Psychological Association[7] which divides the two main essential functions of the counsellor into two broad areas labelled developmental activities and preventive/remedial activities. Both are used in working directly with pupils and also in working with others who work with pupils in the areas of intellectual, vocational and personality development. The programming responsibilities of the counsellor are listed under the headings student appraisal procedures, informational procedures and counselling. (It is suggested that individual counselling should occupy about 50 per cent of the counsellor's time.)

The third view is from Tyler who concentrates her attention on the counselling interview as being the main work of the counsellor. She includes testing, use of occupational information, use of background information and case records and decision-making interviews, but emphasizes that the main role of the counsellor is to counsel.[8]

Present and future functions of the counsellor

The following table sets out the responses of members of the American School Counselor Association to questions about the future activities of the counsellor:[6]

1 Counselling students (developmental, educational, vocational, personal, etc.)	100%
2 Conferences with groups of parents and counselling individual parents	45%
3 Test administration and interpretation	41%
4 Conference with teacher(s), counselling a teacher	37%
5 Student group guidance and orientation	32%
6 Evaluation, follow-up, research	16%
7 Referrals to and contact with community agencies	16%
8 Vocational information, collection and dissemination, contacts with employers	12%
9 Involvement in curriculum development	8%

Counsellor education

Since the training of school counsellors here is based to a large extent on American approaches—both theoretical and practical—there are similarities in the functions and role of the counsellor in the two countries.

The first American graduate course in counsellor education was offered by Harvard University during the summer session of 1911 and by 1967 three hundred and thirty-six colleges and universities were providing graduate courses which led to professional degrees in counsellor education.[9]

Many American universities have departments of counsellor education, the training of counsellors is well established, perhaps even a little insular; the literature on counselling is overwhelmingly numerous, diverse and of varying standards; the theoretical approaches to counselling are well documented and widely practised. In England none of this established security is available. Nine universities offer courses for the training of counsellors, sometimes with help from a different visiting American professor each year. Theoretical approaches are mainly non-indigenous and use an alien vocabulary; the available literature is predominantly American and very expensive.

The method of training counsellors varies slightly in the two societies. In England most school counsellors are seconded from their teaching posts on full salary for one year, during which they take a course which leads to a diploma in the advanced study of education, the subject of their study being counselling. To be eligible for a course of this kind, a teacher must be qualified and have taught for at least five years in a recognized school. This means that all such English counsellors have at least five years' teaching experience, not because they necessarily need it to become a counsellor, but because they need it in order to be eligible to take a full-time course of training in any aspect of education. There are very few part-time courses for the training of counsellors in England, although these are quite common in America.

The first full-time university course for the training of student counsellors, which began at the university of Aston in Birmingham in 1971, has also made good use of American knowledge and experience. The part-time courses for the training of student counsellors in the London area seem to rely more on the psychodynamic approach and the analytical theories of psychotherapy as it is practised within this country, than on the American counselling and psychotherapeutic theories of non-directiveness, existentialism, gestalt therapy and developmental counselling, and the behavioural derivations of rational-emotive therapy and reality therapy. There is a distinct split in the field of student counselling in this country between the traditional psychodynamic 'psychotherapy' approach to counselling and the newer, in some ways more flexible approach of the American theorists, but one hopes the conflict will be a productive one.

Concepts and reality in the counsellor's role

One of the most striking differences in counsellor activity in America concerns the 'reality gap' between what is taught in the universities and what is done in the schools.

> What might be called the counsellors' (and counsellor educators') role conception of themselves . . . stresses personal counselling at a sophisticated, psychological level, although this will include 'developmental' as well as 'therapeutic' counselling. When one looks at what actually goes on in the senior high schools, the picture is rather different . . . the counsellor spends . . . the largest part of his time on educational programming and college advising. . . . Much counsellor time is taken up by quasiclerical and administrative duties. Counselling on 'personal' problems seems to be minimal partly because of student distrust, time pressure as felt by some counsellors and a feeling of inadequacy by a few counsellors. . . . If the majority of counsellors do a great deal of routine work this may be a function of their personality.[10]

At present counsellors in England are struggling very hard to establish in schools the counselling role that is taught in the universities, and although the emphasis varies from course to course, for me it is undoubtedly on counselling for personal problems. Developing from this view is the one that counselling in England will grow alongside and interrelate with other helping agencies in the area, more than the American pattern suggests. American schools seem so isolated from their communities, which is a criticism I have voiced of English schools, and the counsellor is one of the most important links with the world outside the school, which is after all the world in which pupils will spend the greater part of their lives.

It is perhaps regrettable in some ways that much of the follow-up to the initial impetus for counselling in education has come from America, when we have had such perceptive commentators on child development as, for example, Bowlby and Winnicott, together with a talented nucleus of psychoanalysts and analytical psychologists in London and a group as internationally highly regarded as the Tavistock Institute for Human Relations. Despite the fact that the Tavistock does offer part-time courses on counselling in education and the psychoanalysts and analytical psychologists have formed a group known as the Centre for the Analytical Study of Student Problems, I think it not unfair to say that these various groups have, as yet, contributed almost nothing to the development of counselling in education outside the capital. Perhaps they have very good reasons for not doing so, and perhaps, too, we need to be reminded, once again, that London is not England. However those counsellors who seek to restrict the work to a very select group with an expensive analytic training more appropriate for a psychotherapist, should not be too surprised if they become becalmed in the backwater of their own exclusiveness, whilst the mainstream of counselling in education passes them by. I hope that both the National Association of Counsellors in Education and the more recently formed Association for Student Counselling (see appendices) which has a wide and varied membership, may to some extent help to prevent this by making available the opportunity for counsellors of all theoretical persuasions and those who are still searching, to meet for mutual support and an exchange and synthesis of ideas.

Although there are those who think that the American influence on guidance and counselling in education is an unwarranted intrusion, I do not share this view. I have already acknowledged my own personal debt to American colleagues, but would also like to offer a wider appreciation on behalf of all those counsellors who have learned so much as a result of the generous sharing of knowledge and experience in a warm spirit of friendship and enthusiasm which American counsellors and counsellor educators have extended to us. To them all, we owe a gracious and grateful thank you.

The development of guidance and counselling services in American education has not been without its mistakes and difficulties. Because of financial limitations we shall never be in a position to provide such comprehensive services in our own schools and colleges. We must, therefore, learn from the Americans' experience by looking closely at their system to determine which aspects we can best use in our own culture, remembering that fifty years after the Americans we are moving toward a similar comprehensive system of education which is likely to produce changes in our society, reflecting those of America.

Counselling and comprehensive education

The growth of counselling in schools is very dependent upon the development of comprehensive education, for it is usually only the larger comprehensive schools with their flexibility and wider choice of courses which can maintain a member of staff to carry out counselling and guidance activities on a full-time or part-time basis.

In some areas feelings run high about comprehensive education, but one good thing which has emerged from the controversy is that people from all walks of life are talking, and some of them are even thinking too, about education. Instead of being simply something they take for granted, it has become a point of concern, and for some, a point of action.

Brief history of guidance and counselling in America and England

Two kinds of historical development led to professional counselling in America. One was the Vocational Guidance movement which began in Boston when Frank Parsons published his book *Choosing a Vocation* in 1908, and later started a vocational guidance centre. The First World War helped the movement through the development of group intelligence tests by the armed services, for these tests were later used by vocational counsellors to help with individual analysis in vocational guidance.[8]

The second historical development was the growth of the Mental Health movement stimulated by Clifford Beer's book *The mind that found itself*. This drew public attention to mental illness as a social problem, psychoanalysis became a talking point among literate people, and psychotherapy was thought to be something of a magic wand that would dissolve the difficulties of the emotionally disabled by enabling them to talk about their problems. The Second World War helped this movement through the work done by the armed services on the emotional problems of servicemen, which convinced people that emotional difficulties responded to treatment.

The American Mental Health Movement developed the term 'counselling' in its clinics and social agencies. Vocational guidance workers in schools repeatedly encountered personal, social and emotional problems amongst their students. Counsellors in mental health work found a need to concern themselves with their clients' outer life as well as with their inner conflicts. Thus two kinds of service—helping people to make wise choices and helping them to improve their emotional health and well-being came to be offered increasingly by the same person, the counsellor.[8]

In Britain educational and career guidance dates from 1904 when Mrs Ogilvie Gordon put forward a scheme for the establishment by Local Education Authorities in England and Wales and School Boards in Scotland, of Educational Information and Employment Bureaux. Five years later the President of the Board of Trade, Winston Churchill, during the debate on the 1909 Labour Exchanges Act 'indicated that the Board of Trade intended to make the information the Labour Exchanges collected available to Education

Authorities for the benefit of children. He made it clear that it was intended to co-ordinate the exchanges with the educational system for this purpose'.[11]

In 1910, under the terms of the Education (Terms of Employment) Bill, Local Education Authorities for Higher Education were given power to make arrangements for giving help in the choice of suitable employment to young people up to the age of seventeen through the collection and communication of information and the giving of advice—a guidance function.

The present Youth Employment Service was set up under the terms of the Employment and Training Act 1948 to provide vocational guidance for school leavers of any age and other young people up to the age of eighteen, to help them to find suitable employment and to follow them up for a few years after they have left school. The Careers Officers visit the schools to interview those pupils who are in their last year at school, and their job is predominantly concerned with information giving and placement. The bulk of their work has been done with fourteen-year-olds, because until 1973 many of our pupils left school at the age of fifteen. Grammar school pupils and the more able pupils in the higher sets of comprehensive schools receive their vocational guidance from Careers Advisory Officers who are mostly university graduates with some knowledge and experience of higher and further education and related careers. It is all very amateurish by American standards and because the resources are limited the guidance is too little and often too late. 'In the choice of a career there should be an alternative to fate,' said Pascal, but for some of our students there is no alternative to fate, and it is only through the expansion of our guidance services that this situation can be remedied, notwithstanding the disturbing realities of unemployment amongst young school leavers.

In this country the National Association for Mental Health was created after the Second World War. Its work is slowly expanding, but until recently, beginning with the Mental Health Act of 1959, we have not emphasized the community aspects of mental health outside mental hospitals in the way that America has done. Perhaps the need has not been as great, but it is undoubtedly increasing at a faster rate than the facilities for coping with it.

Existing guidance services

In 1913 the London County Council appointed the late Sir Cyril Burt as the first official Child Psychologist in Western society to examine dull, backward and feeble-minded children and to give

24

guidance to teachers and parents on the treatment and education of other problem children attending ordinary elementary schools.[2]

The term educational guidance is often used to describe the use of tests and measurement in education which in the past has been largely confined to the selection process at eleven-plus or to the process of attainment testing for the purpose of streaming, and to the work of the educational psychologists in the School Psychological Services. Until the introduction of trained counsellors into schools, educational psychologists were the only people available who were recognized as competent to administer certain tests and interpret their results, though teachers were of course qualified to use standardized tests of ability and achievement in various academic subject areas.

In 1921, Child Guidance Clinics were established as medical rather than educational services, to offer 'a form of medical treatment for children of normal intelligence whose behaviour has previously been satisfactory, but who begin to behave in a way likely to be detrimental to themselves, objectionable to others, or actually anti-social'.[2] In 1965 the first university courses to train school counsellors were started, the first attempt to provide guidance and counselling for 'normal' children, and by now there are several hundred counsellors in schools in England and Wales.

Thus, in the past, the term guidance in education has been used mainly to describe three distinct and restricted activities—Child Guidance, often provided by a medical service; vocational guidance, provided by the Youth Employment Service; and educational guidance, provided mainly by the School Psychological Service.

Within the person of the school counsellor we have the school's first attempts to provide personal counselling (which may be considered an element of child guidance work), vocational guidance and counselling, together with educational guidance and counselling. This does not imply that the appointment of a counsellor removes the need for the three existing guidance services, but rather that, for the first time, some schools have a member of staff with a working knowledge of these areas who can act as a liaison among and between these existing services and the school.

The development of school counselling was not a direct outcome of the sensitivity and foresight of educators, but was rather a result of the deliberations of the National Association for Mental Health and its attempts to live up to its name. At a conference which the N.A.M.H. held in Bristol in 1963 it was felt that a more preventive and positive approach to mental health might be achieved by work with parents and in schools.

'School counselling is one outcome of the intention to improve the quality of schools as caring institutions with a responsibility for maintaining, protecting and promoting the personal development and well-being of children. . . . Counselling in schools is basically a "preventive" mental health service.' [12]

Work with students

Guidance and counselling in further and higher education have had a somewhat different development. The universities, attempting to emulate the tutorial luxury of Oxbridge, but not quite able to finance the operation, have relied heavily until quite recently on the goodwill of academic staff with no formal training in teaching, counselling or interpersonal skills, to fulfil the combined roles of teaching, guidance and counselling for students as part of their tutorial function. The University Health Services started after the Second World War were probably the first attempts to offer counselling by non-academic staff, though not all Student Health Services make provision for counselling or psychotherapeutic help for students. As far as I am aware the first university counselling service was created at the university of Keele and there are now some nineteen universities and several polytechnics, colleges of technology, technical colleges and colleges of further education offering counselling services to their students, either in a medical setting or as a separate service altogether. University Appointments Boards were developed in response to the increasingly obvious fact that universities had expanded to the stage where they were no longer able to absorb their graduates themselves as postgraduate students, or pass them into the traditional fields of teaching, the church, the armed services or politics and the legal profession. University Appointments Board officers are now changing their approach to careers guidance in response to the paradoxical situation of wider opportunities and the recent increase in the number of unemployed graduates.

Welfare officers in higher and further education were originally appointed to help students with such practical problems as accommodation and finance, and many of these people have developed more of a counselling approach as their experience taught them that, at times, practical and personal difficulties are closely inter-related.

Those colleges created under the auspices of Local Education Authorities usually have available to their students under eighteen, and in some cases to older students, the same external guidance facilities that are offered to the schools.

Thus for many years we have made some provision for the guidance and counselling of children and students. Whilst the quality of that provision has obviously varied, I think it is fair to say that the resources of all the services mentioned have become too stretched for them to provide either the level of help that they themselves would like to offer, or that which is needed. They are all tending to become 'fire-brigade' services and a waiting time of two years for an appointment at a Child Guidance Clinic must inevitably throw the burden of support on to the school, and the parents; on to people who are often not equipped by training or in resources to shoulder it. The Seebohm Report on the reorganization of the Social Services offers little to educational needs, so perhaps the time is ripe for a Seebohm on the provision of social services in education.

2
The need for counselling

> Where no counsel is, the people fall; but in the multitude of counsellors there is safety. *Proverbs, 11: 14.*

Predicted membership of the National Association of Counsellors in Education will pass the four hundred mark during 1973, and of these perhaps about 60 per cent are acknowledged to have the training and experience in counselling which the Council of N.A.C.E. consider acceptable for full membership of that association. The Association for Student Counselling will achieve a membership of 150 to 200 during 1973. In these two groups there are about 600 people who are sufficiently interested in counselling in education to join an appropriate association. There are no figures available of the number of counsellors employed in educational institutions, but it seems unlikely that there are more than three or four hundred throughout the country, certainly not a number to be justifiably considered a multitude.

The advent of professional counselling as a supplement to pastoral care has had a very mixed reception. There has been hostility and resentment from those teachers, tutors and parents who see the counsellor as one who is making a take-over bid for the personal relationships with children and students which hitherto have been their concern. Others feel antagonistic towards the counsellor's acceptance of children as they are and towards the counsellor's efforts to help young people to make their own choices and decisions and, within limits, to take responsibility for their own lives. I remember being sharply taken to task by a school governor because I said that children had some 'rights' of choice. He seemed to believe that children should not have freedom to choose anything. Perhaps a look at some of the objections to counselling which people raise may be appropriate as an introduction to the needs.

Some objections to counselling

Not a great deal is known about counselling in education in this country, and one of the aims of this book is to provide an introduction to the work which may help people to decide what counselling can and cannot do in diverse educational settings. Among those people who know a little about counselling and among those who know nothing there are some who raise strong objections to the introduction of counselling as a specialist activity in schools and colleges, which is what I advocate. Some of these objections merit attention, because they arise from very real fears and firm beliefs about the meaning of education and of life, and they are helpful in the sense that they enable counsellors, indeed sometimes force them, to re-examine their own beliefs and acknowledge their defences.

1. COUNSELLING IS OF NO VALUE

This view is representative of those who believe that any helping relationship is detrimental both to individuals and to society because to need help is a sign of weakness and to provide it fosters deficiencies in character; adversity is the means to strength and people should counter it alone and unaided. Leona Tyler argues that '. . . Counseling is still to a large extent an art, dependent more on shared experience than on reported experiments . . .' and counsellors need to 'distinguish between the things we do simply because they seem to work well and things we do because of some definite research evidence'.[1] Nevertheless counsellors can and should assess the value of what they are doing.

2. COUNSELLING FOSTERS CONFORMITY

This objection to helping professions is being voiced increasingly by some students, who suggest that the counsellor manipulates people for example, into taking up safe, secure occupations instead of 'doing their own thing', which seems to ignore the fact that for some people 'doing their own thing' lies in a secure occupation and conformity. It is true that counsellors encourage people to take into account the cognitive and affective aspects of a decision or problem and the likely consequences, which does to some extent encourage caution. The alternative is action by impulse, which in certain circumstances, such as immediate danger, or in response to another person's distress, may be appropriate.

3. COUNSELLING PERPETUATES THE MYTH OF FREEDOM

Those who object to the self concept theories of counselling suggest that counsellors deceive themselves by talking about freedom of choice, for in reality life is deterministic and each step affects the direction of the next one. Someone described the importance of previous experience by saying that 'as we walk into the future we come face to face with the past'. In suggesting that we have a human capacity to choose between two or more genuine alternatives we should acknowledge that the choice is always limited both by past and by present circumstances. The limits and the freedom have been compared to a game of cards, in which the limits are imposed by the cards which you are dealt and the freedom comes in the way you choose to play those cards.

4. COUNSELLING IS NOT A DISCIPLINE

At the present time in this country, counselling is not a discipline; it draws upon knowledge from many areas but its main subject is people, and to my knowledge there is no subject which attempts to concern itself with people in the way in which counselling does. Psychology is concerned with behaviour, not so much with the people who do the behaving, and sociology seems concerned to a large extent with people in groups and the problems which society creates for them, but not with solutions. Between psychology and sociology there seems to be a gap in our knowledge and our concern which social psychology to some extent may close, but into which counselling as a study of interpersonal relationships, their effects, their development and practice in education may grow. Much depends upon the activity of counsellors and counsellor educators and the importance that they themselves attach to the study of their subject. However, in America Brammer and Shostrom suggest that 'there is an identifiable body of fairly valid techniques and procedures for counseling and psychotherapy'.[2]

5. COUNSELLORS ARE INADEQUATELY EDUCATED

The objection that counsellors are inadequately prepared for their work must inevitably in these early years have some validity. It is of vital importance to assess the needs in a particular school or college which a counselling service may realistically be expected to meet and it is essential to appoint a counsellor who is trained and capable of running the type of service needed. Of course counsellors are inadequately prepared to perform as psychiatrists, as educational psychologists, as nurses, as mind readers or as magicians. Trained counsellors should be adequately educated to counsel students who may wish to talk with them about personal, educational or vocational problems, but they are not trained to solve all these problems; they should be adequately educated in the administration and interpretation of certain tests, and in their liaison work with outside social services and with school staff. Counsellors are always learning and one of the things that a few years' experience as a counsellor reveals very painfully is that the counsellor who tries to be many things to many people sometimes ends up being nothing to anybody.

6. COUNSELLING IS NOT UNIVERSALLY AVAILABLE THROUGHOUT A SCHOOL

The objection that in theory counselling is available to all children or students but in practice is limited (usually because of the size of the school population and the counsellor's own temperament and preferences) is a valid one. Counselling is often regarded as a source of help for those with problems or crises, but it can have a preventive as well as a remedial function, and it is only one source of help; students and children alike will turn for help to any one of a number of people within the institution, according to their temperament and inclination. The relationship and help provided by a counsellor are not for everyone and cannot compensate in the long term for other relationships which may be inadequate.

7. COUNSELLORS PAMPER PEOPLE AND MAKE THEM DEPENDENT

The charge that counsellors pamper students often arises from those who equate understanding with softness and over-indulgence, and acceptance with the sanctioning of any kind of behaviour. The understanding and acceptance offered by a counsellor are an attempt to encourage constructive ways of coping with problems rather than the negative or destructive ones which often seem to occur as a result of the blind application of moral judgments.

8. COUNSELLING IS AN UNWARRANTED INVASION OF PRIVACY

'We are, I fear, getting to know one another. Reticence, secrecy, concealment of self have been transformed into social problems; once they were aspects of civility.'[3] The right to privacy is fundamental to adults and children, and certainly pupils and students should be free to reject our concern, but in most circumstances counselling is not imposed, and therefore privacy should not be invaded without agreement. I think Rieff is right to point out the danger in the increase in over-solicitousness and I hope that counsellors may have the experience to help to balance this rather than to add to it.

My own feeling is that there is a need for professional counsellors in education and I suggest some of the conditions which lead me to hold this view.

Social factors in the development of post-war education

Since the end of World War II the majority of West European countries have revised their educational systems, attaching greater importance than ever before to the problems of guidance (of which counselling is a part) in schools. The introduction of comprehensive education is a development with which, in principle, I am in agreement, and I am aware that change is never made without inconvenience, even when it is a change for the better. Several years ago I worked in a school which was one of three to be reorganized and transferred to a new, purpose built, pleasant comprehensive school. The reorganization of the three schools took place some eighteen months before the new building was completed and during this interim period the school was housed in three separate buildings some distance apart, not an uncommon situation in reorganization schemes. The transfer to the new building was organizationally fairly competent, considering the size of the enterprise and the inexperience and lack of training of teachers in such undertakings, and the school is now well established and bursting at the seams. Yet when I consider the cost of that experience in terms of human distress I have difficulty in justifying it. Everything seemed to be considered except the people; provision was made for the timetable, the furniture, the books, the equipment, but there was no one in a sufficiently detached position to consider the situation and say, 'Look at the way these children are behaving. What are we doing to them?', or 'This arrangement has placed these teachers under intolerable stress, what can we do to help them?' A counsellor is one of those who can be in a position to consider the 'people problems' of educational development.

> There is a significant association between the system of school authority as perceived by the class teachers, both as persons and professionals. In other words, where teachers feel either that they have a hand in the internal running of the school, or that its outside directors are aware of their internal problems, they tend to be both liked by their pupils and to be seen as effective teachers. If the teachers see their superiors as remote or dictatorial, they, in their turn are seen by their pupils as unfriendly and ineffective.[4]

Awareness of the existence of this kind of situation could lead to an easing of the problem, and a counsellor is an appropriate person—though not the only one—to develop this awareness and to help people to cope with the resulting change in relationships.

Communication between home and school

The teacher/parent relationship is sometimes another difficult part of school life which could be made smoother with the help of a counsellor. In evidence given to the Plowden Committee on Primary Education, the Association of Educational Psychologists suggested that many teachers show defeatism in their attitudes towards parents, pleading that the parents who need to become involved in their children's education are the very ones who do not attend meetings, which of course is often the case. Schools must be encouraged, says the Association, 'to go out into their areas and ensure these contacts, without which much educational effort will be wasted'. Suitable teachers ought to be given the job of developing effective liaisons with parents and welfare, industrial and commercial interests in their areas, for 'with rare exceptions, there is a gross under-functioning of the school as a focal point for community interest and activity'.[5]

Whilst I would not dispute this, I would like to suggest to the educational psychologists that to expect a teacher to spend the day with some classes and then seek out parents in the evening is tantamount to inflicting the worst of tortures, and if they do not believe this, they are very welcome to test it empirically by doing it. I am not saying that teachers should not visit the homes of children, but I do think it is an advantage for schools to have a counsellor or social worker to provide a regular means of communication. Joan Clark, in describing her work as a Home School Liaison officer, gives her impression of the unwillingness of some parents to visit schools: 'Parents who had never visited the school at all, I found, were very often people who were genuinely scared of teachers. They felt that teachers "looked down" at them, and however wrong this may be, that is the way that they perceived the situation.'[6]

Pressure of diffuse role expectations

Daws[7] suggests that the teacher's professional image is one of the most demanding of all the professions, requiring, as it does, that a teacher have a knowledge of his subject and a knowledge of his pupils and that he teach both it and them well.

The increased pressure on teachers to be all things to all children, which is often self-inflicted and which, of course, is impossible, nevertheless indicates that it is becoming increasingly desirable for a teacher to have as great a knowledge of himself as he has of his subject and his pupils. This applies equally to the counsellor, but she is

33

given the opportunity to gain self-knowledge during her training—an opportunity not often presented in the course of teacher training.

Social and geographical mobility

This is not to suggest that the socialization of children is solely the job of the schools. It is initially the job of the parents, and most of them succeed, but where they fail or are inadequate then teachers and counsellors can be the safety net between the potential delinquent and his determined drive to self-destruction against the bulwark of society. Bryan Wilson suggests that the creation of large housing estates, large schools and the promotion of social mobility have all weakened community allegiances, and that the important aspect of this development has been the breakdown of the nexus between home and school.

> Once the school ceases to belong to the community, parental moral training is much less reinforced by school training. As education is shorn of its moral concerns, and as teaching becomes subject to greater professional specialisations, so the personal knowledge of particular children by teachers becomes less intense. As school size increases, so this context becomes increasingly impersonal. The individual child learns to look out for himself: if he acquires independence, he also learns the ropes according to the values of the peer groups and—increasingly evident—of the entertainment dominated youth culture.[8]

This impersonal effect is also increased by the greater mobility of teachers. It is not too uncommon for a child to be taught a particular subject by two or three different teachers in one year. The reputation of teachers comes to depend increasingly on their ability to further their own interests by manipulating a fluid job situation, whereas formerly their reputation depended largely on their role in the community as respected persons.

Parental needs

Many adults are well meaning, considerate of and anxious for the welfare of children, particularly their own. However, parents are exhorted on all sides by child care experts, psychologists, women's magazines, newspapers, radio and television to treat their child in this way or that way, to feed him this food or that food in order that he may develop into a strong, healthy, stable-minded adult. So much so that the child is likely to need all these assets by the time he reaches maturity in order to cope with his neurotic parents.

Some timely words of comfort for bewildered parents were given by Alexander Thomas, Associate Professor of Psychiatry at the New York Medical Centre, in presenting the findings of his New York longitudinal study:

1. Children have their own characteristics of individuality from early infancy onwards. Healthy child development can best be fostered by approaches that are congenial and appropriate to the child's temperament. Most parents will have little difficulty in recognising their child's individual characteristics once they free themselves from the stereotyped view that there is only one kind of normal child and only one good way to bring up a child.

2. Any specific temperamental characteristic is in itself no guarantee either of healthy or disturbed development. Some children are easier to handle than others but the course of psychological development always depends on the specific character of the temperament-environment interaction.

3. Parents are not responsible for their child's temperamental characteristics. A 'difficult infant' or a 'slow warmer-up' may require extra attention from the parent but can develop in as healthy a fashion as any other child. To label such children as anxious and insecure, and to blame the parents for this, as is often done by professionals in the child care field, is to stigmatise the child incorrectly and to burden the parent destructively with unnecessary guilt. Currently popular theories that consider behaviour problems in children to arise exclusively from pathological attitudes in the parents are a source of guilt and anxiety for many parents. The fact is that many, many problems can develop in children even with mature devoted parents who have not appreciated the implications of their child's temperament as a guide for themselves. Such parents need insight into their children's characteristics rather than into any presumed 'unconscious' pathological attitudes within themselves.[9]

Is it possible that a counsellor may help parents to see their children differently? Not an easy task by the time adolescence is reached, but not, I think, necessarily too late for some mutual readjustment to take place, as Joan Clark proved in her work with parents.[6]

Needs of adolescence

The need of some young people to have the opportunity to talk to someone like a counsellor was emphasized by James Hemming in his book *Problems of Adolescent Girls* [10] in which he made a study of the letters written to the 'problem page' of a magazine for girls. He studied 787 letters and divided the problems they contained into four main categories instancing the percentage of enquiries about each as follows:

Friendship 36.1 %; Personal 30.1 %; Home 21.9 %; School 11.9 %.

One example from the main letters he quotes reveals several difficulties, none of them desperately serious to the onlooker but each sufficient to cause a sensitive adolescent a great deal of worry and pain.

> My mother doesn't like us to love my father and tells us things about him like him betting his wages away, really it is my mother who makes all the bothers. My life is all worries as I am not nice looking either and the boys call me skinny legs. When we were doing the Merchant of Venice I was chosen for Shylock and I learnt it all and at the last somebody else was put in and I cried every night in bed and I shall never forgive her. [10]

Hemming suggests that we seem to be taking too much for granted in assuming that adolescents will find people to give them help when they need it. He points out that there is a gap in the range of sympathetic adults who can be turned to in need which formerly was filled by adult brothers and sisters, friendly aunts, uncles and grandparents when communities and families were more intimate.

'Lacking in their own community the support they need, adolescent girls turn to the impersonal friendliness of advice columns. We can hardly be satisfied with this state of affairs. What adolescents seek to gain through writing to a paper should be available to them in a personal relationship.' [10]

The vagaries and ambivalencies of this stage of life are well described by Anna Freud, who says:

> Adolescents are excessively egoistic, regarding themselves as the centre of the universe and the sole object of interest, and yet at no time in later life are they capable of so much self-sacrifice and devotion. They form the most passionate love-relations, only to break them off as abruptly as they began them. On the one hand they throw themselves enthusiastically into the life of the community and on the other, they have an overpowering

longing for solitude. They oscillate between blind submission to a chosen leader, and defiant rebellion against any and every authority. They are selfish and materially minded and at the same time full of lofty idealism. They are ascetic but will suddenly plunge into instinctual indulgence of the most primitive character. At times their behaviour to other people is rough and inconsiderate, yet they themselves are extremely touchy. Their moods veer between light-hearted optimism and the blackest pessimism. Sometimes they will work with indefatigable enthusiasm and at other times are sluggish and apathetic.[11]

What do young people themselves feel about their own difficulties?

Here is a plea from a girl for the opportunity to talk to an adult who is willing and has the time to listen.

' "School days are the happiest days of your life," they tell you complacently. But you're bored sick of school, you want to get out into the "big world outside," but you're scared. It would surprise a lot of adults (who seem to have forgotten their own youth) how many of the swaggering and self-confident teenagers they see around are really scared for long stretches at a time. If only we could reach out more, express our feelings and thoughts aloud. But who will listen? Only other teenagers, and they're in the same boat as us!'[12]

The need for realistic expectations

Some bewildered criticism from a university student which expresses the disillusionment and demoralization that a number of them feel when it becomes obvious that their expectations of university life are a long, long way from reality.

The trouble with our educational system is that you enter the upper sixth and they say you are going to go to university. They plan your life out. You don't really know what you want to do, so they give you a choice . . . a very limited choice at that. . . . Going to university is considered a good thing, everyone's proud of you. But I'm disillusioned . . . in a rut. When I went to university I thought I would get an education but all they do is to teach you to pass exams. I feel cheated![12]

Not all young people go on to higher education and of the majority who do not, some find jobs and others are unable to do so. A nineteen-year-old boy from Middlesborough describes his feelings about being unemployed:

I'm on the dole, I have been out of work for four months. I want to work, I feel guilty about not working because I'd like to bring money into the home, to make life easier for my mother. When you leave school you don't think of the responsibility of being on the dole. I worry about a job for myself but I feel even worse about men with wives and families to keep. . . . People don't realise how hard it is up here, they think I'm a layabout. But I do want work. I'm desperate about it![12]

Indeed, he is desperate, for without work his identity as a man in the north-east is negated. As he says, you do not think about the responsibility when you leave school, and there have not been many people who regard it as important to help you to think about it.

Sexual needs

Coming to terms with one's own sexuality is not an easy process for many young and some not so young people, particularly in the face of the unrealistic romanticizing of the advertising media and the façade of many adults.

'My first experience was with an old woman, she was about twenty-five. I'm not really attracted to older women, I prefer beautiful young girls and young boys . . . I didn't get any pleasure from it at all. I was only fifteen.'

'When it comes to it you're scared because they've told you, the other girls have, that it's painful. And you don't really feel anything for the boy, except as a means of getting this wonderful experience that everyone talks about.' [12]

Ambivalence

Ambivalent feelings and attitudes are another difficult area of acceptance for all of us, but educators in particular seem to have a great dread of ambivalence and to deny its existence. It is much easier if things are either right or wrong, good or bad, yes or no, do or don't, and people know their own minds. The failure to recognize and accept ambivalence as normal is perhaps one of the most prejudicial factors against making choices and decisions to which we can have some commitment.

'I was frightened of failure, yet very ambitious. I resented authority because I feared it, and I hated convention, partly because I had a fear of not being accepted.' [12]

Counselling development in response to needs

The extent to which counselling is accepted and developed depends very largely on the work that counsellors themselves do to counteract the inertia of public opinion and/or the apathy of local and government authority. Perhaps the most useful contribution to the growth of counselling will ultimately be found to be the publicity that counsellors themselves give to their own work and problems, and the energy with which they emphasize those important economic, social and above all human issues for which their work is vital.

The quality of life in many of our schools and colleges is sufficiently inadequate to arouse anger in the mildest of counsellors, and as people who are in everyday touch with the pain that this inadequacy creates for children, students, and staff, we could well use some of that anger in a constructive enhancement of our own profession.

The provision of counselling services in education is not seen as a panacea for all our educational ills, nor does a counsellor hope to give children and students a trouble- or problem-free life, but where possible to help them to resolve their difficulties, or if that is not possible, to live with them. I believe that we should help children and young people to cope with their everyday problems, for all lives bring crises which may be unexpected—illness, a death in a family, a missing parent—and most of us at some time suffer shattered dreams and frustrating or distressing experiences. Being aware of a child's stress situations and being sensitive to the individual thresholds of stress within human beings can be a complex and subtle process which requires not a 'nosey parker' intrusion of privacy but the response of an understanding and empathic person. Teachers and tutors have an important task here in knowing when to try to decrease a child's internal burden by reducing his workload or when to recognize that disturbed behaviour may be his way of asking for help. Pain, hardship and failure can offer valuable learning experiences, but not in the negative way in which they are often used in education.

Need for a shared approach

This does not imply that teachers or counsellors should attempt to be amateur psychiatrists or substitute parents, but that they should work together in an attempt to find educational answers to those psychological problems which arise in the educational setting, for even when children are referred for psychiatric help they usually remain in attendance at school and have to cope with and be accommodated by the school community, except for the hour a week which they spend at the Child Guidance Clinic.

The National Association for Mental Health in its proposal to involve schools in a positive mental health approach drew attention to the potential of the school as being of central importance in preventive measures because it is a community which caters for the total population of young people, it can compel their attendance over a long period of their childhood, and it more or less has a commitment to mental health goals.

The N.A.M.H. Working Party set up to review the purposes of counselling and its development in schools offered the following opinions:

1. that schools, because they have a concern for the entire child, should take some responsibility beyond that for the intellectual and scholastic development of children;

2. that current changes in society and in the educational scene, particularly the development of large socially heterogeneous comprehensive schools and the steady postponement of the school leaving age, will create for the schools problems which will emphasize the need for teachers to be actively concerned with the child's total personal development;

3. that, because of the needs for pastoral care and a growing awareness of them by the schools, the services of trained counsellors will be increasingly necessary as an additional resource;

4. that the school's counselling practices will need to find more explicit emphasis on the timetable and in the activities of the school; and that more time must be devoted, both in initial training and in subsequent in-service courses, to giving teachers the skills to discharge these responsibilities;

5. that nearly all school activities, whether pedagogic, organizational or social, both these internal to the school and those related to the external community, have their influence on the personal development of the child. Thus, counselling is seen as a fundamental process and not simply as an additional one.

Furthermore we are of the opinion that ways can be found of achieving this state of affairs which will enhance the efficiency of the school in serving its traditional objectives.[13]

I look forward to the time when counselling by competent, understanding persons becomes available as an integral part of our educational process in all our schools and colleges, but I doubt that this will come about in my lifetime.

3
Guidance and counselling in schools

To incorporate pastoral care under the terms guidance and counselling is not to reduce emphasis on the caring side but to signify the arrival of a more professional orientation.[1]

Introduction

Teachers and heads of schools in this country have for many years concerned themselves with what is commonly known as 'pastoral care', an interest in the well-being of children, over and above their instructional role. The quality of that concern has varied with individual teachers, as have the quality and effectiveness of their teaching.

In the past a teacher's facility for exercising pastoral care depended almost exclusively on his own ability to make personal relationships. It was a 'natural' outcome of his own personality and life experience, rather than anything that he learned academically or practically as part of his teacher training, if indeed he had any training in teaching, which for graduates was not a professional requirement until quite recently.

Several recent developments in secondary schools have shown that this caring aspect of a teacher's work is more important than ever. The introduction of comprehensive secondary education has brought a formal structuring of these, often large, schools into houses or year groups, with a built-in provision of staff in the form of house heads or year heads and tutors, with special responsibility for both administrative arrangements and the welfare of children.

Another aspect of education which has enhanced the personal element of the teaching relationship is the change in teaching approach and method created by curriculum renewal and development, which is demonstrated by the work of the Schools Council and was influenced by the Curriculum Development Laboratory at Goldsmiths' College, London. By increasing the amount of time a teacher spends with individuals and small groups, as opposed to the group of thirty to forty in an average class, methods such as team teaching, and Inter-Disciplinary Enquiry also increase the dependence on one-to-one relationships between teacher and child. This is perhaps the biggest difficulty arising from these approaches to teaching; the personal skills involved in presenting information to a large group (100–200) differ from the personal skills required for effective small group work and one-to-one relationships. Some teachers can work happily in all these areas, but others are more comfortable either with the larger audience or with the small group.

The introduction of a guidance programme makes provision for help in the form of guidance and counselling in a variety of areas and stages of school life, such as orientation to school, educational choices and assessment, vocational choice, and preparation for work or higher education concurrently with personal and group counselling throughout the child's years at school.

The following outline of a guidance programme suggests those areas of need which warrant consideration by secondary schools, ways in which these needs might be met and the people whose combined efforts contribute to the success of a guidance programme. This is a suggested programme which can be adapted to the work situation in different school settings, for example the staff of middle schools (nine to thirteen years) may consider that their emphasis on vocational choice would be less than that of an upper school (fourteen to eighteen years).

Guidance programme

1. Areas of guidance need
(a) Orientation, both to school and within it, and transition from school.
(b) Educational guidance.
(c) Course choice, vocational and higher education choice.
(d) Counselling, personal, educational and vocational.
(e) Home/school liaison, and liaison with outside agencies.

2. Sources of guidance (personnel)
(a) Teachers: tutors, subject teachers, house heads, year tutors, head teachers.
(b) Parents.
(c) Careers teachers, careers advisers and careers officers.
(d) Counsellor.
(e) Education Welfare Service.
(f) School Medical Service, together with Child Guidance Service and School Psychological Service.

(g) Outside agencies—probation service and local social service departments.

3. *Sources of guidance (methods)*
(a) Daily contacts
(b) Interviews.
(c) Individual and group counselling.
(d) Visits to homes, junior schools, school journeys and educational and occupational visits by children.
(e) Curriculum—team teaching, IDE, extra curricular activities.
(f) School records

Within such a programme counselling is one of several activities and the counsellor is one member of a team which provides the personnel for guidance.

Areas of guidance need

ORIENTATION

The purpose of orientation is 'to help the pupil feel emotionally secure in a new setting and to provide him with the information needed to be successful in that setting'.[2]

To an eleven year old the transfer from junior to secondary school is characterized by anticipation probably containing a mixture of fear and pleasure, with some sadness at leaving behind known friends and teachers and the security that they can offer. Such a transition is a process and not an event, just as going to school at the age of five, leaving school to go to work and leaving school to go to college are processes. If each move is treated as a process, children will be prepared for the change before it occurs and helped to adjust to it. If the transition is treated as an event, a child says goodbye to his junior school at the end of the summer term and arrives on the doorstep of his secondary school six weeks later and copes with the situation as best he can. If he had a difficult time when he first went to school it is likely that this will be repeated at eleven and again at fifteen, sixteen or eighteen, for unless the pattern of behaviour at times of transition is consciously changed it tends to repeat itself.

Many children are capable of working through the process of transferring from one educational experience to another with little or no assistance, which is fortunate, because often that is exactly what they receive. Orientation is included in a school programme to provide general help for all the children involved and particular help for those who find the change particularly stressful. An orientation programme may include visits to the junior schools from staff working with first year forms in the secondary school, and perhaps more important, visits by children from those first year forms who are really in a much better position to 'tell it like it is' from their own recent experience. This can also provide useful insight into the personal reactions of children to their secondary school. Usually they present a balanced view between them, but if there is a predominance of negative feedback, the need for some changes ought to be considered. It may also include visits to the secondary school by the junior children and their parents. The purpose of these visits is to make some contact and to give some feeling of familiarity in what is often a large and diffuse environment, very different from the more close-knit community of the junior school. Any guidance programme should include provision for specific help with all the transition processes of school life.

EDUCATIONAL GUIDANCE

The gradual disappearance of selection at eleven plus places on some secondary schools the choice of streaming and assessing children when they enter the school, or of teaching them in mixed ability groups for the first one, two or three years of their secondary school life before placing them in groups to study for examinations, in groups which have a more technical or vocational approach such as commercial subjects, in those which combine these approaches, or in others.

Those schools which choose to stream children according to ability may divide them according to the recommendations of the junior or middle school heads, which may be based on the results of yearly intelligence tests, combined with teachers' and headteachers' assessments of achievement, ability and sometimes of personality; or they may devise their own method of selection.

This area, called educational guidance, covers both educational measurement and testing and the way in which the results of such measurement are preserved and filed in some form of educational record system.

EDUCATIONAL MEASUREMENT AND TESTING

Thou shalt not answer questionnaires
Or quizzes upon world affairs
Nor with compliance
Take any test. Thou shalt not sit
With statisticians nor commit a social science.

W. H. Auden.

Tests reflect the society in which they are found much more than is commonly accepted. The differences in standardized testing in Britain, Russia and America largely represent each society's philosophy and attitudes towards intelligence and ability. Here hereditary characteristics were for a long time considered to have more influence over behaviour and performance than environmental factors. An individual could be highly intelligent regardless of his environment; now we are not sure that this is so. In Russia, environmental influences are considered more important than hereditary characteristics, so there is little need for standardized tests because you need to predict about environments, rather than people. Achievement tests are probably used most. The Americans seem not to be ready to resolve the problem of the relative importance of hereditary and environmental influences, and testing in schools is almost continuous.

Testing has no purpose apart from people; tests are used to help people to solve problems and to make decisions, and they provide one source of information for this purpose. It is not the test that makes the decision, but a person using a fallible piece of information, the test score. Unless you know what you need to decide, there is no point in giving a test; no measurement is useful by itself, but only when used in conjunction with other information.

Tests may be used in education for selection and classification, they may also be used for diagnosis, perhaps of reading difficulty or backwardness, for research purposes and for the evaluation of individuals or groups perhaps at the end of a course to determine whether or not it was worthwhile, in terms of its objectives.

There are several purposes for which tests may provide information and there are different kinds of tests which may be used by teachers, counsellors or psychologists These may be divided broadly into four categories: ability tests, inventories, rating scales, and projective techniques.

Ability tests

An ability test requires a person to perform a task or answer a question to which there is usually a right or wrong solution. Commonly accepted ability tests are tests of intelligence, aptitude and achievement, which are distinguished in terms of function rather than content. Aptitude and intelligence tests are predictive measures of intellectual capacity. An intelligence test usually gives a general prediction about overall intellectual capacity, whereas an aptitude test may provide a measure in a specific area of aptitude, for example Maths or Science. An achievement test is designed to test past performance and usually measures a specific kind of content, such as English or History.

Inventories
The 'test' which forms an inventory does not have right or wrong answers, the person tested being required to give some information about himself, about his interests or his personality. The most popular are those which cover vocational interests, such as the Rothwell-Miller Interest Blank.

Rating scale
In an inventory the person gives information about himself. In a rating scale someone else gives information about him, or he rates himself.

Projective techniques
Projective techniques such as the Thematic Apperception Test (TAT), the Blackie picture test or the Lowenfield Mosaic Test, are also used in an attempt to assess personality. They have not been demonstrated to be as valid or reliable as other types of test, but some people with exceptional skills can use projective techniques very successfully.

There are many criticisms of the use of standardized tests, including the comments that they are not reliable and valid; that they may 'freeze' the curriculum because teachers will teach to the tests; that an intelligence test may place an indelible stamp of high or low intelligence on a child (indeed such tests have been banned by the Los Angeles Board of Education to prevent the erroneous labelling of children as unintelligent); that the use of tests can lead to self-confirming hypotheses about a child. (See the work of Rosenthal and Jacobson in *Pygmalion in the Classroom*.[3]) It is said, too, that tests are limited in scope and do not measure some of the more important things about growing children.

The best rationale for using testing in education is that despite the pitfalls there is no better way to get the information upon which to base the decisions which people consider important. Most criticisms of testing do not seem justifiable when the testing is done and the information is used responsibly. Since a knowledge of what constitutes responsibility in this context is not considered an essential aspect of the training of all our teachers, it falls to the university-trained school counsellor and the educational psychologist, who will have made a special study of testing and measurement, or to the teacher who has had in-service training in this area, to make sure that the administration of tests, the interpretation of their results and use made of the information provided are all characterized by a responsible and ethical approach.

The National Foundation for Educational Research, one of the main agencies for the supply of both American and British tests, discriminates between test users by dividing purchasers into several levels according to the qualifications demanded for users of particular tests.

It is important to avoid the irresponsible mis-administration of tests and the manipulation of tests results which can occur as the result of an insufficient knowledge of testing procedure amongst teachers.

> One important consideration which affects the way in which teachers use tests is that few, if any, tests indicate which sections of their instructions for administration are absolutely critical for the results, and to what extent partial violations are permissible. The reason for this omission is that it is too great a task to link every part of the instructions to the standardization and still allow flexibility in administration. This presents the test user with an 'all or nothing' situation with regard to the test norms that the test supplies. If he wishes to use the test successfully then the test instructions must be followed to the letter. If, however, he is prepared to restandardize the tests, that is, to scrap the published norms, assemble a representative group, test and retest it, and finally link the test scores with the distributed group results, then he can vary the instructions in almost any way he pleases.[4]

There is increasing concern amongst students about the question of assessment and measurement, and the traditional formal examination system, characteristic of many colleges in the higher education system, gives cause for questions about its validity and reliability. A recently published booklet *Marked for life*[5] makes a good case from research studies for a careful reconsideration of the decisions which people think they are making when they use the formal examination system.

EDUCATIONAL RECORDS

> The state of educational records at primary, secondary and further educational level is, in fact, one of the basic reasons for the present low esteem in which teachers are held by the community. Professions that depend on 'hearsay', off-the-cuff opinions and processed gossip do not deserve to be held in

47

high public regard. However, the pressures which social and economic processes will bring to bear on education— larger schools, a more flexible, realistic curriculum, a greater concentration on self-realization rather than on narrow talent exploitation, plus a prospective rather than an apathetic view of vocational prospects—will bring about a change, because without it schools will become chaotic and unacceptably amateur.[4]

Not many years ago the amount and quality of information available to schools concerning past and present pupils was dependent upon the reliability of the memories of the less transient members of staff. The Education Act of 1944 laid down that schools should keep careful and detailed individual records of pupils. The Grant Regulations for Primary and Secondary Schools, 1951, stated that 'whenever a pupil ceases to attend the school and becomes a pupil at any other school or place of education or training . . . adequate medical and educational information concerning him shall be supplied to persons conducting that other school or place'.

The requirements and social conditions of modern educational practice make it impossible for even the most discerning of teachers to commit to memory a reliable, continuous record of information on even one child. The increase in mobility amongst the population generally, which affects both teachers and children, has increased the need for cumulative school records of a semi-permanent nature. Any record system is no better and no worse than its users make it and a mere accumulation of fragments of information does not provide a useful contribution to the guidance of a child. A record system is not intended to give a complete picture of a child, but the information it contains should be used to assist in educational and vocational guidance.

Use and purpose
1. A record can help a tutor with a new group by providing information to increase his knowledge of a child, and to help him to see that child as an individual, though such information is no substitute for knowing the child as a person. We are all more than the sum of the information that anyone might collect about us.

2. A record may help with choice of courses within a school, or with selection.

3. A record may help in educational guidance by providing a continuous academic record, and can save time spent in discovering what someone else has already ascertained but not recorded.

4. The information recorded assists educational and vocational guidance and it can be useful for selective reference in writing testimonials.

5. A record can be useful in the diagnosis of areas of backwardness and in gaining insight into behaviour problems which first become apparent in the classroom but whose causes may lie elsewhere. It can also provide a useful record of the value of remedial treatment.

6. Records should be available for reference by teachers, and their use by teachers, and possibly indirectly by outside welfare agencies or school doctors, can be of benefit. It is only if records are well used that the presence of unused items of information and the omission of helpful ones may become apparent and the form of the record developed and improved.[6]

Some teachers feel that a cumulative record card is undesirable because it may perpetuate an adverse comment on a child. This implies that the people using the system will necessarily be biased against a child because of someone else's opinion, rather than making their own attempt to understand his situation and helping him to remedy any difficulties he might have.

Content and form of educational records
It is realistic for schools to use ways of recording information which meet their particular needs. Some schools prefer information to be recorded on the record card, others prefer a system of separate sheets stored in a file. The choice depends on the amount of time that the head of a school is prepared to make available either to teachers or in the form of clerical help for the maintenance of the system and for keeping it up-to-date. The content of records usually consists of information recorded under broad headings:

Permanent and semi-permanent personal identification details, and family information, including a photograph of each pupil.

A number of children are handicapped in their learning by home circumstances. If no responsible adult in school knows about their difficulties, they struggle with them alone, often with damaging effects. There are occasions on which teachers and counsellors are aware of difficult home circumstances but cannot change them, though they can perhaps help the children to live with their reality. Although it may help to know about a child's home difficulties such information needs to be treated responsibly. No worthwhile teacher would wish a child's personal and family circumstances to become mere common gossip, but teachers are not trained to treat such information in a confidential and helpful way. The head of every

49

school should make explicit the standards expected in this area so that we may more often reach this situation: 'I brought into the school confidential information about homes of the girls. Not once in my seven years did a member of staff misuse this information. We treated the information with respect, but we were very grateful for it. Until you have been in such a situation you cannot appreciate what a tremendous difference it can make to the handling of a child when you understand the difficulties, the everyday routine, the relationships within the home.'[7]

Information which helps in understanding a child's behaviour might include indications of economic hardship, any known parental attitudes towards children such as over-indulgence, anxiety, coldness or neglect, or known parental attitudes towards school and education in general. Language difficulties in the homes of children with parents of differing nationalities can sometimes indicate the need for remedial or extra help. The death of a parent or the break-up of a marriage are situations to which children react in different ways, often coping better with grief after death than with the shock and divisiveness of the separation of parents who are still living.

Personal and social characteristics are difficult to assess and record, but if they are not contained on the record card, there is little likelihood that they will be preserved anywhere else (except in the person concerned). We are becoming aware of the important part which temperament plays in determining the extent to which a child uses his abilities and his educational opportunities. Some records contain descriptions of social relations with adults and peers, and attitudes to work, which are helpful, particularly if they are written in the form of objective rather than subjective reports of behaviour. There is a place for subjective reports, provided that we remember that they contain bias. They may give a good indication of how a variety of people react to a given child and where they tend to substantiate each other, as for example, when half a dozen people independently report that 'John is a habitual trouble-maker', then we can assume that this piece of subjective information warrants attention. When they contradict each other, one saying that John is a trouble-maker and another that he is a good worker, they cancel each other out. The objective report on the other hand should mean the same thing to each person who reads it; it is concerned with facts and not with what the observer thinks or feels, or with what he believes. The subjective report may tell us more about the teacher than about the child, for it is to some extent a portrait of the teacher's own bias. The difference between the two presentations may perhaps be likened to that between a detective story and a policeman's report of an incident; they meet different needs and we must be clear which is which when we come to use the information.

To simplify a difficult assessment, some schools use a check list of personality traits and an entry is made only where behaviour indicates a clearly defined individual characteristic, together with descriptive and objective comments. If such a check list is to be used, a general description of each of the characteristics listed should be given, so that as far as possible teachers mean the same thing when they state that a child's work is accurate, or original or erratic. An example of such a list together with the descriptions which might accompany it is given in Appendix.[2]

Academic record and standardized test results. The academic record often includes a note of subjects taken, assessment, the type and level of course, subject choices where these are offered and subject changes with reasons for the change if these are available, examination forecasts in some cases, and examination results. Most schools do not standardize their marks, which makes them less meaningful than they might be, for example, the use of a ten or five point scale based on percentage marks makes comparisons of performances in different subjects difficult. If eight children in a form get grade 1 for Maths and only one child gets grade 1 in History, does this mean that the children are better at Maths, or that it is easier to obtain a high mark for Maths than it is to do well in History?

Special abilities, interests and activities. Some indication of a pupil's special abilities or aptitudes, including any noticeable bent, gift or talent for a particular subject or activity, for example art, music, practical skills or unusual accomplishments (usually legitimate ones), may be useful in vocational guidance. Outstanding interests, which do not necessarily correlate with abilities, whether they be social, physical, aesthetic, practical, intellectual or a hobby, may help in vocational guidance but might also provide a means of stimulating learning by linking it with personal interests.

Educational and vocational plans. Notes of work experience, educational or vocational visits, careers courses, the pupil's own educational and vocational plans and the parents' educational and vocational plans for their child recorded from the end of the first year can be used to help in the making of realistic vocational and educational choices.

Attendance can provide an important record for guidance

purposes, since absence can be a symptom of some underlying discontent.

COURSE CHOICE, VOCATIONAL AND HIGHER EDUCATIONAL CHOICE

> ... a person to some extent shapes the pattern of his life by the choices and decisions he makes at successive stages.[8]

American secondary education is very much a process of making choices and decisions. In many schools students 'choose' a new timetable, or schedule each term, and although certain subjects are designated 'required subjects', the fact that options are available to a much greater extent than they are in the majority of secondary schools here, has led to an emphasis on guidance as a process of making decisions.

One of the developments which have accompanied the introduction in this country of comprehensive schools on American lines, has been the increase in the range of subjects offered and the related choice involved. Hughes quotes a headmaster in the London area who could provide more than 350 different permutations of the subjects offered in his school.[1] If boys or girls in school are to move from the former narrow choice between arts and science subjects to the wider range of subjects now available in many schools, it seems reasonable to make provision for some kind of assistance for those who feel a need to make their choices on a basis a little less arbitrary than the tossing of a coin. We could do worse than accept the American notion that in the area of educational choice, guidance and decision-making are at least intimately interwoven if not in some cases synonymous. The same approach is as relevant to the vocational choices made by school leavers as it is to the choices made by those moving into further and higher education, because here too there is a wider choice than formerly. For many it is no longer a choice of whether to go to university or not, but a more multi-dimensional choice involving the important question, 'Which of the several different kinds of higher education now available suits me best?'

Child growth and development follow certain patterns and from these we know that certain achievements, for example walking, talking, are likely to be learned at certain stages in a child's life. Decisions are more reasonably made at one level than another, but that level varies between individuals. Some children can make a vocational choice at the age of nine, more at thirteen, still more at eighteen and some not until their early or middle twenties, but circumstances do not readily permit that people delay their vocational choice until they are 'ready' in developmental terms. Choice-making is a part of the total personality; we make choices in the light of our needs and temperament, but we do need practice and the more experiences a child can have in making decisions appropriate to his situation, the more likely he is to develop the ability to make decisions that are integrated with his personality. If a decision is not a pupil's own choice it is unlikely to be carried through when positive reinforcement is no longer present. This is shown particularly in those students who arrive at college rather as a result of a negative choice, in the sense that important people in their lives had great expectations that they would attend university. It can be very difficult for such students to sustain any motivation for academic study once they have left home and school and have achieved the immediate demands of those expectations.

COUNSELLING; PERSONAL, EDUCATIONAL AND VOCATIONAL
Despite the fact that counselling has been delineated under the sub-headings of personal, educational and vocational, the three areas are more often than not closely inter-related. Vocational counselling cannot be effective if it does not encompass the personal and educational aspects of a person's life; it is as much concerned with personality variables as is counselling for personal problems. Educational choices may have a limiting or a broadening effect on vocational choice. It may not be wise to base educational choice at twelve or thirteen on vocational aspirations, which are quite likely to change, but it is realistic to acknowledge the vocational implications and limitations of educational choices.

Hughes[1] talks of counselling that enables people to examine their needs and problems and in so doing to reduce the confusion in their thoughts and feelings so that they may formulate workable plans for themselves. Anne Jones,[9] too, regards counselling as an enabling process which encourages self responsibility and helps people to make choices or decisions or to share an inner burden which is becoming too intolerable to bear alone. Gill[10] sees counselling as helping people to understand themselves with reference to personal, educational and vocational aspects of their lives and in the light of what they understand about themselves to make decisions.

Counselling in schools is for children who are anxious or unhappy, but it is also for children and young people who are faced with choices which have important consequences for their future. It involves the use of information about the person of the child, his temperament, abilities and interests and information about the opportunities which are available to him. The information comes

53

from a variety of sources, but it is the open acknowledgment, acceptance and clarification of the realities of a person's life, his assets and his liabilities, shared within the security of a caring and dynamic personal relationship which is the essence of counselling, whether it be personal, educational or vocational.

HOME/SCHOOL LIAISON AND LIAISON WITH OUTSIDE AGENCIES

Teachers toil to educate children who benefit only partially from their efforts. . . . Similarly social workers labour to pick up the disintegrated or disintegrating pieces of children's lives, and doctors, psychologists, magistrates and juvenile officers add their quota of trained and dedicated effort, backed by public money, to cure, reform, or restrain children whose response to their educational or social environment is inadequate or down-right antagonistic.

How is this wastage of human potential, human effort and money to be arrested? . . . On the one hand, educationalists need to rethink their priorities; on the other, there is the need for closer integration between the educational, welfare and juvenile services which at present function so often in near isolation.[11]

An illustration of this isolation is Barbara Wootton's comment on the White Paper on The Child, the Family and the Young Offender that, so far as the White Paper was concerned, the whole educational system might not exist.

The establishment and maintenance of good relationships between home and school has come to be recognized as an important aspect of education, yet many parents are fearful of contacting the head-teacher or the child's own teacher, and there are several factors which contribute to this fear. One is the fact that whatever our social standing or level of educational achievement, whether we left school at fourteen or completed a Ph.D. at the age of about twenty-four, we have all had experience of teachers. Because teachers are a mixed group, it is likely that some of those experiences will have been good, some forgotten, and some remembered with a range of feelings from mild dislike to strong anger. For example, there used to be a well-known saying in Lancashire in my childhood that you could tell a teacher anywhere but you couldn't tell them much. Everyone has residual memories of teachers, which can and do cause the barriers that exist between some parents and teachers. Most parents do not like to be thought of as interfering, or as fussy, but it must be very difficult for some parents to 'hand over' their children at the age of five and to have them in someone else's care for most of the impressionable years of childhood and adolescence, having little say in what happens to them during that time. Schools and teachers could make better use of parents' interest in their children and many are attempting to do so. Teachers who readily complain that the parents they want to see never visit the school may be interested in the experiences of Joan Clark, a Home Liaison Officer in a secondary school for girls. She set out 'to visit the homes of all the girls, to offer friendship, and to ask for interest'.[7] Repeatedly the efforts of staff had been baulked by the resistance or the apathy of the parents, and the Education Welfare Officers were kept fully occupied dealing with such problems as absenteeism, free school meals and truancy. There are difficulties in liaison between home and school:

> It is easy to stir up trouble between the child and her parent, or between the child and her class teacher. It is easy to increase the antagonism towards the school instead of lessening it. It is easy to become involved in gossip about other people's children, or to be expected to support derogatory remarks about one's colleagues. It is easy to arrive at the door looking like Lady Bountiful arriving to visit the humble poor. It is easy for parents and the visitor to put their heads together and loftily decide what is 'best' for the child, and reorganize her life for her.[7]

Every school needs the courage to face this problem of communication between home and school and between outside agencies and the school. The benefits which can accrue from a team approach which improves understanding and reduces overlapping activities and visits seem to be well worth the time, effort and swallowing of professional pride. One of the advantages which home/school liaison and community liaison offer is the opportunity 'to test the relevance of what is taught and experienced within the school against the occupational and social realities of life as the pupils will live it'.[7] An important result of Joan Clark's work with families was the revision of the work of the school which took place, based on information about the neighbourhood community which she was able to bring into the school from her visits and relationships with the families.

The reorganization and centralization of local authority social services following the recommendations of the Seebohm Report will, in time, provide a co-ordinated outside agency for providing help for children and their families. I hope that the Directors and staffs of the new Social Services departments will recognize the increasing responsiveness of many schools to this kind of work and will find ways of working with school staffs for the benefit of children, even though tensions may arise as a result of differing professional priorities between teachers and social workers. A counsellor comments:

> Most of my cases are self-referrals, but most of the staff referrals are youngsters who are playing up in class, kicking over the traces, showing aggression or in some way or other acting out their difficulties. Social work professions rightly see these cases in the context of their personal histories, of deprivation at home, of breakdown in socialization or so on. Teachers, when they are acquainted with these kinds of considerations —and it is part of my job so to acquaint them—are almost invariably sympathetic, but they also see the children in other contexts; as, for example, a disruptive element in class, as a challenge to the credibility of the school's disciplinary structure, and so on. They may also see aspects of the children's behaviour which is never provoked by the undemanding atmosphere of the counsellor's or the social worker's interview room. It is therefore my job to acquaint social workers with these kinds of considerations. Disturbed children have needs, but so do schools—if they are to remain stable institutions—and so do teachers.[12]

THE LAMENT OF THE NORMAL CHILD

I was strolling past a schoolhouse when I spied
                    a sobbing lad.
His little face was sorrowful and pale.
'Come, tell me why you weep,' I said, 'and why
                    you seem so sad.'
And thus the urchin lisped his tragic tale:

The school where I go is a modern school
    With numerous modern graces.
And there they cling to the modern rule
    Of 'Cherish the Problem Cases!'
From nine to three I develop me.
    I dance when I'm feeling dancy,
Or everywhere lay on
With creaking crayon
    The colours that suit my fancy.

But when the commoner tasks are done,
    Deserted, ignored, I stand
For the rest have complexes, everyone;
    Or a hyperactive gland.
Oh, how can I ever be reconciled
    To my hatefully normal station?
Why couldn't I be a Problem child
    Endowed with a small fixation?
Why wasn't I trained for a Problem Child
    With an Interesting Fixation?

I dread the sound of the morning bell.
    The iron has entered my soul.
I'm a square little peg who fits too well
    In a square little normal hole.
For seven years in Mortimer Sears
    Has the Oedipus angle flourished;
And Jessamine Gray, she cheats at play
    Because she is undernourished.
The teachers beam on Frederick Knipe
    With scientific gratitude,
For Fred, they claim, is a perfect type
    Of the Antisocial Attitude.
And Cuthbert Jones has his temper riled
    In a way professors mention.
But I am a perfectly Normal Child,
    So I don't get any attention.
I'm nothing at all but a normal child,
    So I don't get the least attention.

The others jeer as they pass me by.
    They titter without forbearance.
'He's perfectly normal,' they shrilly cry,
    'With Perfectly Normal Parents.'
For I learn to read
With a normal speed.
    I answer when I'm commanded.
Infected antrums
Don't give me tantrums.
    I don't even write left-handed.
I build with blocks when they give me blocks.
    When it's busy hour, I labour.
And I seldom delight in landing socks
    On the ear of my little neighbour.

So here, by luckier lads reviled,
I sit on the steps alone.
Why couldn't I be a Problem Child
With a case to call my own?
Why wasn't I born a Problem Child
With a Complex of my own?

Phyllis McGinley (1951)
from *Times Three* (Viking, 1960)

'Counseling refers to the help given by one person to another "normal" person toward understanding and solving his adjustment problems.'
(English and English, in *Dictionary of Personnel and Guidance Terms*, edited by William E. Hopke.)

'The psychologist and the psychiatrist are interested mainly in the unusual child; the teacher and the counsellor with the normal child.'
(Jackson and Juniper, *A manual of educational guidance*.)

4
Sources of guidance in schools

Guidance . . . is the total program, or all the activities and services engaged in by the school . . . that are primarily aimed at assisting an individual to make and carry out adequate plans and to achieve satisfactory adjustment in all aspects of his daily life. Guidance is not teaching, but it may be done by teachers. It is not separate from education but is an essential part of the total educational program. Guidance is a term which is broader than counseling and which includes counseling as one of its services.[1]

Teachers

In any school the major source of people to implement a guidance programme is the teaching staff. Teachers have regular contact with large numbers of children throughout the school week and it is they, together with parents, who are in a position to observe changes in behaviour which might signify stress, difficulty or need in children. Often the most difficult part of the observant teacher's work is knowing what can and cannot be done to help. It is sometimes said from the floor at conferences that 'all teachers are counsellors,' or that 'counselling is necessary but counsellors are not'. I am not able to meet the expectations of a teacher/counsellor role though there are those who prefer to do so.[2] I left teaching to train as a counsellor because the pastoral function was taking precedence over the teaching function, yet there had been little in my teacher training or my experience of working in schools and with adults to enable me to work at a more personal level. When I was a teacher I did not regard myself as a counsellor any more than I regarded myself as a social worker or a psychologist. There are some fairly clear distinctions between what I did as a teacher and what I did as a counsellor in a school setting.

Whether teachers without counselling training choose to call themselves 'counsellors' or not, and I should prefer that they choose not to do so, any guidance programme however carefully planned and organized can be only as effective as the personal qualities of the teachers implementing it allow. We must acknowledge that there are teachers whose sole wish is to teach and who see the conditions of their job as arriving in school on the morning bell and leaving it on the afternoon bell. Such teachers often impart knowledge well in the classroom—which is what they regard as the work for which they are paid, but they believe that personal, vocational and sometimes educational guidance too, should not be the concern of teachers or schools. These teachers should not be used as tutors because they do not want the extra responsibility that tutoring involves and consequently they give the minimum of their time and interest to it. However, it is administratively expedient to use the majority of teachers as tutors or form teachers, whether they wish it or not. To allocate a number of children to an unwilling teacher and to inform him that he is responsible for their pastoral care, or their counselling and guidance, may result in the pupils receiving not even guidance of an inferior quality. 'In our view there should be opportunity for all members of staff to engage in pastoral care to the limit of their diverse capacities and enthusiasms, whether in the classroom or in extra-curricular activities.'[3]

There is disagreement about the counselling aspect of a teacher's role. There are those who believe that all teachers are counsellors because of the nature of their teaching work, and those who believe that counselling at its best can only be carried out by professionally trained specialists. Between these extremes are others who support the dual role of teacher/counsellor with or without counselling training, and those who suggest that successful guidance and counselling services involve professionally trained counsellors working closely with interested and capable teachers.

Warters suggests three essential basic requirements for a successful school guidance and counselling programme:

1. leadership by a professionally trained competent counsellor;
2. an adequate number of interested and trained counsellors;
3. sufficient time in which to do the work.

She particularly stresses the importance of trained counsellors, and in America there are many of these. '. . . if the services of professionally trained counselors are not available, much that may be done in the name of guidance may be of limited value or even useless. Some of it may actually prove harmful to the recipients.'[4]

This notion that education, which includes guidance and counselling, can be harmful is one which we do not yet seem ready to acknowledge in this country. The Americans have coined a word, *didascalogenic*, meaning 'harmed by education', at which I used to smile, but, particularly since I have worked with university students, I have not found the concept at all amusing, and it is something which causes me concern.

In most comprehensive schools 'the first line of reference on guidance matters'[5] is the tutor, who is usually a teacher who does not actually teach the members of his tutor group. This is a deliberate policy to remove guidance from the academic setting and to make it possible for a tutor to help with personal guidance without being hampered by any specific teaching relationship or overtones from the classroom situation. This places an extra responsibility on the tutor, namely that of developing a 'guidance' relationship with children he does not teach in a limited weekly or daily tutorial period.

Parents

... it is naïve to imagine that any great reorganisation of the school system will automatically cause children and parents who are incapable of taking fullest possible advantage of educational opportunity, to do so. Ultimately greater attention will have to be paid to the motivations which are the product of the home environment, despite the difficulties which are involved.[6]

Miller goes on to say that his research showed clearly that both working-class and middle-class parents can unwittingly deprive their children of educational opportunity.

Where parents and the school agree as to the best interests of the child, there is little conflict, but when parents take an opposing view, or none at all, it is in the interests of the child that some process should be available for working towards a mutually acceptable solution or an agreement to differ. We tend to over-organize children's lives in the sense that important decisions are often made for them by parents and teachers who believe that it is their responsibility to know what is best for young people. This attitude curtails the opportunity for personal growth and choice-making which guidance seeks to introduce, and has several possible consequences, ranging from emotional immaturity, depression or apathy to aggression in young people.

Although teacher/parent relationships are important, it can be difficult for a teacher, who is personally involved in a child's success or failure, to remedy the attitudes and behaviour of both parents and school, where difficulties have arisen. In such cases mere liaison between teachers and parents hardly seems adequate and we may conclude that:

> While enormous budgets are being invested in better buildings, and in implementing new forms of school organisation, it would seem prudent to invest further comparatively small funds in greater numbers of workers who are properly trained in counselling, guidance and social work, competent to work within a professional relationship with families in seeking to reduce the social and psychological obstacles that make it difficult for so many children to benefit from their educational opportunity.[6]

Careers staff

> It is not many years since careers officers (formerly Youth Employment Officers) were attempting to carry almost the whole burden of the task [of vocational guidance] in secondary schools, their work, partly of necessity and partly by design, being concentrated largely upon 15 and 16 year old school leavers in secondary modern schools ... in any reasonably self-respecting secondary school today, one can expect to find a wide range of careers literature (even a library section) indexed and regularly up-dated, frequent talks by careers officers and employers, films and T.V. programmes on careers, work visits, involvement in work experience schemes and careers conventions, and separate pupil careers records.[7]

The attitude of some head teachers that the limit of a school's function in vocational guidance is twofold, namely to provide a room in which the careers adviser can interview pupils, and to supply the information required on the Youth Employment Service form, seems not only to misinterpret the scope of the work of the YES, but also to miss completely the importance of an early approach to vocational guidance, which can only be met from within the school itself. The whole concept of vocational guidance in schools must alter radically, in a situation in which the obligation of the school is to prepare boys and girls for life in a world where 'vocational pursuits are irrevocably linked with personal self-fulfilment'.[7]

The trait and factor approach to vocational guidance which attempted to accommodate square pegs in square holes is of limited value, given today's social and economic circumstances and opportunities. Leading American psychologists have studied vocational development extensively, and there is general agreement that a person progresses occupationally through a developmental process involving a series of choices, rather than on the basis of a single decision at a particular time. Where the current theories differ is in the emphasis placed on the different aspects of the developmental process. The major theories include Anne Roe's personality theory of career choice; John Holland's career typology theory; Ginzberg's developmental stage theory; Bordin's psychoanalytical conceptions of career choice; Donald Super's developmental self-concept theory and Tiedeman's choice and decision-making theory.[8]

In this country Rodgers's 'planned procrastination' offered a developmental approach to vocational guidance some thirty years ago, but regrettably we have paid too little attention to it. Taylor summarizes the role of the teacher in process of careers guidance as follows:[9]

1. disseminating information about occupational requirements and opportunities (by for example, providing relevant books, periodicals, pamphlets, private talks, lectures, film shows, group discussions and group visits to places of employment . . .);

2. collecting data (by interviews and written reports) from parents, doctors and colleagues about boys and girls seeking advice;

3. adding to these data (by making sensible use of tests for general intelligence and special aptitudes, and by planned interviewing);

4. interpreting all the data available in the light of his general knowledge of occupational requirements and opportunities;

5. co-operating with placement organizations in their task of making specific suggestions and finding suitable openings (and, when and where necessary, undertaking this task himself);

6. instructing young people in appropriate methods of applying for posts; and

7. following up those he advises (by obtaining regular progress reports on their satisfaction, and, if possible, on their satisfactoriness).

There is enough activity here for a full-time job, yet in many schools such work would be done by a careers teacher in addition to his teaching, and often in his lunch-hour, which is representative of the approach to vocational guidance which educators have had for many years. I would reject the placement role allocated to the teacher in item 5, as an insidious and at times unethical practice. Placement is not the job of teachers or counsellors, but should be left to those agencies whose prescribed function it is.

The National Association of Careers and Guidance Teachers[10] has made the following suggestions about the minimum requirement of time and facilities for vocational guidance in secondary schools.

1. Timetabled periods for teaching and discussion of careers and educational guidance from the third form upwards. [Personally I feel that vocational guidance should begin in the first year at secondary school and that guidance should be timetabled from the first year onwards.]

2. Administrative time required for the organization of the careers team, organization of records and information about pupils and for liaison with other bodies, including local careers officers of the Department of Employment.

3 Interview time for personal discussion with pupils. One 15/20 minute session each year for each pupil in 4th grade and above seems a minimal allowance.

4. Visits outside the schools: 8 half-day visits a term, equivalent to two or three periods a week for an average school.

John Russell, an American school counsellor, had some interesting reflections on the process of vocational choice, as he observed it in several English secondary schools.

I did note with some concern . . . the fact that preparation for school leaving in England seemingly does not begin until quite late and the selection of a career is often accomplished with a finality and irreversibility that does not seem justified, in view of the student's lack of maturity and sometimes awareness of what is involved in his decision. In some cases I had the feeling that the career choice was almost managed for the student by a panel of adults such as the career teacher, employment officer and parents. While this constitutes the most negative observation I made of the English system, I found many who were aware of it and I had the feeling that steps are being taken rapidly to improve the situation through improved training, earlier approaches to students, and more counselling services.[11]

The counsellor

It is possible for a school to have a programme of guidance covering the areas of guidance need mentioned in Chapter 3, without having a school counsellor on the staff. I have become so accustomed to thinking of guidance and counselling as integrally related concepts that to have a guidance programme without a counsellor seems like staging Hamlet without the Prince. Nevertheless, it is salutary to be reminded that it is possible and indeed usual. In studying systems of guidance in comprehensive schools, Moore looked at three schools without counsellors in which the heads felt that 'pupils' personal guidance needs were sufficiently well met by an active teacher-staffed pastoral care system'. The two schools which employed counsellors 'could point out that it was all too easy to take for granted that the personal problems which were affecting the educational progress of some pupils, and the numbers affected, were adequately met by a decentralised pastoral care system whose members already had a great many other commitments to teaching, administration and school social organisation'. [5]

In 1973 the National Association of Counsellors in Education (see Appendix 3), the association to which most school counsellors belong, produced a paper on the work of the school counsellor.[12] This set out a range of counselling objectives some of which are summarized here. As society changes, so do schools, and these changes have advanced beyond the point where traditional pastoral care and guidance provision in schools is sufficient. One significant aspect of recent change is the larger size of schools, particularly secondary schools, bringing increased problems of organization and communication. The intention to make a school a community in which each child can actively and constructively participate as far as he is able, is hindered by the sheer bulk and complexity of the work which the school is called upon to do. These hindrances may be more keenly felt by those children who are unusually shy or fearful, or who are inclined to respond to stress with hostility or aggressiveness. The tendency is that the larger the school the greater is the proportion of its children who feel alienated from the education system in one way or another. Whatever other means a school might use to respond to the demands of expansion, a school counselling service makes a significant contribution by helping to improve the communication of the school to the child and the child to the school, and by making the school a more meaningful and accessible place to certain children. Such a service might represent the care of the school for those children for whom traditional means of guidance and support may not be constructive.

There is a growing trend toward providing for the prevention and the care of breakdown in family and social life, through community care for individuals and families for whom the pressures of life prove unbearable. The school is for most children the second most important socializing influence in their lives, and as such is well placed for the early identification of children at risk. A school which

65

is aware of such children can help to facilitate contact between itself, the families and the appropriate social agency of support or care, as well as providing its own community support. A trained counsellor in a school can improve communication between the school and the local social services and the efficiency with which they are used.

A counsellor in a school would not wish to offer all the pastoral and guidance support which all the children need. Although a counsellor may be accessible to all the children, the personal emphases which are built into the way she works will tend to be on children in certain kinds of difficulties or at certain stages of development; a counsellor might initially concentrate on working with first-year pupils so that as children enter the school they learn about the purpose of the counselling service. The counsellor's role is a supplementary one, not replacing but supporting existing provision in the school with differing knowledge and skills.

One of the limitations on the work of existing staff is that, because there are other severe demands made upon their time and energy, it is difficult for them to be accessible to children who need their help, at the particular time when they seem to need it most. In theory a counsellor should have time to be available at the moment when a child senses his need for support and help and is perhaps most ready to benefit from it.

The staff of a school are responsible for sustaining discipline and thus maintaining some kind of social stability. This limits the range of matters about which they will be consulted by certain children. For the counsellor to attempt to sustain school discipline or to communicate moral approval or disapproval to the child, would be to erect unnecessary barriers between herself and some of the children she is trying to help. It is quite unrealistic for a counsellor to work as though the school made no disciplinary demands upon children or staff; it is perhaps the counsellor's task to interpret, where it might be helpful, the school's discipline to the child, and the child's misdemeanours to the school.

Many problems of young people are concerned with feelings and experiences which are unacknowledged or only partially acknowledged, and threaten their sense of security. In the context of a secure relationship these personal and often threatening feelings can be expressed. A trained counsellor should be able to help a particularly insecure child—whether the insecurity manifests itself in withdrawn or in aggressive behaviour. This suggests that a counsellor is equipped to help, not that she has a magic wand.

A counsellor's training makes available in school a range of professional skills which may not be generally offered, for example, in addition to her training in counselling skills, she would be equipped to administer, score and interpret a range of standardized tests of intelligence and personality inventories—though not such a wide range as would be available to a trained psychologist.

Much successful teaching, pastoral care and guidance is related to the personal meaning that a child places on his experience. It is a matter of emphasis rather than exclusion to say that a counsellor is more concerned with the internal world of the child than with communicating facts and ideas originating in the external world, which is often the province of a teacher. A counsellor will be less concerned with giving information and advice and more concerned with helping someone to find their own resources in terms of needs, capacities and talents through which they may constructively resolve their problems in their own way.

These features of counselling require of a counsellor certain minimum standards of training and perhaps certain characteristics of personality. It is thought that practice in the development of counselling skills calls for a fairly lengthy period of training because the acquisition of those skills involves the trainee counsellor in some sensitivity training through which her self-awareness and awareness of others may be heightened in particular respects. A one-year, full-time course of training is considered to be minimal for this purpose, and this is not regarded as a completion of training but as a foundation upon which further in-service training can be built. The National Association of Counsellors in Education has as one of its major priorities the promotion of opportunities for continuous in-service training for practising counsellors.

If a counsellor is to work successfully within the complexities of a modern school, it is an advantage for her to have been a teacher and to have a teacher's understanding, both of children and of how schools work. Not every successful teacher will make a successful counsellor, for the personal demands of these two professions are comparable in intensity but different in kind. I think that there is a place in schools for counsellors or social workers who have not been teachers, but who often bring the benefits of a less insular view of life. The introduction of such 'outsiders', although difficult, might be helpful.

Comparison of teaching and counselling

One of the essential differences between teaching and counselling concerns the development of relationships. Teaching usually starts with a group relationship and individual contacts develop from and return to group activities. A teacher often uses the skills of group work, and uses individual interviewing skills less frequently. A teacher is responsible for the welfare of many pupils at any one time and works mainly with children.

Counselling usually starts with an individual relationship and may develop into group situations for greater efficiency, to supplement the individual relationship, or as valuable experiences in their own right. Individual counselling skills are a basic technique of the counsellor and although the skills of group work are also important the emphasis is more often on the one-to-one relationship.

Most teachers know their objectives in teaching and they have to know children in order to attain these. They encourage children to behave in ways which will help society, by teaching accepted, though not always realistic, values of morality, honesty and good citizenship, and in this sense they have a responsibility for the welfare of society. Many teachers are concerned with the day-to-day growth of children and with their general development.

A counsellor often knows children in terms of specific problems, difficulties or plans for the future. The subject matter of the interview, unlike that of most lessons, is unknown to the counsellor and sometimes unknown to the child. Although a counsellor is not opposed to the values of society, she is probably more concerned with and responsible for the welfare of a child in helping to resolve personal problems, to make immediate choices, or to develop workable long-term plans.

A teacher has a compelled relationship with children who, up to the age of sixteen, are required by law to attend school. Many of the children a teacher meets are well adjusted and fairly happy, unless there are particular difficulties in the school or neighbourhood, and this would certainly be so in some schools.

Counselling is probably most effective when the association is voluntary, when a child wants help and feels that the counsellor can be helpful. Although counselling is theoretically for 'normal' children, a counsellor quite often deals with children who are disturbed by problems, sometimes characterized by emotional upsets or lack of confidence. Teachers meet such children, too, and sometimes in an apparently more demanding situation than the counsellor. When this happens teacher and counsellor can often work together to decide how best the situation may be handled.

Teachers have books, visual aids and syllabuses to increase their effectiveness, and they use lists and records to assist them. A skilful teacher uses information and develops abilities which increase her effectiveness in helping children to learn.

Counsellors have no similar aids to use with all children. They first establish a relationship within which both may discover problems, and sometimes causes, and within which individually appropriate ways of helping may be worked out. Counsellors use tests and records, but mostly to help them to look at particular individual problems. A skilful counsellor tries to develop some of the abilities used by a variety of specialists, forming an amalgam of some of the skills used in psychology, social work, psychotherapy and vocational guidance. Counselling involves learning and is person centred rather than subject centred. The counsellor tries to provide an experience through which children may be enabled to learn about themselves and their particular situation.

In a school with a well-established guidance programme which includes a counselling service, the work of the teacher and that of the counsellor are often complementary. Occasionally a counsellor may feel that it is in the interests of a particular child that he should not be taught by a particular teacher and would suggest a change. Some teachers do not favour this manipulation of the environment in the interests of themselves or of the children. Although such a move can change the atmosphere of a class completely, and remove some of the stress involved, it needs consultation and discussion.

Some functions of people in a guidance programme

Activity	*People who may be involved*
Orientation to school, and at other transition periods	Junior school staff Staff of colleges Teacher/tutor Counsellor Parents. E.W.O.
Maintaining liaison between school and home	Some teachers/tutors Counsellor E.W.O. Parents
Establishing ways of helping children to have experience of choices in preparation for choosing educational courses and careers, e.g. using opportunities for individual decision-making from first year upwards	Teachers/tutors Counsellor Parents

Activity	*People who may be involved*
Providing educational and vocational guidance and counselling	Teachers/tutors Careers teachers Counsellor Parents Careers Advisers Careers Officers
Ensuring that ALL pupils are informed of the means and meaning of further education	Teachers/tutors Counsellor Parents Careers Advisers
Establishing and maintaining educational records system	Teachers/tutors Counsellor Clerical help
Liaison between school and other agencies, school psychological service, local social services	Counsellor E.W.O. Some teachers/tutors

Individual and group guidance and counselling in the area of personal problems	Counsellor
	Some teachers/tutors
	Some parents
	  according to choice
	Some outside
	  agencies

Aspects of a guidance programme which may be particularly relevant to the work of the counsellor

Individual counselling according to need on matters of personal, social, educational and vocational development.

Group counselling and group guidance.

Work with children who seem to have special needs.

Links with contributory primary schools and assisting with orientation of first year pupils, together with orientation help at other points of change.

Case conferences with tutors and teachers.

Liaison with parents and outside agencies.

Vocational guidance where there are no careers teachers.

Assisting in the establishment of a cumulative educational records system.

Use of standardized tests where appropriate.

Curriculum development and renewal.

To be available during process of choice making to help tutors, and pupils with particular reference to both the personal and the possible future implications of the decisions.

Education Welfare Service

The Education Welfare Service is one of the oldest statutory social services. It was born shortly after the introduction of the first Elementary Education Act of 1870, when it was realised that . . many parents then, as now, and largely for the same reasons, showed little interest in education, and compulsory school attendance had to be introduced. In order to enforce attendance, the School Boards which had been set up under the Act, were empowered to appoint School Attendance Visitors, whose job was simply to chase children into school.[13]

The bowler-hatted School Board man, with his official-looking file of absence records, has now been replaced by the Education Welfare Officer. Although many of these workers have as little training for their work as had the 'School Board man', there is a slowly increasing number who qualify for the Certificate in Educational Welfare awarded by the Local Governments Examination Board.

Many Education Welfare Officers are still kept busy doing the work of the School Attendance visitors and chasing children into school, but the scope of their work has broadened considerably to include the provision of such welfare facilities as clothing, transport and maintenance allowances and free school meals. The E.W.O. provides a triangular link between the local authority, the home and the school. Although some E.W.O.s are now attached to schools they do often act as independent interpreters of the school to the parents and similarly may represent the views of the parents to the school. Their function may overlap with that of school counsellor in this area, but the role of the E.W.O. is perhaps more often and more accurately defined as advice-giving rather than counselling.

The Education Welfare Service is developing into a helpful

guidance service for schools and its usefulness should increase as more and more E.W.O.s become trained for their work.

School Medical Service together with Child Guidance Service and School Psychological Service. Other outside agencies, probation service and local social service departments

In many areas the relationships between the staff of schools and the staffs of the School Medical Service, the Child Guidance centres and the School Psychological Service together with other outside agencies have been tenuous and marginal.

The roles of teacher and parent differ and influence their attitudes to children, so, too, the differences in role-expectations of teachers and social workers, probation officers or School Medical Officers affect the way in which they respond to children and to each other. Often the counsellor, who has had teaching experience and whose counselling training has provided some insight into the work, attitudes and vocabulary of workers of other agencies, is a useful link between the views of the school and those of other people working with a child, to the mutual benefit of all, even if it is only an agreement to recognize crucial differences in approach. This link between the counsellor and other agencies has to be built up by personal contact and by working together over a period of time in much the same way as the counselling relationship itself is developed, and this aspect of liaison is one of the most important contributions a counsellor can make.

Sources of guidance and methods

There are several methods which might provide sources of guidance, including interviews, individual and group counselling, visits, and using the curriculum. Hemming [14] suggests a broad foundation upon which to create a comprehensive programme of guidance for schools, and although schools will vary in the extent to which they wish to implement elements of such a scheme it offers a basis for discussion. The elements recommended cover several areas including the curriculum, in which he asks for a humanizing of subject teaching so that pupils receive insight about people and about society from many different sources, and have the opportunity to discuss informally things which concern them about growing up. English, religious education and home economics lessons are mentioned as appropriate for such informal discussion, especially on personal problems and sex education, supplemented by visits from people outside the school, such as marriage guidance counsellors, health visitors or doctors. However, there is a limit to the use we can make of the curriculum for guidance purposes, for the curriculum is concerned with the common needs of a group of children, whereas counselling is concerned with the unique needs of an individual.

A second element covers the provision of facilities and opportunities for private talks between staff and those pupils who seek their help, and specifically requires small rooms for group discussion and counselling, together with an allotment of time for these.

The third element involves regular staff conferences at which the only item on the agenda is the discussion of pupils who are being difficult or who are in difficulties Periodic discussion meetings are suggested between counsellors and the Staff of the Child Guidance Clinic and the School Psychological Service for the sharing of experiences and ideas and to foster the development of mutual respect and understanding between the school and these helping agencies.

A fourth element to supplement the schools' existing provision for guidance is the training of teachers to specialize in guidance and counselling. There is also a suggestion that some provision should be made to inform parents about the normal developmental problems of adolescence.

There is a growing interest in education in the potentiality of guidance, illustrated by the increasing number of local education authorities who have set up a Working Party to report on guidance and its educational, vocational and personal aspects. Schools, too, are beginning to build 'guidance' into their work by making provision within their timetables for guidance activities.

In this country, the majority of teachers accept a pastoral responsibility towards their pupils; moreover, this aspect of the teacher's role is generally accepted by parents and by informed public opinion. The demands made upon the teacher in this regard are certainly increasing; at the same time the schools' response in meeting the challenge is increasingly beset by the difficulties imposed by large classes, re-organisation, the movement of families and teachers, unsuitable accommodation and so on. In many schools, Heads and their colleagues are pressing forward with a great deal of experimental work, in changed patterns of teaching and learning, in non-traditional forms of organisation, in curricular reform, in programmes specially designed to help prepare young people for entering the world of work and future parenthood. The provision of a systematically organised guidance programme, including the centrally important service of counselling, might contribute significantly to the success of many schemes of reform and re-organisation that are already launched. Such success should be judged in terms of a better educational opportunity for every young person. Nothing in the provision of a guidance programme can be construed as relieving or taking away from the teacher any of the responsibilities he now holds. Rather, specialist help within the school would be supportive and co-ordinative. There is no panacea in guidance. But there is abundant evidence of growing areas of need in which trained counsellors could provide, within the school, a new dimension in the help available to children, young people and their parents.[15]

A PLANNED GUIDANCE PROGRAMME FOR A COMPREHENSIVE SECONDARY SCHOOL

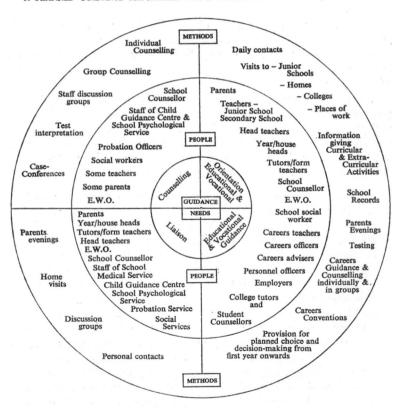

Guidance and counselling in primary schools

'The most dramatic and consistent finding of this study was that many behaviors exhibited by a child during the period 6 to 10 years of age, and a few during the age period 3 to 6, were moderately good predictors of theoretically related behavior during early adulthood.' [6]

The child coming to school for the first time brings a pattern of development which has evolved over the first five years of his life, and the primary school is for many children their first major exposure to a large society. The way in which a child adjusts to this new life within the school establishes adjustment patterns which are likely to be repeated each time the child encounters a similar situation.

Developmental psychology suggests that children learn and develop through a process of action which is slow and proceeds in stages and that, if attention to a particular process is received over a period of time, a pupil has a better chance of achieving his potential, of making reasonable choices appropriate to his situation and of meeting the educational requirements of subsequent stages. The child who learns to read in the infant school has an adequate foundation for the work expected of him throughout the junior school and later education. The child who does not learn to read in the infant school starts his junior school life with a handicap; not only does his lack of reading ability affect his academic efforts and sometimes cause him personal problems, but it is difficult to remedy because many junior school teachers do not expect to have to teach children how to read and, indeed, are not trained to do so. The further the non-reading child progresses through the junior and secondary school the more pronounced are the academic and personal difficulties he experiences. We offer remedial education with varying success. If we had more facilities, and people with time and skills, to discover why children do not learn reading or other appropriate developmental skills when we expect them to, we would be spared some of the juvenile delinquency, truancy and other social problems in our secondary schools.

A recent study by Lawrence [17] offers some findings relevant to this problem. In a small experiment using counselling with backward readers, junior school children retarded in reading were divided into four groups. Group 1 received remedial reading from a specialist teacher, Group 2 received remedial reading and counselling, Group 3 received counselling only, each child being seen individually for 20 minutes each week and allowed to draw pictures or talk about his worries, fears, attitudes to school and himself and his personal

75

relationships. Group 4, the control group, received no special treatment. Over the six month test period the overall improvement in reading ability by children in Group 4, the control group, was slight: 0.2 years. Group 1, remedial teaching, improved by 0.33 years; Group 2, remedial reading and counselling, by 0.47 years. Group 3 (counselling only) was the most successful: two of its members gained a year in reading ability and one almost to 2 years. The average improvement in the group was 0.61 years.

The primary school is charged with the task of providing an adequate academic, psychological and personal foundation for each of its pupils, and we now understand more clearly how inter-related these areas are and how their development may affect intellectual accomplishment.

Guidance in primary schools is probably best seen as a process which is primarily concerned with helping the child as a learner. It is concerned with the early identification of each child's needs and interests, some interpretation of these to teachers and parents, and also with helping the child to understand and accept himself in relation to those needs and to the demands of his environment.

Counselling is as significant an aspect of guidance in primary as it is in secondary schools, but there are differences of emphasis and approach because of the differences in physical and psychological development in the children at various school levels, and the limitations of verbal communication. The counsellor in a primary school is likely to be more directive and active in her approach because of the greater dependence of younger children and their undeveloped conceptual skills, and a behavioural approach to counselling, rather than a Rogerian or analytical one, may have particular value. The counsellor is a specialist helping the child to reach a better understanding of himself and his environment, and because the primary responsibility of the school is instructional the counsellor is concerned with the various aspects of physical development, relationships with children and adults and self-understanding which affect a child's ability to learn. Three main roles seem appropriate to the work of the junior school counsellor: counselling with children, teachers and parents; consulting and advising teachers and parents and co-ordinating by means of case-conferences, the collection of information, and liaison with outside agencies and orientation activities. The work of the junior school counsellor may be divided into several categories.

1. Consultant to teachers (including matters concerning individual children, learning disabilities and curriculum development).

2. Consultant to parents (including home visits).

3. Counsellor to children on a group and a one-to-one basis probably over problems concerned with academic disability or social adjustment within the classroom and school.

4. Counsellor and co-ordinator to bridge the gap between home and school and between junior and secondary school.

5. Co-ordinator of case-conferences with teachers, and liaison with staff of outside agencies.

ASPECTS OF THE WORK OF A COUNSELLOR IN A PRIMARY SCHOOL

A counsellor in a junior school in a difficult area said:

> . . . having undertaken [counselling] training while still teaching at the junior school level, and as a result [having] developed a

programme over a 3½ year period, I am more than ever convinced that there is a definite need for more trained counsellors to be on the staffs of primary schools, because at this stage more preventive work can begin. . . . At the beginning of the autumn term, a letter introducing the [guidance and counselling] service was sent to all families connected with the junior department: a reply slip on the bottom of the letter stated the times I would be available, either to make a home visit, or see parents in school. Considering the general apathy of the community towards the school we were amazed to find that 92 of the 272 families contacted requested a visit and that we had a 95 per cent return acknowledging receipt of the letter.[18]

This was the beginning of a guidance programme which has been particularly successful in co-ordinating home/school and community interaction, and in 'parent education' at the junior school level. One hopes that these benefits will not be lost when the children transfer to secondary school.

5
Student counselling

There is clear evidence that children who show aggressive, delinquent or neurotic traits at school, most of whom come from disturbed home backgrounds, are unlikely to realize their full intellectual potential. For this reason the university population, selected for intellectual achievement must also be selected to a considerable extent for psychological health. Looking at the range of emotional problems encountered among students, one can only murmur, 'God help the others'.[1]

The scope of student counselling

A survey of the field of counselling with students presents an interesting and diverse picture. Within the membership of the recently formed Association for Student Counselling (see Appendix 4) there is a variety of people who have in common an interest in the development of counselling in higher and further education. Among them are people who have entered counselling from a welfare officer role; others who find that part of their work as personal tutors, chaplains or wardens of student residences sometimes involves them in a counselling capacity; those who have moved into student counselling from various kinds of social work appointments; counsellors trained by the National Marriage Guidance Council; counsellors like myself who came into work with students via teaching and school counselling; counsellors who would describe themselves as psychotherapists, and yet others who have medical training as doctors or nurses and who have moved away from the strictly medical role into more of a counselling approach. Some student counsellors work in a combined appointments and counselling service, some in the field of student progress and achievement, others in combined medical and counselling services and some in counselling services independent of other departments. Counselling with the student age group includes many levels of counselling and types of counsellor working from a variety of theoretical approaches. The diversity shows that in this field, as in school counselling, there is 'no "pure" type of counselling from which all others are not only deviant, but to which they are inferior'.[2]

The scope of counselling with students outlined is very broad and its all-embracing nature will cause offence to some student counsellors. Although I do not believe that counselling is a catch-all category which can legitimately be used to describe all the help that people extend to each other, within higher and further education it does cover a wide field. At this early stage in the development of student counselling we could probably obtain as many different descriptions of the work of the student counsellor as we have individual counsellors. This is not necessarily a bad thing, since it is important for counsellors to try to meet some of those needs which actually exist in a particular situation and these will vary according to the needs which are already being met by other people in the college. It is important, too, for those who appoint student counsellors to be clear about what they expect from their counselling services. Not only would it seem to be a waste of talent to put a counsellor who seeks to work solely as a psychotherapist into the kind of counselling service which I shall describe, but it would probably result in some apparent needs of students not being met.[3]

When the Student Counselling Service was started in my own college in 1969 there existed a well-established Student Health Service which offered both medical help and psychotherapy. There was an equally well-established tutorial service within the departments and faculties and the Tutor to Women Students had offered women students help with a wide variety of personal and practical problems. On her retirement those people concerned with the appointment of a Student Counsellor, a service which the students had been requesting for two or three years, indicated that they would like the services formerly provided by the Tutor to Women Students extended so that they were available to both men and women students, and that there was a need for a further source of help with personal problems, to fill the gap which they felt existed between the resources of the tutorial system and the work of the Student Health Service. The Student Counselling Service was started with these expressed needs in mind, to offer help, or information on other sources of help, for people with a wide variety of practical and personal difficulties.

One aspect of the work of the service is the provision of information and practical help on such matters as where to obtain legal advice; what to do if the ceiling of your flat falls in, or the landlord changes the locks on your door and deposits your belongings on the pavement; where to go for help if you are an overseas student and your father, who is financing your course, has a heart attack and has to retire, or your country is plunged into civil war and both your parents are killed, or what to do when your father embezzles your grant cheque. Sometimes there is a student faced with the dilemma of an ultimatum from worried parents that they will withdraw their financial support if a relationship which they consider unsuitable, immoral, or both, is not ended.[3] Some of these difficulties are not entirely practical, they have a personal element which often has to do with the relationships involved; the landlord who locks out students may want to let their room for more money, or he may be quite at the end of his tether and know of no other way to deal with noisy and inconsiderate adolescents. The overseas students whose country is at war are often faced with financial difficulty, but there is also the conflict and concern which may make it harder for them to cope with being thousands of miles away and in comparative safety, than it would be for them to face the danger of being in the actual situation.

Thus, in addition to counselling, the Student Counselling Service offers guidance and information on some accommodation and financial difficulties. This could be offered by other people, for it does not constitute 'counselling' as such. The advantage of offering this kind of help within a counselling service as opposed to providing it within a purely administrative service, is that both financial and accommodation matters can make useful 'presenting' problems. It is recognized in counselling that the problem which a person first mentions may be a matter which he feels he can safely bring to a counsellor without feeling too threatened, yet which ultimately is found not to be his main difficulty. The first problem is then referred to as the 'presenting' problem and some students, like other people, find it easier to present with a practical difficulty or a request for information, than a more personal problem. This gives them a chance to proceed from the presenting problem if they feel the counsellor can help, or to withdraw with their practical 'answer' if they do not. For example, one counsellor discovered that a student who 'presented' with a request for vocational information had a terminal disease. If there is a difficulty other than the one presented, a counsellor, because of her training and experience, may be in a better position to recognize this than a tutor or an administrator who is not trained to do so. This does not imply that counsellors can invariably discriminate between 'presenting' and 'real' problems. I would hope they are sufficiently human to disclaim any such infallibility.

The main disadvantage of offering practical help and information

81

within a counselling service is that some accommodation problems are purely practical and could well be taken to an administrator, but until the counsellor has listened carefully to the student, it is usually not possible to find out whether or not the difficulty presented is the only problem. In a busy service a counsellor could spend much time talking about practical difficulties which could be helped by someone else, while students with more pressing problems of a personal nature have to wait for an appointment. If the counselling service is adequately staffed—and very few seem to be so—the problem is not so immediate, and this applies if there are other dependable and consistent sources of help for students with practical difficulties.

'Other branches of higher education are usually less fortunate than the universities in the facilities which they can offer for medical and counselling help. Too often they have to rely on part-time medical officers or over-worked local G.P.s for the former and the goodwill of academic staff untrained in counselling skills for the latter.'[4] The newer polytechnics are likely to provide better facilities for helping students because they are in a position to build this provision into their organizational structure at the planning stage, rather than adding it piecemeal to supplement the tutorial system, as many of the universities have had to do.

The need for student counselling

Millers has concisely summarized a number of considerations which point to a need for full time counselling services for students. He suggests that

> specially qualified people are needed for the full-time counselling of students, which is too important to leave entirely to enthusiastic amateurs, however good many of them may be. Easy accessibility to a well-qualified counsellor can enable relatively minor needs of students to be met before deterioration begins. Normal developmental processes can create problems; it is not only the ill or maladjusted who need help.

The growth of institutions of tertiary education, the increased number of young inexperienced staff and the greater diversity among school leavers themselves all point to the pressing need for counselling services. Miller uses the adult status in law of the eighteen year old as a reason for considering that *in loco parentis* is outdated, and that the pastoral role of tutors is seen by some students as implying an unacceptable paternalism. The increase in the numbers of school leavers with university qualifications, which rose from 6.9 per cent in 1961 to 10.9 per cent in 1967 and which is still gathering momentum, will result in increased pressures for the teaching staff of large institutions.

To confine the counselling role to doctors would be too expensive in terms of medical salaries to make counselling available to all the students who want it, and it is not valid to assume that physicians have the counselling skills that are required. Counselling should be available in diverse settings including careers services, health services, counselling services as well as in teaching contacts and in residential settings, as in the past. Because people are diverse no one of these settings is likely to meet the full range of student needs.

Pointing to the economic value of counselling, 'if one counsellor could prevent the wastage of only four "student years", each costing £800 to £1,200, he would be earning his keep. Similar savings of graduate salaries foregone as a result of failure or delay would benefit students as well as the tax-payer.'[5]

Areas in which students may need help

PERSONAL PROBLEMS

Adaptation
Disillusionment with and unrealized expectations of academic, social and personal aspects of college life have a demoralizing effect upon a number of first year students, and these adaptation problems may be quite difficult concerns to express to a tutor. 'How do you tell a tutor that his lectures are lousy and this college is a dump?' said one student. Well, how do you? Behind this particular student's disaffection with college life lay the fact that he did not understand the material in the lectures, he was missing his home and his friends, he did not like his accommodation and his grant cheque had not arrived.[6]

Schools can do much to help fifth and sixth formers through the process of transition from school to college and an increasing number of teachers and school counsellors are recognizing the value of this work. They are handicapped by a dearth of useful information from colleges and universities upon which boys and girls in schools may make informed choices. The typical college prospectus tells you almost nothing that you really need to know in order to be happy there, and perhaps it is unfair to expect that it should, but it does make it difficult for schools to prepare young people for the realities of student life. Student unions and to some extent student counselling services have a useful contribution to make in this area, partly because they are in closer touch with the various aspects of student life than most academic or administrative staff.

If it is recognized that adaptation to college may create stress, there is less likelihood of the demoralizing sensation of alighting from a familiar train at a station in a foreign country where nobody speaks your language, which seems to overwhelm some students on going to college.

Many students are living away from home and are in the position of being wholly responsible for their own behaviour for the first time. Their years in college provide a period in which they can begin to work through their emotional emancipation from their parents, which they must do if they are to begin to become mature and responsible people with their own sense of personal identity and system of personal values which give meaning to their lives.

Although many students adapt well to college, we should neither minimize, nor attempt to shrug off, the loneliness and utter desolation which some of them experience. The purgatorial intensity of this feeling of being abandoned often leads to all kinds of unrepresentative and sometimes rather bizarre behaviour. Students who have been apparently stable throughout their school lives become withdrawn and depressed, or become involved with a peer group whose values and actions are often morally and personally alien to those they previously held. This creates a 'double bind' for those students whose need to feel a sense of belonging to some group of people is so consuming that it leads them to behave in the group ways, which then make them feel guilty. Such students, whether they are withdrawn or acting out, may eventually reach the counsellor in a desperate attempt to find a reason to go on living, to pick up the disintegrating pieces of their lives and begin to build something worthwhile from the chaos and despair which they feel. Counsellors have no answers, no guarantees, no instant solutions, the way to meaning may be slow and painful but students have great potential for personal growth and a remarkable resilience which serve them well, if they can be helped to get in touch with their own resources through the sharing of their experience in an accepting relationship.

The search for satisfying relationships

One of the main problems of adaptation to any new situation is the search for friendship, for relationships with other people which often leads to intense emotional entanglements.

On the whole students underestimate the effects of what is popularly known as 'emotional involvement' and what I have heard aptly likened to a fly being 'involved' with a piece of flypaper. It seems that the only way in which these very dependent exclusive relationships can grow is toward painful extinction. Like the fly which can only release itself from the flypaper by leaving its legs behind, these couples appear to either tear themselves apart or to expire slowly.[4]

It is in this way that students may become emotionally mutilated by an intense need for a close involvement with another person, usually of the opposite sex, which may have less to do with real feeling for the other person than with dependency needs, or the need to be independent of parents. This need for a close relationship may arise from students' needs to prove to themselves their feminine or masculine identity or as a reaction against their normal homosexual feelings, or as part of their normal basic need to be involved with other people.

The breaking of such a close relationship and the accompanying unhappiness bring both men and women students into counselling. If they can have an opportunity to talk about the situation and to acknowledge and freely experience their emotional upheaval in the privacy of a counselling relationship they can often use the pain as a positive learning experience.

Choice of career

It may appear a strange choice to place the subject of careers counselling under the heading of 'personal problems', but it is not my intention to write at length on this specialized area of counselling and I regard the choice of a career very much as a function of personality.

Whilst there is a great deal of careers guidance in the form of information giving and careers advice for students, there are few colleges, the University of Keele being a notable exception, where the ratio of careers staff to students makes careers counselling, which requires much more time than careers guidance, anything but a Utopian fantasy. However, this is an important area of counselling and in the future it is likely that appointments officers and careers advisers will press strongly for the facilities and training which will enable them to extend their counselling function.

Developmental difficulties

Some students encounter developmental difficulties associated with late adolescence which arise mainly from the emotional, physical and intellectual needs of this particular age group. A familiar one is the

85

search for some meaning to life and the attempt to work out a set of personal values, which involves examining and perhaps replacing some of the values learned in childhood. Often linked with this is the striving for personal independence, encompassing the emotional and intellectual needs which are sometimes closely linked with economic factors. Some students seem not to have the need or opportunity to think for themselves until coming to college and they can be adept at persuading other people to do their thinking for them by giving them advice. Such students find counselling a difficult experience which makes them quite angry, an example of the fact that it is not just a cosy chat to a sympathetic ear which provides the answers to all problems, but that counselling may at times be a painful and demanding process provoking comments like 'I came here for advice, you make me think for myself and I don't like it. If I get advice I can't lose because if it's what I want to hear then it makes me feel better, and if the advice is not what I want to hear, then the person who gave it is a fool, and that makes me feel better too!' There are not many students who say it aloud in that way but I suspect that similar thoughts go through more than a few of their heads when they come face to face with something about themselves which is unacceptable.

Developmental psychologists suggest that there are emotional difficulties or disturbances characteristic of each stage of life, which are largely determined by the particular tasks that life presents at that stage. These difficulties are most effectively dealt with during the period in which they emerge, and if regarded as crises of inner growth which may be aggravated by tensions created by social conditions, they can be worked through. To deal with these emotional problems at the appropriate stage in life may prevent them from becoming chronic ailments in the future.

Emotional disturbance
A small number of students are suffering from quite serious emotional disturbances which may have a detrimental effect on their academic work, and psychiatric help from sources outside the college may be needed, but they are often able to return to complete their courses successfully after treatment.

The degree of emotional disturbance among students and the incapacity it creates vary widely, and it is tempting to divide student problems into overlapping categories. There is a large group of students who are able to handle their development through late adolescence and early adulthood using their own resources and those of people with whom they come into contact, without needing to seek specific help. At the other extreme there is a smaller group of students, estimated at about one in every ten, who will encounter emotional disturbance serious enough to give them symptoms which necessitate psychiatric help. Somewhere between these two groups in nature and size, and probably overlapping with both of them, is a group of students with problems less severe than those needing psychiatric help, which may be helped by counselling. This is a neat way of looking at students and their emotional and personal problems, but I feel that, although it has value, it is an artificial distinction, even taking into account the overlap between the three groups, because we all have unconscious feelings, thoughts and problems which vary both in their intensity, in the way in which they affect us and our behaviour and in the amount of incapacity that they cause. Students who are unable to function academically or are incapacitated socially would appear to be in need of professional help. But there are students who perform adequately or sometimes very well academically, who are nevertheless emotionally distressed and whose incapacity manifests itself in other areas of their life, such as a final year student whose marriage broke up about three or four months before finals and who was extremely depressed, yet gained a first class honours degree.

There are students who, in the experience of the counsellor, might benefit from psychiatric help, but who decline to be referred to a psychiatrist. Such students may remain in counselling, and the counsellor can work with the psychiatrist, which happens in the school situation when parents refuse a referral to the Child Guidance Clinic.

ACADEMIC PROBLEMS

Academic difficulties involving lack of organization in study habits and ineffective use of time may be a symptom of some psychological stress, or they may be a practical result of the inadequacy of schools in teaching students how best they as individuals may learn, and result from an inability to read quickly and sensibly, or to make discriminating lecture and reading notes, or they may arise from a combination of these. If the inability to study has psychological origins, it may be helped by counselling or psychotherapy which concentrates on this area of the student's life with the expectation that once the personal difficulties are resolved the academic ones, because they were symptomatic, will also be resolved. If the inability to study arises from ineffective study habits, then the counsellor may be able to help the student in a practical way by organizing together individual study patterns.

Academic pressure arising from an environment which grades people on the basis of their performance in a highly competitive situation is one of the 'occupational hazards' of being a student. The effects vary and are closely related to personality and temperament, to the student's expectations and those of significant people in his life, as well as to the actual academic standards of any particular department or college and the pressures which they exert. If a higher than average number of students from a department indicate by their self referral to the counselling service that the level of academic pressure in that department may be unrealistically high, or low, the counsellor may offer this information to the staff of that department without revealing the identity of the students.

An aspect of academic difficulty which is too frequently ignored is the quality of the teaching offered to students, who are now the only section of our population in full-time education to be taught by untrained and unqualified teachers. It is a rare but exquisite experience for a student to feel the intellectual stimulus of being lifted out of his seat by the sheer power of the spoken word during a lecture. American research[7] indicates that a *good* lecturer can expect about 40 per cent of his students to learn about 40 per cent of the material he presents in a term. The majority of lecturers assume that the reason that the percentage is not higher is a function of limited intelligence or effort on the part of the student. The research indicates that in the majority of cases the area which accounts for a greater proportion of the variance than either student intelligence or student effort is the style of delivery of the lecturer. If lecturers paid attention to the style of their presentation and thought more about their audience, they could increase the proportion of material learned and the proportion of students learning it. Many colleges claim to have the single purpose of the advancement of learning, or the development of the intellect, and this is of course enhanced and sustained by the creation of new knowledge, emanating from research. In the last analysis, learning depends on the capacity and commitment of students to learn, which are dependent upon the talent of scholars to teach.

PRACTICAL PROBLEMS

Some counselling services offer help with practical problems such as accommodation and financial difficulties, and mention has been made of the use of practical difficulties as 'presenting problems'.

Teaching, counselling and psychotherapy

In addition to the overlapping nature of some student problems, there is an overlap in the provision of help. In colleges which have a psychotherapist, teaching, counselling and psychotherapy may be seen as learning situations based on personal relationships. We are beginning to learn that even in the rarefied atmosphere of a university, the emotional climate has implications for the effectiveness of the education which is offered. One of the most important factors affecting this climate is the emotional status of teacher-student relationships. In some cases a student's capacity to accept information, and to learn it, is affected by those events and relationships which have no apparent connection with what happens during the factual presentation of a lecture or the interchange which takes place in a seminar or tutorial. Since any school or college succeeds to the extent to which it creates an atmosphere which enables students to learn, it seems reasonable to look at the teaching relationship in a personal way.

Teaching students involves learning as a cognitive activity, with little or no consideration of the 'affective' content of the relationship. The emotion is present in the teaching situation, but it is not overtly acknowledged. Particularly in the seminar or tutorial setting this learning relationship may develop into one in which feelings are acknowledged and used to facilitate learning. When this occurs, the relationship could be thought to overlap with counselling, although the content of the learning will differ.

Counselling involves a learning relationship which is both cognitive and affective; the intellect and the emotions are deliberately acknowledged and used in the learning process. The content is personal to the student, he is the 'subject' about which learning takes place. A student with emotional difficulty requiring perhaps continuous weekly counselling for a term, or more frequent sessions over a shorter period which some counsellors term brief psychotherapy, is an example of how counselling overlaps with psychotherapy.

Psychotherapy is similar to counselling in that it involves a learning relationship which emphasizes the use of the intellect to understand the emotional aspects of a student's life, but it often seems to be more intensive and interpretative than counselling and may seek to invoke personality change through the use of the unconscious and childhood experiences, though this depends upon the theoretical orientation of the therapist.

Thus there is some overlap between teaching and counselling and between counselling and psychotherapy, and possibly between some teaching and psychotherapy. The majority of students do not need psychotherapy and many do not need counselling. If the resources of a college provide helping relationships which may be illustrated thus:

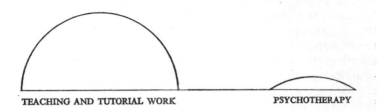

TEACHING AND TUTORIAL WORK   PSYCHOTHERAPY

the personal difficulties of some students are likely to go unaided. Perhaps a more comprehensive provision to aim for would be this:

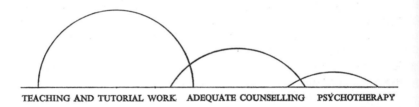

TEACHING AND TUTORIAL WORK   ADEQUATE COUNSELLING   PSYCHOTHERAPY

Some teachers and lecturers regard counselling with students as an isolated service which has no bearing on the teaching function of the college. If we consider that a counsellor may be the first adult representative of the college with whom a student has an opportunity to talk at length, together with the emphasis on counselling as a learning situation, it seems unwise to disregard the possibility that counselling may provide motivation for academic learning.

Working with others who work with students

A school counsellor is one member of a guidance team, and in addition to her counselling function she works with parents, other staff and also with the staff of social agencies outside the school. A student counsellor is primarily concerned with counselling either individually, in groups or both. In school and college the fundamental task of the counsellor is to counsel, but there are other guidance activities which encourage a healthier emotional climate within a college which can prove both therapeutic and preventive.

One of these areas of concern for a counsellor is that of disciplinary procedures. A school counsellor is not part of the disciplinary structure of the school and a student counsellor does not take part in the administration of discipline in a college, but in both situations the philosophy which underlies the discipline and the way it is implemented may well be the concern of the counsellor. Students' relationships to authority have been aptly called the 'battleline of adolescence' and it has become apparent recently that the imposition of punitive or arbitrary restrictions upon or the adoption of censorious attitudes towards individual students or the student body are likely to provoke a reaction of rebellion and hostility. Children and students react more positively in a situation in which they can maintain or enhance their self-respect. This is not intended to imply that students are always 'right'; they are not: they have this in common with us all; nor is it intended to imply that students should be permitted to behave exactly as they please without regard for the consequences of their behaviour both for themselves and for others. It does imply that if we behave towards people in a way which undermines their self-respect we should not be surprised when they react unfavourably to the pain we thus cause them. This is a lesson for students and staff alike.

CONFIDENTIALITY

The confidentiality observed by the counselling service is as important to some students as it is irksome to some academic staff. Sometimes confidentiality may work against the interests of a student and this is the criticism of some academic staff against counselling and student health services, because some tutors think, occasionally justifiably, that they could help if they knew the details of the problem. Nevertheless there are students who welcome the opportunity to talk through a problem, in confidence, on 'neutral ground' with someone who is not connected in any way with their academic progress and assessment, which is what a counselling service provides. If a counsellor sets out to offer a confidential service, then anything a student might say must be in confidence. Individual counsellors vary in the limits to which they can maintain confidentiality on information which they feel might threaten their own values, or the good of the college, other students or society, and this ethical aspect of counselling is one which prospective as well as practising counsellors need to think about very carefully. There is a practical and personal safety aspect in which I personally would not be prepared to maintain complete confidentiality.

91

I am not prepared to maintain confidentiality in a situation where there may be danger to life, such as would occur from the planting of a bomb. I would, however, talk to the student about what I would do and why. Other counsellors may react differently in a similar situation. I once saw a distressed student who threatened suicide and then rushed from the room. I could not retain this information knowing that the student had recently consulted the Student Health Service for sleeping tablets. I decided to talk to the psychiatrist who had prescribed the sleeping tablets, but I did so for my own benefit, as much as for that of the student. I have counselled other students who have talked of suicide and have maintained confidentiality, but in this particular case, I made a professional judgment to break it, after careful thought.

This illustrates another problem of the counsellor, namely that of support, sometimes put as the question 'who counsels the counsellor?' which will be raised later.

CENTRALIZATION OF STUDENT SERVICES

The counselling service in which I work is independent of other sources of help for students such as the Student Health Service, the Careers Adviser, the Students' Union, and the administrative and academic departments of the College. This independence is geographical as well as actual, since the service is housed in a temporary building together with some research scientists. To be seen to be separate is helpful but as students become more accustomed to the idea of having available non-academic staff whose job it is to provide help of various kinds, it may be more feasible to concentrate these services in a central area, which would make them more easily accessible to students and would facilitate professional liaison between them, bearing in mind that such an arrangement might raise questions about confidentiality in the minds of some students.

> I think the thing that excited me most of all in America, when I was there, was to see Kansas State University, where all the student services, with the exception of health, have been merged into one great centre and it is no longer known as the welfare place, it is called the Centre for Student Development. The whole notion of this centre is that it is a large building with all kinds of resource people inside it—psychiatrists, counsellors, appointments officers, a nurse, an orientation officer, a campus information centre. In other words, it is a great big supermarket of places where the students can get help. . . . It has diffused the pathological element in these helping services by making it

a place where any student could walk in, and as far as I can see, the students there are delighted.[8]

Another important part of the counsellor's work is liaison between the counselling service and the academic and administrative staff of the college. The task of working towards staff acceptance of a counselling service is delicate.

> There has been for a very long time, and there still is in some areas of universities, an attitude that there ought not to be within their walls problems of a kind which are incapable of solution by the investment of intellectual ability. If such problems dare to occur then they should be tackled by the assumption of a stiff upper lip, a kick in the pants or a stiff dose of academic sherry.[9]

Some tutors think that because of their traditional pastoral care, or moral tutor role, students should seek help from them whatever problems they might have, that tutorial services are quite adequate if only students would use them, and that it is an unnecessary expense to provide counselling services. Others concede that perhaps students with personal problems may be helped by seeing a counsellor, but that other problems, particularly those of an academic nature, should be taken to a tutor.

There seem to be several reasons why some students prefer to talk to a counsellor. One is the nature of the problem; the student who came in, and before he had even sat down blurted out 'I've got a sex problem', clearly had felt that this was not something that he could take to his tutor, yet it caused him concern which could have affected his academic work and may already have done so. Another reason may be the tutor's role as teacher and all that this implies to some students, especially those who are sceptical of a teacher's ability or his wish to separate his teaching/assessing role from his work as a personal tutor. As one student succinctly said: 'It doesn't matter what I say to you because you have no power.'

Perhaps a third reason why a student may prefer to talk to a counsellor rather than to a tutor may be when the conflict between the values of the college, as represented in the student's eyes by its academic staff, and the values of the student reaches deadlock. Conflict in these values can often be productive, but in some cases resolution is difficult because of differences in perception. Generally the values of the college are best served if a student is encouraged to choose the long term goal of a degree, certificate or diploma, rather than the short-term goal of recognizing the importance of his own feelings and perceptions of reality and his right to express these in his own terms. The student's dilemma comes in assessing the consequences of choosing the short term goal or making a compromise and choosing the long term goal. There is current concern about the number of students who discontinue or fail their courses. Some students find that they have chosen the wrong course, others struggle to achieve an academic standard which they feel is beyond their capacity or find themselves in a course which does not make sufficient demands on their abilities, while some students seem to be searching for identity before success. Failure is still too often regarded as a major disgrace rather than a minor set-back, and while it may not be economically sound for a student to 'drop out' of college, that does not necessarily make it irresponsible, in some instances it is more beneficial for the student and for society that he should choose something else.[6]

There is a real need for agencies like the Educational Redeployment Service set up by Dr Nicolas Malleson in London (see Appendix 7) and the Student Progress Office run by Mrs Jean Mackintosh at the University of Aberdeen, which make available counselling help together with a wide range of information on a variety of courses for students who discontinue their studies.

Students' experiences of counselling

The effectiveness of any counselling relationship varies according to the circumstances, the nature of the difficulty and the personalities and life styles of the people involved. Counsellors should ask questions of themselves and of the students they counsel about the helpfulness of the relationship. The following contributions from students are of necessity anonymous, and present differing reactions to the counselling experience ranging from the very positive to the negative.

The first piece of writing offers a vivid description of the kind of turmoil and searching which some students undergo in their attempt to give meaning to their lives and illustrates how deep and intensive this search can be. It is unrepresentative in the sense that it is written by a particularly imaginative student, but it shows a counselling relationship from a student's point of view. My approach to counselling, although basically Rogerian, is eclectic in that I use whatever behaviour seems ethical and appropriate. In this particular relationship, I moved out of the counselling setting into the social world of the student. This is not something I usually do, and it is not generally considered to be acceptable behaviour according to the tenets of some theories of counselling and psychotherapy, but it seemed helpful to both of us.

MY EXPERIENCE OF COUNSELLING

I had always been wary of psychologists or psychiatrists and preferred my own versions of dealing with my inner mind and problems. I had experienced an intensive inner life from first adolescence of conflict and anxiety, but had always dealt with it in my own way. The problems were about my parents and family, and my own relations to boyfriends and of adjusting my own personality to the world of people, of ethical ideas, and of goals and situations that had to be dealt with. I had evolved over the years a very elaborate system of secret values, almost a code with terms of private reference, for giving order and direction to the things that troubled me.

A crisis came when I was about 26 and a postgraduate student: I was suddenly frantic for help, and ran forcing back tears to the college's Student Health Centre. I began to pour out my problems to the doctor there; he interrupted me, and sent me to the Student Counsellor in her office nearby. Crying, I ran over to see her, and crying sat in the office. The secretary let me in to her room and not stopping crying I began to pour out my deepest anxieties—hardly hoping for comprehension in my listener, and enough aware of the external situation to be apprehensive. But I was in great crisis: it was an absolute appeal for help.

She responded briefly and quietly, but almost at once I found myself uttering fervently, 'Thank God, you *are* understanding.' My fear had always been that no-one would ever be able to understand the terms of my deepest troubles, and in fact I was very lucky that at this time of most pressing need to unburden my mind at last, I had actually found my way or been directed to someone who was understanding.

My audience was someone of rare sensitivity and wisdom. During the months that followed, my former secrecy, pent up from years of complex and intensive self-absorption and mastery of self, was gradually eased, aired, and brought into the open community of human converse. It was as if she reached her hand into my troubled mind and helped me to sort out its strands. This idea was very much present to me: the strong, tactile presence of a hand, guiding the anxious *mêlée* of the contents inside my skull.

This period of intensive counselling began as two sessions a week and lasted that way for several months. I was able to believe in them and bring my most honest and deepest ideas and troubles to the open and to her, because I was able to believe in her ability to understand and her wisdom. Otherwise I would not have been able to enter the counselling relationship and it wouldn't have worked. As it was, I was able to speak myself out; to speak to another human being as I had never spoken of things that are beyond the range of normal communication even with one's most intimate friends. This was a special and an artificial relationship; not so much between two people, as between a soul and a mentor. I had always searched and longed for a mentor. When I found one I was ready and knew what to do with her. The terrible privacy was dispelled.

The strain of these sessions demanded from her what no ordinary person in a normal life situation could give. They were conducted in utmost tension. Every gesture or muscular move, every glance, that either of us made, seemed crucial to me: it was the intense earnest of someone at confession battling for solutions and real answers to be able to go on living. At this period I was in fact severely dislocated in myself. I had violent waking nightmares of resentment I had never dared to formulate, and other disturbing images from the past. In my own introspections over these things I had never been able to face them as I was forced to face them now because they rose to the surface and forced themselves on me. I woke up one night from a dream of such matters and wrote a very long letter to her, confident that she would read it and respond to it, about the anxieties of my life. It was like talking to a superhuman friend. During this whole time together with my distress I had a sense of special privilege, of lordly importance and privilege, of being indulged and of drawing on someone else's living fibre to be so indulged and sustained. I was abashed at being so greedy and ruthless in my use of her to help me; but I needed the help and took it without too much compunction. I would go to the meetings with a sure sense of being drawn toward help, and leave them trembling for half an hour afterward, exhausted, emptied, and fearful, but sure in my dependence on her.

The dependence was real because it was a period of decisive change in myself. However complex and peculiar to myself its elements were, it was no more than a necessary surge of growth in myself out of what I had been and into what I must become:

a further and more mature stage of being myself. It seemed to me like a time of great peril in the terms of the mind but a time of peril that could be traversed because I had the support of her counselling and knowledge of me and my progress. I had often been depressed but never so really in trouble and frightened and at this time the counsellor was able to know me as no-one on earth knew me. Without this intimacy and support I do not know what would have happened to me. It was so significant or essential a step in my life to have had this period of dislocation supported by counselling that I can't imagine having gone through any alternative to it as I look back on it now. If this crisis in me had not been met, presumably it would not have developed into the large scale and intensive period of chaos, gradual relief of lifelong tension, and transition to a more peaceful state of mind. I was lucky to have the opportunity to have it all out at once in that way. Certainly the problems that were raised then and eased if only by raising them would not have gone away by themselves; and I had come to the point myself of being no longer able to deal with them; I had had 'a deadline'.

Gradually our sessions became less intense as the first revelation of the problems eased and I was able to become more relaxed and rational in looking them over. I remember the time when I was able to think, and say—'but after all, you can't help me about *everything*—life is hard; there's nothing you can do about that'. I think this must have been the point of strength returning to me, and ability to go on living on my own again without any further prolonging of my sharing out the responsibility for my very existence with her.

At this point I am not clear about the details of what we dealt with together. I remained shaky and nervous for some time after that main counselling time, and kept seeing the counsellor irregularly. There was hardly any immediate happy ending, or conscious grasp of the solutions for my problems or even an emotional enlightenment of greater balance or orientation in life resulting from the counselling. But these things have begun to come now because of taking steps to improve the actual conditions of my life to effect solutions for myself. At the time of my counselling sessions with her I was unable to do this for myself or even to continue as I was with any equilibrium at all. So I think that the experience was that she was there when I was in crisis and helped me to have the crisis and get through it, so that I could go on from there. This was a moment of human help in need: not a revelation of solutions to existence. But the quality of the help was both steadying in its great, calm sense, and consoling as I needed to be consoled then in order to have faith in life and people. In fact, it was an emergence from solitude, and a highly developed sense of isolation, into the world of living among people. The counsellor's understanding proved to me that the facts contained in my privacy were not abhorrent, or alien, or impossible in the terms of this world. For a highly strung and extremely intellectual and introspective person, it seems to me that this is an experience which can happen once in life, and make all the difference in this life. Otherwise the tensions and unbroken mental solitude would dominate and torment the personality more and more through life; but without the special and artificial situation of dealing with a trained and specially gifted counsellor there would be no outlet available for their relief. Without the one time, the first time, of such relief, I do not see how a person troubled as I was by these things could go on to grow.

Very strong in this experience was my counsellor's sense of care. As the intensive sessions wore off she responded to my need to experiment *with her* as a friend and a person to know; I felt that I was taking too much from her and giving nothing back, and she simply agreed at that point to become less superhuman in her role toward me and to take up the role of a friend. We arranged some outings and she told me some things about herself, and we talked about other things besides my problems. But even in this she was gently reminding me about the fact that I did, still, have problems to deal with; she asked if I was thinking about them, and said, 'You should'. The delicacy with which she could relate to me in the ordinary terms of friendship made a transition for me—and perhaps for her too —away from the over-wrought and strained terms of the period of counselling with its stark confession and appeal from me. This transition was back into the more relaxed ways of normal living and human relationship: after a period in which my upheaval of mind had made everything uncertain to me except her voice as a counsellor.

There is an excellence in this experience which remains a significant emotional fact to me. The disinterested and objective care of another human being at this depth of life—when it is as honest and fine, as inspired, as this was—is not only consoling and healing and helpful at the time it is given but it remains as a basis for faith and ease, confidence and relaxation about life.

This kind of counselling is surely a modern form of the ancient wisdom of providing elders or guides in the community who teach and guide people toward the love and communion that they need.

Briefer comments from students offer a different picture, as the following extracts show:

> Yesterday
> I learned how to live for today
> with an eye to tomorrow,
> And the next days . . .
> For tomorrow is important
> today
> And yesterday adds up to experience
> Which is useful
> today and tomorrow.

This is my own story. It may not be typical, but it may be useful as illustrating a point.

My grant had run out, but my work was not finished, I was living (just) on my savings. I could not apply to my parents, although they would have helped, because they are very poor themselves. I had applied for literally a score of jobs and got nowhere, not even an interview. This had been going on for several months.

I now think, looking back, that I was in a state of depression in the medical sense, but I did not realize it at the time. I was sort of numb, and had no initiative left. This is my point. I was no longer looking for jobs because *I could not*. Had the Student Counselling Service been merely an extension of the Careers Office, I should probably still be in that state now, but you found me a job in the library. The fact that this was only two evenings per week, and that I would receive no money until the end of term was quite irrelevant. Once I had that job, I bucked up enough to choose a different career; I wrote letters of application, and I got a job!

My whole point is this: one minute piece of practical help is worth hours of advice and instruction to somebody in my state then. I *could* not act on advice and instruction, however good; if you had told me to go and *ask* for a job in the library I probably wouldn't have done it. I desperately needed someone to present me with something on a plate, and although I suppose that morally this is a bad thing to the 'pull yourself together' school of thought, it did restore my self-confidence or whatever it was, enough to take up the cudgels myself.

When I first saw [the counsellor] she appeared to be a very understanding person, I would say very helpful to most people with typical student problems. However, my problem was not so, and she voiced her own opinion on the moral aspect of my problem, which differed somewhat to my own. After establishing this difference, I realized I could obtain no further help and so had to sort it out myself.

When I first consulted the counsellor I was a first year student with strong feelings of inadequacy and failure to tackle my personal problems. The counsellor seemed to accept these feelings as correct, i.e. our conversation was directed towards how I could be less inadequate, etc. I now think that my problems were very largely the result of external factors beyond my control, e.g. I was being exploited sexually and emotionally in a fairly commonplace way. I do think the counsellor could help a lot of people by suggesting that their difficulties are not of their own making, and perhaps imbue them with a little therapeutic indignation. Then a few very real evils might be changed.

I found the Student Counsellor to be a pleasant, understanding and humane individual. She was easy to talk to and managed to make me verbalize my thoughts. When advice was needed as to the proper course of action she seemed to have the necessary information within her reach. Nothing more could have been asked for and although it sounds as though I'm describing a product I will say nevertheless that I was completely satisfied.

The essence of counselling should be to listen and guide people to face things themselves, not to tell them, as so often happens at school, or with parents, what to do. I am very grateful for the help I received . . . and now I know myself, as far as one can, and hence can cope adequately without now feeling the need for counselling aid. Keep up the good work.

Finally a view of counselling, not from a student but from a counsellor educator.

Counseling is not helping a person either to adjust to society or to fight it. It is helping him to come to see who he really is, what he has and does not have; what he can do easily, what he can do with difficulty and what he probably cannot do at all. . . . [It] is a close sharing of a human relationship with one who has for him a high regard; one who can offer him unconditional acceptance, but one who has no guarantees, no answers; one who can help him to see freedom, but freedom with risk; one who can help him to come to see that freedom and self-integrity are the same thing, that they are within the grasp of each of us and that we are the ones to determine whether we wish to hold them tightly or to let them fall.[10]

The pattern of higher and further education in Britain has changed in some ways quite markedly during the past decade and I would predict that the provision of effective and adequate student counselling services is one of the challenges facing British higher education during the coming decade. The opportunity to provide these is within our grasp. It remains to be seen whether we wish to use it or to let it fall.

6

Philosophical and social implications for the work of the counsellor

Philosophical bases for counselling

> When life does not find a singer to sing her heart, she produces a philosopher to speak her mind.[1]

A philosophical basis for counselling involves asking the question why we do counselling, and perhaps this has priority over the question of how we do counselling. Thus I have chosen to write about the philosophical rationale for what one does as a counsellor —the why of counselling—before discussing the theory and practice —the how of counselling, although to some extent the two overlap and the philosophy involves some discussion of the theory.

The ways in which people behave, think and feel is the province of psychology, but why they behave as they do, the meaning of man's behaviour and the meaning, purpose and value of man's existence, involve the use of philosophical constructs. We can relate the aims, the processes and the criteria for evaluation which we use in counselling theory and practice to philosophical assumptions.

The philosophical influences affecting the various approaches to counselling are of sufficient importance to be studied in greater detail. All that I shall attempt to do is provide an outline of several positions as an introduction.

Every counsellor needs a set of philosophical beliefs which form a basic and integral part of the counselling relationship and give direction to her counselling. These are based on what she believes about the nature of man, the universe, reality and being and the philosophical enquiry in which she marshals evidence to support such contentions results in values of importance and worth, which may lead her to direct the means of counselling towards the vision of ends which those philosophical deliberations reveal.

It is possible that a counsellor may find that a particular theory of counselling assumes something that she does not believe, and this disbelief will have consequences for her counselling. Thus the first questions for the counsellor concern personal beliefs and values which then lead to the search for ways of implementing those beliefs in a counselling setting.

ENVIRONMENTALIST AND HUMANIST PHILOSOPHIES

The point of view in which philosophy precedes theory is open to argument, since the founders of most of the schools of counselling developed their theories without any direct relationship to the formal philosophical ideas and labels by which I shall represent them. Freud, who for the purposes of this chapter is classified in philosophical terms as an environmentalist, because of his leanings to scientific determinism, put forward his own view about the influence of the thinking of philosophers upon his work when he said:

> The large extent to which psychoanalysis coincides with the philosophy of Schopenhauer—not only did he assert the dominance of the emotions and the supreme importance of sexuality but he was even aware of the mechanisms of repression —is not to be traced to my acquaintance with his teaching. I read Schopenhauer very late in my life. Nietzsche, another philosopher whose guesses and intuitions often agree in the most astonishing way with the laborious findings of psychoanalysis, was for a long time avoided by me on that very account; I was less concerned with the question of priority than with keeping my mind unembarrassed.[2]

B. F. Skinner's methodology of experimental behaviourism can be aligned with the philosophical position of logical positivism, but he disavows any such relationship. Similarly Carl Rogers, who for the purposes of this chapter is classified in philosophical terms as a humanist, developed his theory of client-centred counselling without reference to the formal philosophical ideas of phenomenology and existentialism, although he has been rather scathingly referred to by some empirical psychologists as 'nothing but a philosopher'. However his work has undoubtedly drawn attention to the relationship of counselling to philosophy.

Barclay[3] suggests two classifications, environmentalist and humanist, which provide a broad basis upon which to develop philosophical approaches to counselling. The environmentalist approach is largely object oriented, and the counsellor is concerned with bringing the person into better conformity with the forces of external reality.

In practical terms, a counsellor working from this environmentalist philosophical position might use a realist, problem-solving or a behavioural approach and may try to change students' attitudes in the direction of more conformity to school values such as wearing school uniform or studying hard. Such a counsellor might believe that the main difficulties of students arose because their learned patterns of behaviour were maladaptive when considered in relation to the values of the school. This resistant behaviour would have been learned because of wrong reinforcement in the past, and the purpose of counselling would be to change behaviour through operant conditioning and manipulation of the environment.

The humanist approach is subject oriented and the counsellor is concerned with the internal phenomena of the person. In practice the humanist counsellor may work from a client-centred approach in which she is concerned with the student as a unique individual whose problems arise from the fact that he has been unable to integrate his feelings about other people, school and reality, and this relates to his poor self-concept. The emphasis is on the counselling process and the chief concern is to help the student to come to terms with reality, to recognize the need for communication through an inter-personal relationship characterized by emotional dialogue in an accepting, non-threatening atmosphere. Such a counsellor is not aiming to improve the student's attitude to school (though this may be a by-product). She is not trying to probe into the inner dynamics of the student's past life, nor is she attempting to help the student to adopt new patterns of behaviour through learning theory.

The philosophy discussed in this chapter has an American orientation because counselling and psychotherapy have been related to philosophical thinking and are more widely accepted as part of American culture than is the case here. Until recently the counselling and psychotherapy carried out in this country have been based largely on Freudian theories of psychoanalysis or on Jungian analytic psychology, which seem to have had little influence on the study of philosophy.

These two major philosophical positions, environmentalistic and humanistic, often differ quite substantially in terms of their goals, their methods and their criteria of evaluation.

Environmentalism specifies goals which are oriented to a correspondence between an individual and his society which is the least handicapping and leads to the clarification of individual problems. It stresses cultural norms and scientific reality.

The humanist approach specifies goals which are oriented towards self-understanding and self-acceptance and the clarification and establishment of a wholesome self-concept. It stresses individual understanding and subjective reality.

Agreement on the need for valid criteria of counselling would be a factor uniting all the theoretical positions in counselling; where they disagree is in how to determine the nature of the criteria and the dimensions within which they should operate. If counselling makes any difference in a person's life, this should be shown in more effective and adequate human behaviour which can be used as evidence. Behaviourists might use test information, statistical inference and scientific research designed essentially with reference to an external or cultural criterion of assessment. Humanists are more likely to use measurement theory and statistical analysis or a method of self-report by the person receiving counselling, together with an evaluation of the counselling and perhaps an evaluation by the counsellor.[3]

Origins
Environmentalism and humanism have their historical roots in the traditional psychoanalytic thought of Freud or rather in his theory of personality, which in simple terms, put forward a model of human behaviour in which sexual repression and neuroses had to be transformed to conform with acceptable social behaviour. Freud, the scientist, was interested in how the individual could learn to live effectively in his society. He says of the application of psychoanalytic knowledge to education, 'I myself have contributed nothing to the application of analysis to education It was natural, however, that the analytical discoveries as to the sexual life and mental development of children should attract the attention of educators and make them see their problems in a new light. . . .'[2] Freud goes on to talk of the application of analysis to the prophylactic education of healthy children and to the correcting of those who, though not actually neurotic, have deviated from the normal course of development.

Knowledge, reality and values
Although humanist and environmentalist counsellors may use some similar practical ways, there is a dichotomy in their thinking between the subject and the object of knowledge. For the environmentalist, counselling is a means of bringing about the best congruence between an individual and his culture and offers the clearest perception of how that person may most effectively operate in his environment by using learning procedures to shape and mould his behaviour, so that it comes as close as possible to the criterion of effectiveness set up. Though many environmentalists do not deny the inner world of subjectivity, they believe that it is incapable of being evaluated by the scientific method.

The humanists, whilst generally not denying the validity of science or the reality of the environment, nevertheless believe that a person should move towards some social criterion through his own purposeful action rather than through the moulding or shaping of the behaviourists. Effective human behaviour for them occurs through an understanding of the individual and his subjective experience and the development of an individual approach to cultural problems of identity and meaning.

Knowledge. Scientific realism is one of the philosophical bases of behaviourism and may be related to the behaviour learning therapy of Eysenck in this country and Wolpe in America, and the directive counselling of Williamson.

Experimentalism, which has a distinctly American derivation and has been identified with the philosophy of John Dewey, places great emphasis on pragmatic utility, weighing philosophy against the criterion of social experience and placing knowledge, reality and values in a subordinate role. It is an antecedent of the behavioural engineering approach to counselling represented by Krumboltz, Michael and Meyerson.

One of the philosophical positions which underlies the humanistic approach is phenomenology, conceived originally by Brentano and later developed by Husserl, which emphasizes the world of subjective phenomena and facts and is characterized by the method of description and comparison. The approaches of Rogers, Patterson and the neo-Freudians, such as Sullivan, offer examples of a phenomenological philosophical basis to counselling and psychotherapy.

Briefly, the environmentalist approach relies heavily on scientific method and on the correspondence theory of knowledge in which the subjective world of individual experience can correspond to the objective world of reality and the truth of any idea is determined by its correspondence with objective facts and laws. The humanists on the other hand would argue that the problems of the subjective world are not always amenable to solution by the scientific problem-solving method because they are not always available to conscious verbalization.[4]

A bright sixth former who has done well at O level, takes part in the extra-curricular activities of the school, and seems socially well-adjusted, is referred to the counsellor because she wants to leave school to work in a shop and the staff feel that she is obviously 'university material'. The counsellor working from a behavioural philosophical standpoint might listen, look at her abilities, present alternatives and conclude that the intelligent and sensible thing for her to do would be to continue in school, because all the available information suggests that this is the rational choice. This is what she 'ought' to do and it will be justified by the success she will experience. When after several interviews the sixth former still insists that she wants to leave school to work in a shop, it might be assumed that the counsellor had failed to achieve the school's objective, which was to influence the sixth former to remain in education. The counsellor working from a humanist philosophical stance might suggest that the behaviourist had failed to take into account the subjective aspect of the problem, she knows about the sixth former but does not know her as a person and perhaps she has not acknowledged that people have the capacity to feel on a non-cognitive level the truth of certain experiences. A humanist counsellor would not necessarily accept the school's objective for the sixth former as a valid personal objective for her and might also feel that the search for a personal identity is a more common problem in counselling than the behaviourists care to acknowledge.

Reality. The humanistic view is that perception is reality and what we perceive is real, whereas for the environmentalist reality is something which exists outside of human knowing or perception.

Values. The environmentalist would argue that moral issues must be considered in the context of the social setting in which they arise.

The humanist philosopher is likely to place a higher value on the intuitive aspect of moral insights and universal laws of nature.

> Humanism has as one of its strengths a recognition of the subjective nature of man, his internal states, feelings and concerns. Its preoccupation with the individual as an individual makes counselling a highly personal kind of encounter that focuses on the individual communication or transaction that takes place between counsellor and client. In a very real sense, this kind of counselling process reveals a kind of mystical relationship that in its highest form, approaches a spiritual and charismatic quality. This meets one of man's greatest human needs, the need for communication—and for reassurance and forgiveness. Whether we like the concept or not, counselors often function in the role of a priest. They mediate on the conscious level, and whether or not they recognise their conciliatory role, they often deal with guilt, anxiety and fears that need psychologically to be forgiven. . . .[3]

The behavioural environmentalist approach is particularly useful in coping with specific needs and in particular in answering questions such as 'What constitutes effective learning behaviour in a classroom, or in a social setting?' or 'How may ineffective behaviour be changed?' Several aspects of learning theory such as reinforcement, shaping and modelling are used by a variety of people in education to produce behaviour which meets certain values, and behavioural counselling can be a means of identifying criteria and specifying techniques for achieving these.

It is inappropriate to imagine that we can import the American system of counselling in education to our own peculiar culture, and possibly just as inappropriate to imagine that we can be entirely successful in building a philosophy of counselling on the same framework. Perhaps what is needed is a philosophical approach to counselling which is more indigenous. Existentialism, with its European origins may offer a basis. It has done so in the U.S.A. The field of philosophical analysis may help us to describe, explain and justify our thinking about our development of counselling in education.

Philosophical analysis
Philosophical analysis is concerned with the use and function of language and suggests that philosophical problems are at least in part linguistic problems; in so far as these problems are capable of solution it is through some sort of clarification of language.

Positivists think that philosophical analysis is not a process which provides answers to philosophical problems but rather that it is a preliminary process in which the philosopher must first analyse the question in order to discover what it means and thus to discover how one would go about answering it. Such philosophy

> makes no claim about the world—it merely attempts to unravel those perplexities of everyday life and science which bother people and which people cannot sensibly answer without first discovering what sort of an answer would be relevant. In so far, then, as philosophy solves puzzles and clears heads, its function is therapeutic. Those who advocate the use of philosophy for such purposes have often been described as 'therapeutic positivists'.[5]

The ordinary language school of philosophy, instead of trying to define the meaning of terms through the method of analysis, suggested that 'the function of the philosopher was to indicate the significance of these terms by showing how they are in fact used'.[5] Wittgenstein characterized this activity when he said, 'Don't ask for the meaning, ask for the use.'

The ordinary language philosophers believe that certain problems can be solved by philosophy itself, thus going one step further than the positivists, who felt that once philosophy had clarified the questions involved in a problem they could then be better answered by other disciplines. The activities of ordinary language philosophy give knowledge of the use of certain concepts in everyday life and since they use everyday language they can be used to help us to become clearer about the nature of the concepts of education and of counselling.

Philosophy and education
The relationship of philosophy to education is a complex one which is characterized by an attitude of informed scepticism in a systematic form in which one is sceptical, suspending judgment or final conclusion, but in this process of suspension searching for all available information to enable one to arrive at a conclusion. Philosophy provides one method for studying, clarifying and seeking solutions for educational problems, psychology and sociology are other methods for doing the same thing. It is a method seeking to get beyond the surface phenomena. Why did the teacher behave that way? What are the assumptions behind the curriculum? Philosophy offers a way of analysing ethical problems, problems of behaviour, problems which ask the question 'Why?' 'The relationship of the guidance aspects of education to philosophy is a fundamental one, though philosophical issues tend to be underestimated in an age dominated by admiration for technology.'[6]

In turn philosophy benefits from education because people interacting in education generate problems and education holds in high relief basic problems of philosophy such as: What is real? What is ethical? What is knowledge? However, the relationship between philosophy and education is not just one of systematically working through a life philosophy and trying to implement it in an educational setting.

A detailed analysis of the relationship between philosophy, counselling and education would be worth pursuing. Perhaps others will undertake the philosophical analysis which the development of this tripartite relationship requires.

Tyler suggests that '... the very fact that he witnesses the resolution of such difficulties and the working out of strong satisfying patterns of faith and conduct makes the counsellor less pessimistic than many writers and thinkers are about the chaos in our values and a lack of unifying philosophy. He knows that human individuals have the capacity to face confusion and organise it in meaningful ways.'[7]

109

Some social and sociological implications of the work of the counsellor

'Unless our society sees fit to create a new institution devoted exclusively to the exploration and amelioration of social conflict, the school will not be free to pursue academic ends without first unravelling the strands of disorganisation which inhibit its task.'[8]

The counsellor in education is often considered as a person who works predominantly with individual students or children, and teachers faced with large classes may look enviously over their shoulders as the counsellor goes off to his one-to-one interview while they battle on with Form 4C, or go to lecture to 200 students.

While it is true that much of a counsellor's time will be spent with individuals, there is an increasing recognition of the value of group guidance and of group counselling, both as valid endeavours in their own right and as a supplement to individual counselling. Sociology seeks to provide organized knowledge about group life in society generally and particularly about group life and individual roles in the institutions of our society.

To relate this to education, it is unrealistic to discuss home/school liaison simply in the context of providing more educational opportunity through the meeting of certain needs or the removal of certain handicaps for individual children. Although these aspects are important, this liaison embraces one of 'the most fundamental relationships in society, that between the primary socialising agency of the family and the inducting agency of the school . . . a context within which the occupational roles are assumed and social character built up'.[9] In many ways the interests of the individual child, his family, teacher, school and the state coincide, there are also many ways in which there will be conflict between what each believes is the best action to take in a particular situation, and it will not always be possible for the various parties to agree, however good the links between home, school and community.

Historically, socially and psychologically one of the school's functions is to emancipate children from their parents in the sense of preparing them for their adult role in society. The roles of teacher and parent differ in this enterprise, the teacher's function being mainly objective and the parent's largely subjective with a corresponding difference in the criteria against which situations are judged. Taylor illustrates the problem of conflicting criteria by describing a situation in which a teacher is talking to a parent in the classroom when a fire breaks out. If there were time to save only one child, the parent would have no difficulty in deciding that it should be hers, but the teacher would have no relevant criterion by which to select one child rather than another. Whilst supporting the liaison work of linking home and school we need to acknowledge the differences in role, expectations and criteria, because this may help us to tolerate the failure of some of our efforts and to remind us that 'a technique that does not have its roots in an adequate theory is, in the long run, unlikely to be either helpful or enduring'.[9] It is unfortunate that the fields of education and sociology have been too infrequently related. The sociology of education would seem a relevant study for prospective teachers, and it is encouraging that courses in this particular area are increasingly being offered in teacher training. It is rarely a strong foundation in the subject that is offered, but, like this chapter, an introduction to the field. It would be slightly ironical but not untypical if the problems of adolescence and the administrative problems caused by student unrest were to be the factors which encourage educators to begin to take account of the social forces which contribute to both these areas. The tendency is for counsellors to rely on psychological information to explain student problems, but sociology has a demonstrable contribution to make toward a more complete understanding of individual student problems, and behaviour which may seem to be highly idiosyncratic and based on the unique psychological make-up of individuals can have a valid sociological interpretation. The competitive ethos of education may well provide the motivation which it is used to accomplish, but its unintended, or perhaps in some cases intended, consequences for those who do not succeed in a competitive environment may be highly detrimental. Social class or social position is a social psychological reality having important consequences for attitudes and behaviour in that religious attitudes, racial acceptance, attitudes toward sex, aspirations and some forms of delinquent or deviant behaviour may be related to social position.

The notion that sociological concepts possessed the potentiality through which we might explain the source of some individual problems was greatly enhanced by the French sociologist Emile Durkheim in his book, *Suicide*. Several of his followers put forward and tested the theories that individual acts are linked to and can be explained by cultural or social facts. By comparing the thought processes of primitive and civilized peoples, Levy-Bruhl developed his system of attaching social meanings to individual acts. This was extended by Blondel, who analysed the way in which human feelings were attached to social life, and Halbwachs showed how the structure of group life influences those selective perceptions that evolve as memory.[10] More recent work of this kind is illustrated by the intensive analysis of Leighton who investigated how the mental

111

health of members of a community was related to the community organization.[11]

ROLES AND CONFLICT

Role expectations and role conflict are two areas of sociological analysis which have an important bearing on the work of the counsellor. Role expectations occur, for example, in considering the role of the student in relation to the complex network of expectations and demands of his home, his school or college and his peer group. Role expectations also occur in considering the role of the counsellor in relation to the network of allegiances expected by students, administrators, parents, teachers, tutors and the counsellor herself. Role conflict is generated for the student perhaps when the formal demands of his school are incompatible with the demands of his peer group, or his home. When two or more of these sets of expectations come into conflict a choice must be made and a counsellor may be able to help some students to accommodate the expectations of both the school and the peer group if she has some understanding of the social structure which helps to produce that conflict.

I once counselled a student who told me that he came from a working class home and a secondary modern school and was finding it very difficult to 'settle down'. He was a Londoner and was living at home, but not finding it easy to work because his dad liked to watch television in the evenings and he felt that neither of his parents really wanted him to go to university. He came for counselling two or three times and one of the things he told me was that his 'mates' laughed at him for coming to see me, but that he found it helpful to have his thoughts and feelings 'bounced back' at him. He stopped coming for counselling and I used to hear of him periodically as he won beer drinking races in the students union. Beer drinking was for him a working class accomplishment at which he was very successful, while academic achievement was less highly regarded in his social group.

AUTHORITY

A counsellor, too, has ostensibly incompatible demands to meet concerning her own role. The head of her school may expect her to encourage children to remain at school, or to go to university for their own and the school's benefit. The counsellor herself may feel that her responsibility to the school is in conflict with her responsibility to an individual pupil with the ability to cope with a university course but with interests in other areas.

A teacher may expect a counsellor to support his authority and

vocational experience in counseling the student'. The gap between tomorrow and yesterday is greater when the rate of change is more rapid. 'Most of our experience was valuable for our yesterday, but not for the student's tomorrow. . . .'[14]

Sociological analysis may also be of value to the counsellor in evaluating the work she is doing, or may enable others to make an evaluation. An example of this approach is to be found in Cicourel and Kitsuse's book *The Educational Decision-makers*.[15] In time, when counselling is an accepted part of education rather than an excepted one, sociologists will seek answers to the questions that have already been raised in American education. What is the process by which young people decide to consult counsellors? What important social difference has the counsellor made in a school or college? Do students studying English experience greater role stress than those studying Chemistry? If so, what are the implications for the departments concerned and for the counselling service?

SOCIAL STRATIFICATION

When a student walks into a counsellor's room he walks into a highly structured social situation. The individuals, student and counsellor, form a social group which is governed by the conditions peculiar to any group, conditions which may be analysed in the way that other social groups have been analysed by sociologists or social psychologists. The counselling process within this social group may be considered as it usually is, in terms of psychological concepts such as defence mechanisms or conditioning according to the counsellor's theoretical vocabulary, but it may be also considered in terms of sociological concepts such as norms, roles and role-set.

SOME RECENT STUDIES

There are a number of longitudinal studies carried out in this country which provide sociological material of interest and help to counsellors. The studies initiated by the Population Investigation Committee and directed by Dr J. W. B. Douglas since 1945 have been published in chronological stages from *Maternity in Great Britain*[16]; *Children under Five*[17]; *The Home and the School*[18] and, more recently, *All our Future*.[19]

The various publications on education by official bodies which have appeared in the past decade, the Plowden Report on primary schools,[20] the Newsom Report on secondary schools,[21] have shown increasingly the need for school and community interaction, and the Newsom Report, for example, suggests that there is a need for teachers to have some training in 'some realistic sociological studies' (para. 204). Hughes points out that it was the Newsom Report which was the first official government paper to make specific reference to school counselling by suggesting that 'in large schools, it may not be fanciful to look forward to a stage where there is a full-time counsellor available to advise the pupils throughout their school course and to prepare them for going out into the world' (para. 233.3).

Sociology provides some guidance for the preventive role of the counsellor, and a counsellor's sociological and philosophical understanding, together with her personal experience of life, determine both her choice of theoretical orientation and the way in which she works with students.

All those working in an educational setting as we approach the final quarter of the twentieth century seem to need a much wider perspective than used to be thought desirable. Social problems arising from drug usage, schoolgirl pregnancy and V.D. amongst school pupils, delinquency and the increased hostility towards education which seems to occur partly as a result of unrealistic expectations on the part of both educators and students, are responsibilities that schools and colleges must increasingly cope with as other social agencies increasingly fail to do so.

THEORY VERSUS PEOPLE

Finally a reminder of the dangers of over-reliance on theoretical concepts at the expense of respect for the integrity of the adolescent. Friedenberg, an educational sociologist, after suggesting that counselling for adjustment can be dangerous for a young person's self-esteem, goes on to elaborate the point.

> He already thinks ill of himself and is miserable about what he believes to be his deficiences. He has reason to be; we all contribute a large measure to our own difficulties; they are the difficulties of being *us*. ... If the guidance staff can imaginatively conceive the youngster's problem, it can help him to outgrow the defensive and neurotic dynamisms that may cause most of his trouble, and contribute to his strength in dealing with those troubles that, as a man and himself, he ought to live with. This is not only a difficult and time-consuming technical speciality; it is a course of action that only a person with a deep and trustworthy respect for the integrity of adolescents can see any reason to undertake.
>
> Lacking this respect, the guidance staff proceed to classify the case; the boy is emotionally immature; he has problems with sibling rivalry; he comes from a broken home. He needs

116

sympathetic and understanding handling. Normally the guidance worker establishes partnership gently, he helps the lad understand why he needs to be so hostile; studiously, he ignores the boy's resentment, turning if need be his ultimate cheek; patiently he introduces him to a peer group in which his new personality may find acceptance. Sympathetic handling, indeed; this is too often dextrous manipulation. During the course of it the guidance worker may be sustained by a glow of helpfulness, but he is rarely illuminated by any vision of his client as a unique human being. The goals of such guidance come not from the client, but from the staff member's idea of what a nice boy should be like.

The boy is now in a dangerous position. His self-image had originally been painful and distorted; otherwise he would not have come for treatment or acted in such a way as to be referred for it. It now becomes blurred and confused. Driven by dependency and the promise of warmth, he abandons himself further in the process of turning himself into what the school believes he ought to be. ... It quietly links his self-esteem to the attainment of the virtues of a petty bureaucracy, helping him to think well of himself whatever his self may be, if he becomes more responsible, a better citizen, and especially estimable in the eyes of others.

Well, these are virtues, but even if one accepts them as virtues, this process of imparting them is a process of alienation. It takes advantage of a disturbed youngster's confusion and feeling of inferiority, cultivates his dependency, and manipulates his immediate emotional needs—sometimes even stimulating them—to evoke behaviour and attitudes which are quite inconsistent with his deeper feelings. These deeper feelings must then be further repressed. The youngster's power to build his self-esteem from self-appraisal is thus further weakened; his dependency on external success and esteem strengthened.[22]

Friedenberg is writing from a penetrating perception of the American situation and he has a tendency to over-state his case; nevertheless, his argument is a valid and thoughtful one.

The individual and the society may be viewed as two distinctly different units of cognitive analysis. To change individuals may result in change in society, to change society is likely to result in change in individuals, for the dynamics of change lie both within the individual and society. Weinberg concludes that 'The counselor has many

117

choices, most of which are fraught with the difficulty of changing institutional patterns and values, but if he is to play a preventive role in line with a conception of culture as the determinant of adolescent disjuncture, the disruption of these patterns and values is necessary.'[8]

7
Theoretical approaches to counselling

Theories derive from bases which are personal, historical, sociological and philosophical. In the field of counseling we know so
little about the accuracy and usefulness of theoretical formulations
that we must look inward to needs and desires rather than outward
to data to understand why, from among many, a particular theory
is chosen by an individual.[1]

Counselling is in many ways a synthesis of approaches from related
movements such as social casework, psychometrics, clinical psychology, and psychotherapy. Although human difficulties appear to
lie in specific areas, for example vocational, personal or marital
difficulties, it is people who need help. Consequently the person, not
the problem, is the main focus of the counselling process. This applies
even when the counsellor is using a behavioural approach, which is
specifically problem centred.

To work effectively to help a person it is important that the
counsellor should analyse what is happening in the counselling
sessions. The theories upon which her approach to counselling are
based offer the conceptual tools and provide a framework for this
thinking. Although theories provide a framework, this does not
imply that they are rigid and inflexible; they are working assumptions
which offer provisional ways of analysing and organizing evidence in
a search for something better.

Theory helps to explain, predict, evaluate and improve what
happens in the counselling relationship and to answer questions such
as 'What is happening now?' 'What accounts for this?' Using her
particular theoretical orientation with its underlying philosophical
implications, each counsellor attempts to answer these questions
with her own unique yet limited perception. There is no satisfactory
general theory of counselling, although Carkhuff seems to have come
close to one in his work on helping through human relationships.[2]
Theories of counselling are drawn from a number of schools or
approaches and although they differ in emphases, they all acknow-

ledge acceptance, rapport, the need for support, some limits and the professional status of the counsellor.[3]

It is possible to trace two historical bases for counselling theory, one depending on psychoanalytic principles and emphasizing the emotional 'feeling' aspects of personality, and the other on learning theory, concentrating on re-learning some adaptive ways of behaviour in response to the demands of life. Some writers such as Barclay[4] trace learning theory back to psychoanalytic thinking.

Psychotherapy and counselling

It has been suggested that there are three elements which are either explicit or implied in all systems of psychotherapy or counselling: a theory of personality, a social philosophy concerning the relationship of individuals to society and a body of therapeutic skills which influence behaviour.[5]

American writers vary in their approach to the problem of delineating the differences between counselling and psychotherapy. Some suggest that they are viewed as overlapping areas of professional competence, counselling being characteristically short term, educational, supportive, situational, problem-solving, with emphasis on conscious awareness and normal people, while psychotherapy is long term, supportive (in a more particular sense) and reconstructive; it has a focus on the unconscious, and an emphasis on 'neurotics' or other severe emotional problems. The scope of both counselling and psychotherapy can be subsumed under the framework of therapeutic psychology, and the distinctions between them often seem to be quantitative as opposed to qualitative.[3]

In the area of personal problems counselling and psychotherapy are most nearly synonymous.

> What is most likely to trigger the request for a counseling appointment is unhappiness or dissatisfaction with the course one's life is taking. There may be problems in relationships to other people. There may be feelings of boredom and general meaninglessness. There is likely to be anxiety, along with vague or well-defined fears about the soundness of one's own personality. The treatment given to persons in such states of mind has frequently been labelled psychotherapy: it is in such cases that therapy and counseling are indistinguishable. Most of the controversy that has arisen . . . over whether there is or is not such a distinction can be resolved if we think in terms of what a counselor is eligible to do.
>
> What a counselor should be equipped with, if he is to serve

clients of this sort well, is some tools that will enable him to make visible in its main outlines the present patterns of a person's life and the possibilities this pattern provides for future development. Whether members of the professions giving such assistance decide to label such tools 'counseling' or 'therapy' is not really a very important matter.[6]

The theoretical orientation of the counsellor may well have some influence on whether she calls her work counselling or psychotherapy. Some people working in student counselling base their approach on an analytically oriented theory, and frequently refer to their work in the Student Counselling Service as psychotherapy.

A thought-provoking comment suggests that

It may be, however, that we no longer need to worry about what counseling is, or what psychotherapy is, or if and how they differ. There has been increasing recognition that counseling or psychotherapy is not enough. It will not solve all our social problems. It is not applicable to many people, at least as presently practised or, more accurately, in the hands of our present practitioners.[7]

There are several personality theories which have useful implications for counselling.[3]

1. Psychoanalytic theory.
2. Self theory.
3. Trait theory.
4. Field theory.
5. Behaviouristic learning theory.

Not all these are applicable to the present approaches to counselling in this country, but they are worth a mention, since no theory has been found as yet to explain completely the process of counselling. Some of the main points of each theory are suggested below.

Psychoanalytic theory

The 'talking cure', first used extensively by Freud, forms the basis of the counselling relationship for all the approaches, although they vary in the way in which they use it.

The psychoanalytic concepts of levels of awareness are significant for the 'dynamic' approaches to counselling, though not for the behaviourist or learning theory approaches which place no value on the concept of 'depth' of the unconscious. Both use the conscious level of awareness consisting of those ideas of which the person is at present aware, and both utilize the preconscious ideas which, although not in the individual's present awareness, can be recalled. Although Freud regarded the unconscious level of awareness as having a powerful influence on behaviour, the behaviourists prefer to think that the explanations of and solutions to human problems are to be found within the perceptual capabilities of the individual without recourse to the depths of personality.

The Neo-Freudian theorists, Adler, Horney, Fromm and Harry Stack Sullivan in America have moved away from traditional Freudian theory in so far as it postulates a personality based on a biological drive concept, mainly sexual in nature, the satisfaction of which is the goal to which all behaviour is directed. For the Neo-Freudians personality is a social product 'possessing needs which arise as much from the individual's society as from his biology'.[8] Whilst the American approach is sociological in the sense of approaching human problems and conflicts as social ones, European practice seems to have retained the biological individual approach: 'in Europe . . . the approach is not only predominantly biological, but, under the influence of Melanie Klein and others, increasingly so'.[8] The scientist's social background and his culture influence psychological theories but although the American approach is having an increasingly active influence on European psychology, the interest is selective rather than complete.

> For example, Britain has been interested in behaviourist theory but accepted it from Pavlov rather than from Watson; the Neo-Freudians Horney and Fromm have proved to be almost scientific best-sellers here—but were read by the intelligent layman rather than the analyst or psychiatrist; American work in social psychology has aroused interest too—but is perhaps better known to industrial management trainees and social workers than to academic psychologists.[8]

The American approach to counselling in education may be added to this list of increasingly active interests from across the Atlantic, for 'the general acceptability of a scientific theory is not wholly dependent upon its validity as a science, because history shows that its relevance to the contemporary situation and the degree to which it conforms to the contemporary approach are equally important. In a world which increasingly sees all human problems as social problems, psychoanalysis as a method of treatment may well fall into desuetude, not because it does not work, but simply because it is inapplicable to the problems of the day'.[8]

Self theory

Self theories are much newer in counselling and psychotherapy than analytic theories. Carl Rogers is credited with having collected the most systematic assumptions and constructs on self theory and is recognized for his application of the theory to counselling and psychotherapy in his client-centred or non-directive therapy, recently re-named experiential therapy. This is one of the main theories taught in the departments of counsellor education in American universities and it is one of the main approaches to counselling in American schools. It also has a strong emphasis in several such courses in English universities, although it is only one of the theories which are studied. It seems particularly appropriate for counselling in education because it was initially developed whilst Rogers, a psychologist, was Director of the Child Guidance Clinic at Rochester, in New York State. He observed that certain administrative structures and policies in schools and colleges prevent maladjustment, while others contribute to it. It is important to know how to prevent maladjustment in schools and homes, in addition to knowing how to treat it. Rogers stressed the need for more concern with the teaching of reading to prevent the costly effects of reading disability, as well as emphasizing the psychological, social and economic loss which results from wrong vocational choices, and the consequent need for education about vocations and course choice.[9]

Client-centred counselling derives from its time and its cultural setting, but Rogers acknowledges its debt to the appreciation of unconscious striving and the complex emotional nature of man contributed by Freud; to the therapy of Otto Rank; to the scientific method of psychology, which submits all hypotheses to a process of objective verification or disproof; and to Gestalt psychology for its relationship of the cluster, or various phenomena which make up the individual, to the whole. Rogers suggests that this approach is rooted in the educational, social and political philosophy of American culture, though he does believe that behaviour in the counselling relationship transcends to some extent the limitations of influences of a specific culture.[10] To this list, Barclay[4] adds the antecedents of liberal Christian theology, existentialism and pheno-menology.

Carl Rogers is in some ways the Martin Luther of psychotherapy, not philosophically or temperamentally, but in the sense that he has challenged the dogma and extended the scope of participation in the work to make it available to a much wider range of people. Counselling is not the appropriate approach to the problems of all children or all parents, but it is one significant method of dealing with adjustment problems.

Adjustment begs the question 'adjustment to what?' but used in the context of self-theory it signifies a person who is acting in accord with his self-concept, which is learned progressively from birth. When a person's awareness and experience are closely matched his behaviour may be described as congruent. Where there is incongruence between a person's awareness and his experience, if he is aware of trying to communicate a feeling of love but experiences hostility his communication is defensively distorted. The implication for counselling is that the communications of both counsellor and client should aim at a state of congruence.

A further assumption of client-centred counselling is that the individual's reality is that which he perceives, and external events are only significant in so far as the person experiences them as meaningful. Thus the counsellor must try to work from the client's 'internal frame of reference' if she is to accept his feelings and attitudes.

The most significant therapeutic element in this view of counselling is the emotional quality of the relationship. Information, diagnosis, historical understanding are all secondary to the climate created by the counsellor through her sincerity, warmth, acceptance and sensitive empathic understanding. The client is believed to have the capacity and motivation to solve his own problems and it is suggested that these will emerge in the freedom and safety of the counselling relationship.

Although Rogers's early work was with children, adolescents and families he later moved from the Child Guidance field into the academic world, constantly researching the results of his counselling and revising his theory. Since then the scope of client-centred work has extended into hospitals and Rogers's present position is probably to be found in this comment on schizophrenia.

> What does the word schizophrenic mean to me? To the extent that it has any definite meaning at all, it means that here is a person who is highly sensitive to his own inner experience and also to interpersonal relationships with others, who has been so defeated and traumatised in endeavouring to make use of his sensitivities that he has retreated both from his own experiencing and from any real contact with others. In addition to this fairly basic understanding, the word schizophrenic also means to me that anyone whose behaviour is deviant and who cannot easily be understood is tossed in this all encompassing basket.

I try to remain open-minded to the possibility that there may be specific genetic, chemical or nutritional factors which may bear some causative relationship to the behaviour that is called schizophrenic. But thus far I have seen no evidence that would convince me.[12]

More recently Rogers has concentrated his attention on encounter group work.[13]

Trait theory

The trait and factor theorists see personality as a collection of interdependent factors, abilities, attitudes, interests and values and temperament together with social traits. This approach is mainly used by counsellors working with educational and vocational problems, in which some prediction of success in school or job is of value, rather than by the therapeutic counsellor concerned more with feelings which have become debilitating. It is in this theory that the influence of psychometrics on counselling is greatest.

Williamson regards it as equally unfortunate to underemphasize the rational aspects of the counselling situation as it is to understress the emotional, for he believes that counselling should help people to learn to think logically and constructively about themselves, their relationships and their situation. He is an exponent of the directive counselling approach, which because of its emphasis on learning, the collection of information, diagnosis, prognosis, counselling and follow-up within a caring relationship, and his view that counselling and discipline are not incompatible seems to offer a way of counselling appropriate to the dual role of teacher/counsellor, which other approaches do not offer so readily.

Cattell's factorial work on the organization of personality, and Allport's psychology of the individual have both contributed to this approach to counselling; indeed it is perhaps more appropriate to term this an approach to counselling rather than a theory of personality.

Field theory

Any theory of personality wide enough to encompass the vital aspects of man's behaviour was recognized by Kurt Lewin (a leader in the development of field theory) as one which would be multi-dimensional. Field theory revived the concept of man as a complex energy field, a set of forces operating in conjunction with an environment which is also a set of forces. Lewin's work on group dynamics, social conflicts and re-education has particular relevance for counselling.

Gestalt psychology, another approach to field theory, has made two main contributions to counselling theory through Gestalt therapy which applies the principles of Gestalt psychology to psychotherapy. One contribution is the principle of the organization of perception and the other is the 'phenomenon of insightful learning'.[3]

The implications of these principles are that a person in a disorganized state will organize his perceptions as completely as possible to reduce the tension. Behaviour is construed as a primary function of the person's present perceptions and it is therefore important first to understand a person in terms of his own unique perception or his phenomenological field, not in terms of his past history, as in the psychoanalytic approach, nor in terms of past learning, as in the behavioural approach.

Insightful learning is achieved in counselling by a 'reconstructing of the field', or a review of past experiences with a loosening of the rigidity of former thinking through re-experiencing past or present feelings and ideas, so that over a period of time the reorganization and freeing of perception which results in insight may take place. This is also an important element in the work of the self-theorists and to some extent the psychoanalytic orientation, both of which lean heavily on insight.

Behaviouristic learning theory

The learning theorist is characterized by his assumption that most human behaviour is learned and can be modified. The stimulus response model is an important explanation of behaviour, and this approach is sometimes known as the stimulus-response theory of personality. Stated simply, in order to learn, a person must want something (drive), notice something (stimulus), do something (response) and get something (reward). It is the reward which acts as the reinforcement, so that the S-R pattern tends to be repeated under similar circumstances. A response which is not repeated and rewarded or reinforced from time to time tends to disappear, or be extinguished. Substituting one stimulus for another to get the same response is known as reconditioning or, when used in therapeutic terms, re-education.

This emphasis on how behaviour was acquired and how it can be changed offers a way of helping students with some practical difficulties, such as study problems. Whilst some students cannot study because other things worry them, there are students who cannot study well because in the past they learned to study badly.

Krumboltz is another theorist who sees behavioural counselling as the application of learning theory to counselling. He defines counselling somewhat broadly as 'whatever ethical activities a counselor undertakes in an effort to help the client engage in those types of behaviors which will lead to a resolution of the client's problems'.[14]

Krumboltz considers that the goals of behavioural counselling can be achieved by the use of several approaches including the operant learning process, the use of imitative learning, classical conditioning and emotional and cognitive learning. He views the counsellor as an active helper in the learning process working towards specific and precise kinds of behaviour change through the use of techniques and procedures which are experimentally tested to determine their usefulness. The goals of counselling must be defined in terms of specific behaviour so that these behaviours may be recognized and reinforced when they occur. The counsellor is seen as one who arranges conditions so that the student may learn more adaptive ways of coping with his difficulties within the setting of a warm, friendly and secure counselling relationship.

Michael and Myerson[15] relate the experimental analysis of behaviour to counselling and suggest that the phenomenon with which counsellors deal is behaviour and that the independent variable which controls that behaviour is the environment. They accept that behaviour derives from the interaction of hereditary and environmental variables, but point out that a behavioural approach attempts to specify those conditions and processes by which the environment controls human behaviour. The example of students who discontinue their studies is used to illustrate that by their behaviour such students are showing that they are not being 're-inforced' by those influences which keep other students at college, or that the educational reinforcement they are receiving is weaker than reinforcement coming from other sources. In such a case, it is the job of the counsellor to discover what reinforces student 'drop-outs' and to make these reinforcements contingent upon learning. They make the provocative claim that 'Under appropriate environmental conditions, which man can create, almost anyone can be motivated to do anything'.[15]

It is perhaps unfortunate that the vocabulary of behavioural theorists often appears to be so technical, and so removed from the experience which most of us have of human interaction. The behavioural approach has much to offer to guidance and counselling

127

but it is difficult not to share the feeling of exasperation which led an American student to write the following Skinnerian scenario.

JOHN Marcia.

MARCIA John.

JOHN Marcia, the sound of your voice, the very mental image I hold of you, have become conditioned stimuli which evoke a wide range of pleasurable physiological responses in me.

MARCIA Do you mean . . . ?

JOHN Yes, you have become a very potent stimulus . . . each of my behaviors has as its goal some indication of your acceptance.

MARCIA How fortunate, excuse me, how inevitable . . . that even in this unscientific world of change contingencies we found each other. Two human beings upon whom our microcosmic environments operated to produce a complementary set of emotional needs and response repertoires! You have been both stimulus and consequence for so many of my behaviors, both overt and covert, ever generalising, far longer than I dared exhibit. My conditioning led me to believe that you might question the freedom of your will [both chuckle] if I were to reveal to what extent I find your presence rewarding.

JOHN And to think the efficacy of negative reinforcement was ever in doubt! No matter how aversive the immediate consequences, I would perform any act, undergo any punishment, for the ultimate reward of a word or even an expression of approval on your face. It's been that way since the first barrage of continuous reinforcement.

MARCIA You perceived . . .

JOHN Oh yes . . . and the way that your overt rewards became intermittent . . . extinction did not follow . . . rather, increased intensity and generalisation were concomitants of the schedule you established. Oh let us continue to manipulate each other through eternity.

MARCIA Oh yes, John, or at least until some potent unforeseen contingency factor with the power to alter our mutually reinforcing response patterns do us part! [16]

Behaviour therapy has evolved in this country in opposition to psychotherapy. Hans Eysenck, Head of the Department of Psychology of the Institute of Psychiatry, London University, has written critically of the ineffectiveness of psychotherapy and has claimed successful outcomes for behaviour therapy.[17]

New ways of helping people in difficulty have recently been developed in America. They are not new theories of personality and tend to be derivatives of some of the older approaches. However, there is no longer just a triadic conflict of psychoanalytic versus client-centred, versus behaviour therapy, but a series of new developments which have arisen in part because of a disaffection with existing methods and in part as a result of renewed efforts to provide help for the poor and the disadvantaged. Role playing, psychodrama, sociotherapy (a form of personality adjustment through social action) and reality therapy—which seems to have been particularly effective amongst delinquents and in schools—are some of these newer approaches. There has been a change, too, in the range of people offering this therapeutic help. Whereas formerly the therapeutic role was held primarily by the psychiatrist, therapist, psychologist, counsellor or social worker, an increasing number of lay therapists or 'paraprofessionals' are working in hospitals, schools and in the local communities with heartening success: 'this burgeoning of new practitioners has presumably terminated the search for the "one" most effective way of helping troubled people'.[18]

Developmental counselling

Developmental counselling is an approach which aims to change behaviour in order to facilitate human development and is based on the assumption that students are capable of choosing the desired direction of their own development. Blocher has suggested a number of basic assumptions about the nature of developmental counselling which are summarized as follows:

1. Students are not considered to be 'mentally ill', but capable of choosing goals, making decisions and generally assuming responsibility for their own behaviour and future development.

2. Developmental counselling is focused on the present and the future and is primarily concerned with where the client is going, not where he has been.

3. The student is a client, not a patient. The counsellor is not an authority figure, she is a partner of the student as they move toward mutually defined goals.

4. The counsellor is not morally neutral or amoral, but has values, feelings and standards of her own. She does not necessarily impose these on students, nor does she attempt to hide them.

5. The counsellor focuses on changing behaviour not merely creating insight. She is a helping person, a teacher, a consultant

129

and a confidante as these functions are seen to be appropriate in meeting mutually defined goals.[19]

Developmental counselling is educational and is based on the assumption that human personality develops in terms of a mainly healthy interaction between the growing person and the environment. It aims to maximize human freedom, whilst recognizing that such freedom is sometimes severely limited by reality, and that few people are prepared to exercise the freedom which they do have. It also aims to maximize human effectiveness and suggests that the effective human being strives for control over those aspects of his environment which he can manipulate and also for control over his affective responses to those aspects of his environment which he cannot change.

Blocher admits that the psychology of human effectiveness is a relatively neglected area and acknowledges that psychology knows little about the behaviours which thousands of people employ to lead satisfying and effective lives. Despite the poverty of knowledge about human effectiveness, this approach to counselling may have particular appeal to counsellors working in educational settings.

Leona Tyler points out that the dominant personality theories of our time have grown out of the intensive study of abnormal individuals. Analytic theories offer useful conceptual tools to consider what is wrong with a student and how it might be set right, but not to consider what this person might do. Learning theories are useful when there is an identifiable behaviour which needs to be changed, but are perhaps not as helpful to the student who is not seeking obvious change so much as to plan his future. The increasingly popular counselling characteristic of promoting full potential ignores the human imperative that for most people some potentialities must be closed so that a few may be actualized. None of us use our full potential and such an objective is in many ways illusory.

Developmental counsellors may also help those who are not troubled by confusion or anxiety but who might benefit from doing some serious thinking before taking important steps in their lives such as choosing a college course or a career.

A theory made up of what we know about the way in which individuals use human possibilities leads to a definition of counselling as a process of helping an individual to make his choices in such a way as to maximize the probability that his future development will be satisfying to himself and useful to those around him. A counsellor is seen as a specialist in developmental possibilities.[6]

Reality therapy

Reality therapy was developed by Dr William Glasser, an American psychiatrist, as a result of his dissatisfaction with what he saw as the ineffectiveness and unreality of those methods of counselling and therapy which dismiss morality from the focus of treatment. Reality therapy holds that people are responsible for their behaviour, and Glasser believes that man's basic problem is moral, in the sense that being responsible is the requirement for mental health. He defines responsibility as 'the ability to fulfil our needs and to do so in a way that does not deprive others of the ability to fulfil their needs'.[20] Glasser postulates that all people who come for help have identified in some way with failure and that the way to help them is to try to involve them, through the counselling relationship, in behaviour which will lead to success.

Reality therapy is based on the need which people have for love and constructive activity, and requires from the counsellor an involvement through which she confronts the student with what he is doing and helps him to plan better choices and obtains a commitment from him to work towards those choices. It says that people who are failing have chosen to fail. They have chosen to identify with failure because they believe that they have no other choice, and the counsellor has to try to help them to understand that a better choice is possible. It is a method which guides people towards making those choices of behaviour which help them to move in the direction of successful involvement with others.

Glasser quotes case-histories of seriously delinquent adolescent girls, of psychotics, including chronic schizophrenics, and of disturbed ex-servicemen and students, and indicates that discharge rates from mental hospitals have risen fairly dramatically following the use of Reality Therapy as a form of treatment. He has written of the use of his approach in schools and believes that schools, more than anywhere, are places in which children become convinced that they are failures and locked in a failure cycle which is difficult to break.

This behaviouristic method of counselling has been criticized for its apparently naïve approach to the subtle realities of human personality and motivation. I think that we would be ill-advised to be deceived by its simplicity for this is an approach to counselling which has proved that it can be effective and its moral precept perhaps makes it more attractive to teachers and educators than other methods.

131

Rational-emotive counselling

The rational-emotive approach to counselling was developed by the American Albert Ellis. His theory is that everyone has emotions but that some of us have emotions which are either too intensive or last too long for our own good. He suggests that intense emotions should last only a few moments and if they are more enduring than this, then the person needs to look closely at his philosophy of life.

Ellis has evolved what he calls an ABC theory of events and emotions in which he suggests that events themselves do not cause emotions, it is rather what we learn to believe about these events which creates the emotion.

'A' represents the existence of a fact, an event or the behaviour or attitude of another person.

'C' represents the reaction of a person, perhaps an emotional disturbance of unhappiness which most of us presume to follow directly from 'A'.

'B' represents the self-verbalization of the individual about the event 'A', his definition or interpretation of it as awful, or terrible.

Ellis's theory is that 'A', the event, does not cause 'C', the emotion, but 'B', the interpretation, does. He further suggests that emotion which is so intense as to interfere with normal life for any length of time is sustained by some irrational belief about an event. Below are several examples of the irrational beliefs which most people commonly hold but are unable or unwilling to specify verbally, although they consistently behave as though they hold such beliefs:[28]

1. It is essential that one be loved or approved of by virtually everyone in one's community.

Comment
It is desirable to be loved, but the rational person does not sacrifice his interests and desires to this goal.

2. One must be perfectly competent, adequate and achieving to consider oneself worthwhile.

Comment
The rational person strives to do well for his own sake rather than to compete with others: to enjoy the activity rather than the results, to learn rather than to be perfect.

3. Some people are bad, wicked or villainous and therefore should be blamed or punished.

Comment
The rational person does not blame others or self. He tries to under-

stand mistakes and stop them, but if he cannot, he tries not to let it upset him.[21]

The rational-emotive counsellor attempts to show the student that his thinking is illogical, to help him to understand how and why this is so and to demonstrate the relationship between his irrational ideas and his unhappiness. The aim is to help the student to change his thinking and to abandon his irrational ideas by directly contradicting these and by encouraging, persuading and at times insisting that the student try some activity (perhaps one which he fears) which will counteract what Ellis considers is the nonsense the student believes. Although the counsellor attacks the beliefs of the student, this approach can be very supportive of the person of the student and the most important aspect of the counselling is the positive aspect of getting the student to try new ways of thinking about himself and to examine the subsequent emotional and behavioural responses which occur. As in reality therapy, one of the main tasks of the counselling relationship is to encourage the motivation to try new behaviours.

There have been attempts to present a more united front. Dollard and Miller have attempted to integrate Freudian psychotherapy and the behavioural drive theory of Clark Hull.[22] Bronfenbrenner attempts to translate Freud into Lewin's field theory.[23] Rogers has attempted to explain his construct of the self in terms of learning theory.[10]

In view of this it might seem attractive for the counsellor to select appropriate parts from each theory of approach and use them as he thinks fit. Yet eclecticism can be superficial and is often a cul-de-sac approach, for it seems unlikely that concessions from various theories will result in truth. At the same time it seems equally inappropriate to disregard the work of counsellors of differing orientations, for even though we work from a basic theory of our own choice we have much to learn from each other.

What does seem to be meaningful is for counsellors and therapists, regardless of their theoretical orientation, to attempt to apply the principles of their approach more widely to the situation in which they are working. '. . . in a decade we have seen client-centred therapy develop from a method of counseling to an approach to human relationships. We have come to feel that it has as much application to the problem of employing a new staff member, or the decision as to who is to get a raise, as it does to the client who is troubled by an inability to handle his social relationships.'[10]

8
The counselling relationship

I would willingly throw away all the words of this manuscript if I could, somehow, effectively point to the experience which is therapy. It is a process, a thing-in-itself, an experience, a relationship, a dynamic. It is not what this book says about it, nor what any other book says about it, any more than a flower is the botanists' description of it or the poet's ecstasy over it.[1]

The helping relationship

The developing field of counselling is presented as a helping relationship in which counsellors, in common with members of other helping professions such as psychiatry, psychotherapy, social casework and some branches of psychology, seek to use a combination of specialized knowledge and skills, within a relationship, which will enable people to cope more effectively with the ordinary and extraordinary dilemmas and paradoxes which are characteristic of human life as they experience it. The counselling relationship is only one in a series of helping relationships which people may enter into throughout their lives; the mother-child relationship, husband-wife relationship, the doctor-patient relationship, the teacher-pupil relationship, together with friendships, are perhaps the more commonly experienced ones.

The nature of a helping relationship has an elusive quality and some people seem disinclined to differentiate between a 'helping relationship' of whatever nature and a 'counselling relationship', wishing to see no difference in the quality and outcome of a chat between a teacher and a pupil, or a mother and child, and a counselling session. Sometimes this viewpoint is entirely valid, for in a very real sense the interpersonal relationship which is developed through counselling is an attempt to provide a synthesis of those qualities which make our personal encounters valuable and meaningful. Yet, at the same time, we must grant equal validity to the perceptions of those observers in any school or college who cannot fail to notice some children and students for whom existing relationships are not sufficiently adequate to help them to use their resources, either to cope with a particular situation, or in response to the general responsibility of living. Whilst one of the aims of the counsellor is to work with individuals and groups in ways which may be helpful, another important aim is to work with others who work with students, in an attempt to suggest and find understanding approaches which those who wish to do so may bring to their relationships with students. The creation of a counselling service is sometimes seen as a panacea for all the educational, psychological and personal problems which befall the institution or its members. The dichotomous view that all teachers or tutors are counsellors, which precludes any necessity to create a counselling service, is in my experience equally unrealistic. Somewhere between these two extremes lie the appropriate benefits which a counselling service can provide for each institution.

Some characteristics of a counselling relationship

Helping relationships of whatever kind have, by definition, some common features, but I will suggest some of the characteristics of counselling, recognizing that some and in certain cases all of these may be appropriate to other situations.

A CASEWORK APPROACH
Biestek [2] has listed seven overlapping principles of the casework or counselling relationship which derive from seven basic human needs of those with problems, and Moran [3] uses these as the basis for a discussion of the characteristics of the early 'social casework' approach to counselling.

1. Individualization
A recognition of a student's need to be considered as an individual rather than as a case or category.

Not many of us want to be classified or numbered, and each person's uniqueness, identity and need to be treated as an individual are heightened at times of emotional stress; when one feels threatened in some way, this uniqueness is not only a need, but a right.

2. Purposeful expression of feeling
A recognition of a student's need to communicate at a time when his problem is partly or predominantly emotional.

Only the student knows how he feels, and it is important that he is able to express this. This sharing of the burden gives him strength, allows the tension to subside and enables him to view his problem

135

more realistically. The giving of advice and information at this stage is likely to be unhelpful, often accentuating rather than relieving the distress. Advice and information are forms of knowledge, whereas tension, anxiety and depression are forms of dynamic or emotion. Once the emotional build up of tension has been released, it may be possible to move on to the different process of guidance, if it is needed.

Counselling shows that if a person can be helped to express his feelings he will often prove quite capable of finding a solution for himself, though many children are handicapped by their immaturity and some adults by their incapacity. Expression of painful feeling often brings relief, whether it be through words or tears, and in counselling it need not be suppressed. The ambiguity and tension which accompany such affective behaviour can provide the material from which the student enhances his self-perception.

3. Controlled emotional involvement
A recognition of the student's need to receive an appropriate response to his feelings.

Counselling is something of a warmly human, professional relationship which gives the best of ourselves without becoming too deeply involved in an unhelpful way. If we look at over-involvement and controlled involvement we may compare them to a situation in which someone who cannot swim plunges into a river to save a drowning man instead of trying to rescue him from the bank. The intention is admirable and the result disastrous.

4. Acceptance
A recognition of the student's need to be accepted as he is and not as the counsellor would like him to be, thus helping to maintain a sense of dignity and personal worth.

Acceptance does not necessarily mean approval of all the student's behaviour, nor does it imply the right to judge. Although it may involve some objective evaluation of the student's standards, attitudes and behaviour in the light of the counsellor's responsibility to the student, to herself and to society, throughout it all the student must feel that he is received as he now is. This threefold responsibility may be considered as follows:

To the student: It is unrealistic and harmful to condone 'deviant' behaviour, but since the counsellor accepts the student as he is, it is important for her to try to help him to acknowledge and recognize the likely consequence of his behaviour for himself and others.

136

To herself: The counsellor has her own values, personal and professional, and whilst acceptance involves not imposing these on the student, it also involves the self-acceptance on the part of the counsellor which enables her to be authentic and true to herself.

To society: Both counsellor and student are subject to the laws of society and if they choose to work outside the law or the basic values of society (and I believe that occasionally this may be necessary) they should each be very clear as to the likely consequences for both of them.

Acceptance can be expressed by warmth, courtesy, listening, respect, concern, interest, consistent maturity and firmness as well as a willingness to enter into and share the life and experience of the other.

5. *Non-judgmental attitude*
A recognition of a student's need to be understood and helped rather than condemned.

A counsellor is not a judge and has no right to pass sentence. Even praise or approval can be subtle forms of judgment and may prevent a student from revealing his positive and negative feelings freely because he may feel compelled to remain within the good grace of the counsellor by presenting himself in a favourable light. The expression of approval carries with it the implication of a right to express disapproval. There are others in education whose concern it is to assess and to judge, to fail or to pass. It is the counsellor's concern to accept.

6. *Self-determination*
A recognition of a student's right and need to make his own decisions.

If we impose our decisions on a student we are encouraging a relationship of dependency. Counselling is rather an attempt to foster attitudes of maturity, resourcefulness and independent thinking within the student's own capacity for these. There are of course limits to self-determination, for human freedom is not licence, the right of self-determination begets duties, and the rights of any one person are limited by the rights of others. The actual possibilities for action available to a student may be limited by three factors:

   i. civil and criminal law;
   ii. moral law; if the counsellor and student have differing moral standards, which is probably likely to occur more frequently, the student has a right to follow his own conscience, but the counsellor has a similar right and is under no professional

obligation to co-operate in conduct which she considers wrong. Self-determination is a counsellor need as much as it is a student need;

iii. personal capacities; the student's liberty may also be limited by his actual capacity for constructive decision making, as is often the case with children, disturbed adolescents, mentally retarded people and those affected by drug dependence. Such people are not always able to bear the full responsibility of decision-making for some time during counselling, though they may be helped to do so. It is perhaps this principle of self-determination which makes counselling a long-term rather than an instant process.

7. *Confidentiality and confidence*

A recognition of the need to keep confidential information about oneself as secure as possible. The student does not want to exchange his reputation for the help he receives.

Only when the student can really trust the counsellor on this point will he feel secure enough to bring out his real problems. It may sometimes be necessary to consider certain points with others outside the counselling relationship, but this should be discussed with the student first and if he is not willing for this to be done, his right to confidentiality should be respected. Confidence includes more than confidentiality, it includes a respect for the counsellor's competence and a liking for her as a person, and the counsellor has constantly to work at becoming the kind of person in whom confidence can be placed, demonstrating this by word and deed.

A CLIENT-CENTRED APPROACH

Rogers,[4] in discussing the characteristics of a helping relationship, presents a series of inter-related, tentative hypotheses, similar to Biestek's principles, which have guided his behaviour in relationships with students, staff, family and clients. Although open to change, they are in my view crucial to any consideration of the counselling relationship.

1. 'Can I *be* in some way which will be perceived by the other person as trustworthy, as dependable or consistent, in some deep sense?'

The suggestion here is that being trustworthy does not demand that we are rigidly consistent but that we are dependably real or congruent.

2. 'Can I be expressive enough as a person that what I am will be communicated unambiguously?'

Here is a basic question for anyone hoping to form a helping relationship, namely, that it is safe for us to be transparently real. If we can be aware of, sensitive towards and accepting of our own feelings, it is very likely that we can establish a helping relationship with another person.

3. 'Can I let myself experience positive attitudes towards this other person—attitudes of warmth, caring, liking, interest, respect?'

We tend to fear these positive feelings because they may lead to demands being made upon us, or we may be disappointed in our trust. We react by building a distance into our relationships, making them more objective, professional or impersonal, until we learn that there are times in all relationships when it is safe to care and to relate positively to others as people rather than as objects.

4. 'Can I be strong enough as a person to be separate from the other?'

To be helpful we need enough strength to respect our own feelings and needs, and at times to express those feelings as our own, as separate from the feelings of the other person. We need, too, to feel sufficiently separate so as not to be 'downcast by his depression, frightened by his fear, nor engulfed by his dependency'.

5. 'Am I secure enough within myself to permit him his separateness?'

This point is concerned with the extent to which we can allow another person the freedom to be himself, not to follow our advice, to depend upon us, but to *be*, whether we like the aspect of himself that he is being, or not.

6. 'Can I let myself enter fully into the world of his feelings and personal meanings and see these as he does?'

Whilst having the strength to be separate and the security to allow the other person to be separate, can we at the same time see and feel the world as he does without needing to evaluate or judge?

7. 'Can I be acceptant of each facet of this other person which he presents to me? Can I receive him as he is?'

Many of us have the capacity, perhaps the need, to accept others conditionally, receiving some aspects of their feelings and disapproving of others. When our attitude is conditional, it becomes difficult for the other person to grow or to change in those areas in which he is not received. Our ability to be helpful is closely related to the extent to which we can accept our attitudes and our fears concerning those aspects of the other person of which we disapprove.

8. 'Can I act with sufficient sensitivity in the relationship that my behaviour will not be perceived as a threat?'

Rogers's hypothesis here is that if we can free the other person as far as possible from external threat in the helping relationship, then he can begin to experience the internal feelings and conflicts which threaten him, and subsequently to deal with them.

9. 'Can I free him from the threat of external evaluation?'
External judgments are a part of our lives and have some social value in education and the professions. It is preferable to keep the relationship free from evaluation, in order to permit the other person to recognize that the important evaluation and the centre of responsibility for his life lie within himself.

10. 'Can I meet this other individual as a person who is in the process of *becoming*, or will I be bound by his past and by my past?'
If we accept the other person as fixed, irrevocably shaped by his past, if we deal with him as a neurotic person, or an ignorant student, these concepts set limits on what he can become and limit the extent to which he can be helped to become something different.

When we can answer in the affirmative all the questions which Rogers raises, he believes that the relationship in which we are involved is a helping relationship. Often we cannot answer positively, but can only work towards such answers, and thus towards our own psychological maturity. The extent to which we can create relationships which facilitate the development of other people as separate persons is a measure of the growth we have achieved in ourselves.
The counselling relationship is initiated in some way by the student's need. He may be anxious, vulnerable or distressed; he may need understanding, information or both. The counsellor may be helpful because of her personality, her greater maturity, knowledge or competence or because she is trusted. She is not a mind-reader nor a worker of miracles, but perceptive, experienced and trained to develop a relationship which focuses on the needs of the student. The relationship only develops with the explicit or implicit mutual consent of both counsellor and student. It is characterized by volition and the absence of pressure or coercion. Help cannot be forced and the student should have the option of not responding to the counsellor's concern just as sometimes the counsellor may need to suggest more appropriate sources of help because of her obligation to benefit and not to harm the student.
Looking at the optimum conditions under which counselling is likely to be most effective, we see that a student or pupil would be sufficiently aware of feelings of distress or anxiety to accept the emotional character of his problem and voluntarily to seek counsel-

ling, with the expectation that this would result in a change in his life situation, whilst recognizing the possibilities and limitations of the counselling relationship. Few people come to counselling with such knowledge, but it is to be hoped that they leave it with this understanding.

Counselling in relation to education

Education is only a voluntary, chosen experience after the age of sixteen; young people below that age are required by law to undergo education, and for the majority this means to attend a state school. Counselling is probably most effective when it is a voluntary experience, although school counsellors in particular will have had experience of working with the initially unwilling pupil—the one who has been 'sent' for counselling by teacher or parent—and once the natural defensiveness and resistance have been worked through there can be gains. The directive or behavioural counsellors may be in a better position to initiate counselling with unwilling pupils, because they tend to take more responsibility for what happens in counselling than they allow the student, and suggestion and advice are more natural outcomes of their approaches. Where the responsibility is shared, or is offered predominantly to the student, as in Rogers's client-centred approach, the voluntary element of the counselling process becomes more crucial, for it is obviously not easy for a student to accept responsibility for an experience which he may feel he neither wants nor needs. The student who accepts responsibility for initiating counselling himself is in a better position to accept responsibility for working at his problems.

Boundary definition and approaches to the encounter

It is incumbent upon counsellors to define the counselling situation for the student as a part of the process. For example, the client-centred counsellor tries to make it clear that this particular time is set aside for the student to use, to take responsibility for, that the counsellor does not have answers, but will assist the student to work out his own solutions to his problem, the aim being to help him to understand who he is and what he can do.The behavioural counsellor, after talking and listening to the student, defines the problem and sets out to eliminate or modify it by conditioning techniques, working on the assumption that it is the counsellor's responsibility actively to help the student to alleviate his problem by facilitating and directing his behaviour.

141

Experience suggests that it takes a little time for English children to adjust to the responsibility and relative freedom of the client-centred approach because generally they have had little previous experience of a non-directive relationship with an adult, and some find it ambiguous and difficult to tolerate. I think this same difficulty arises in a non-counselling setting in higher education where, for the most part, students are expected to take more responsibility for their study and their lives as students than they have previously known, and some of them find this experience demoralizing, attributing the giving of independence to a lack of concern on the part of staff.

Regardless of the theoretical approach, or the voluntary or involuntary movement of the young person into counselling, the relationship is based on a sincere interest in and acceptance of that person as he is when he presents himself for counselling and as he proceeds through it. This acceptance by the counsellor is, as far as is humanly possible, unconditional in the sense that it involves neither approval nor disapproval of the person who comes for counselling. For me counselling begins with the offer of warm hospitality, not to be confused with general conversation, for counselling is not conversation and it need not be maintained or even begun on a pleasant level, but I prefer to start with a brief greeting such as 'Hello, would you come in' and if the student is wearing an outdoor coat 'Will you keep your coat on, or would you like to hang it up?' Sometimes I might say 'You seem very wet and cold, would you like a cup of coffee?' If the student remains standing I would suggest that he sit down wherever he likes. The student then chooses his own seat from three easy chairs and one upright one round a table, and I choose one of the remaining easy chairs. Then I might say something like 'What is it that you'd like to talk to me about?' or I might say nothing if the student seems ready to talk without the question. Thus, from the beginning the student is offered choices, they are limited and they are not vitally important, but they have a value in that they enable me to pick up cues and signals, and they provide a means to communicate that although I am friendly, interested and concerned, I am unlikely to tell the student what to do. This is not the way in which all counsellors start a counselling relationship; like most people, they use behaviour which is appropriate both to the situation and to their own and the student's needs. A student once rushed into my room in a very agitated state and put her feelings into words with remarks like: 'I hate this place. I wish I'd never come here. My sister told me not to choose that subject. I want to do medicine and I've talked to my tutor and he says it's practically impossible for me to get in and I've walked the streets for hours going to the medical schools and . . .' ending in a flood of tears, 'NOBODY CARES'. My first response to this was, 'Have a hankie', offering her a box of paper tissues, followed, after a pause, by a quiet, 'Why don't you sit down and tell me a bit more about it?'

I think John Wilson describes this adaptiveness on the part of the counsellor when he says of his own approach:

> There is no one type of counselling used and no one technique to apply to all the students. Each student is a person having a particular problem and requiring a particular approach to his problem. The counsellor's approach is not from a dogmatic stereotype, but is rather to be described as empirical or particular. However, one has certain preferences. . . . First and last, the treatment depends not so much on the client, but on the relationship which can be established between the counsellor and the client and what can be worked out within that relationship.[5]

I also feel that it is the meeting of the personalities of the counsellor and the pupil in school or the student in college which is at the heart of the counselling process, and I think this holds whether they meet for twenty minutes or an hour, four times a week or once a week, whether they talk about symptoms, discuss facts, or explore feelings, whether it is a group counselling session or a one-to-one situation. Whatever influence counselling may have relates most closely to the nature of the relationship which grows out of the encounter of a person and his counsellor.

Characteristics of the effective helping relationship

Truax and Carkhuff[6] made a study of research findings on the effectiveness and ineffectiveness of counselling and psychotherapy, and concluded that an effective counsellor is one who provides a relationship characterized by accurate empathy, non-possessive warmth and genuineness.

Since these three characteristics seem to be critical elements in an effective counselling relationship, it is appropriate to look at them more closely to find out what is meant by the terms accurate empathy, non-possessive warmth and genuineness and then to discuss how they may be conveyed by the counsellor. I think it is important to begin by pointing out that these are not 'techniques' of counselling so much as interpersonal skills which the counsellor uses in applying his knowledge and they are of value whether the field be personal, educational or vocational counselling.

143

EMPATHY

Accurate empathy can perhaps be called understanding with the heart as much as with the head. Responding to the feeling which a person is expressing, rather than concentrating solely on the intellectual content of what he is saying, is one of the most difficult of these interpersonal skills which the counsellor needs, partly because we are educated to respond to ideas and to ignore feelings. In many ways the training which a counsellor receives has to do with replacing our over-reliance on the intellect by teaching us to respond also to the emotional content of our lives. It may be that the skill of recognizing and acknowledging feelings is partly intuitive, but it is also a skill which can be taught, just as we already teach people to pay attention to ideas.

Having sensed the other person's private world and understood what he means, the counsellor needs to be sufficiently sensitive to the current feelings to be able to communicate this understanding in a language which is attuned to the student's world. Here it is often helpful to use the student's own words, even when they do not form a part of the counsellor's own normal vocabulary, but this needs to be done with care and feeling if it is not to become merely an artificial and parrot-like reiteration. For example a school girl once came to see me in a very agitated state because her period was late and she'd been 'having it away' with a boyfriend. To talk to her in terms of 'sexual-intercourse' would have been accurate, but not empathic. It would have taken the counselling relationship out of the field of her meaning. It is not sufficient for the counsellor to achieve empathy she must also communicate it.

Longfellow said, 'If we could read the secret history of our enemies we should find in each man's life sorrow and suffering enough to disarm all hostility.' In a similar vein Truax and Carkhuff suggest that 'it is through this process that we come to feel warmth, respect and liking for a person who in everyday life is unlikeable, weak, cowardly, treacherous, vile or despicable.'[6]

UNCONDITIONAL POSITIVE REGARD

Non-possessive warmth is what Rogers calls 'unconditional positive regard' and both these phrases add meaning and quality to the concept of acceptance. This is acceptance without conditions. It is a warm caring, not one which is offered under threat of withdrawal if the other person's behaviour does not match certain standards, but a complete acceptance. The counsellor tries to accept and recognize both her own positive and negative feelings as well as those of the student. This non-possessive warmth involves respecting the integrity of the student and accepting his right to make decisions that may be contrary to those the counsellor might make under similar circumstances. Cultural mores are not always right for all individuals at all times, and the counsellor's primary responsibility is to the individual in the relationship with her rather than to other students, teachers, or the community. But we need to remember that a counsellor who works for the students or children does not necessarily work against the staff, the school or the college. It is rarely an either/or situation.

Truax and Carkhuff[6] have developed a scale which provides insight into those aspects of the behaviour of the counsellor which indicate high levels of unconditional positive regard, where she accepts the student's experience warmly, as a part of that person, without imposing conditions. The scale also measures those aspects of counsellor behaviour which indicate low levels of unconditional positive regard where the counsellor evaluates a student or his feelings and expresses disapproval. The scale runs from 1 (Low) to 5 (High).

When at some stage the counsellor experiences a warm caring which is not possessive and does not demand personal gratification, which accepts both the negative and positive feelings and expressions of the student and accepts him as a separate person with his own experience and his own meanings for these experiences, then the counsellor may be said to be offering the high level of unconditional positive regard associated with Stage 5. When a counsellor assumes that a student's basic difficulty is a lack of information and refers him to appropriate books without giving him the opportunity to talk freely about anything he wishes to raise she may be said to be offering the lower level of unconditional positive regard described in Stage 1. Tyler suggests that whether it takes two minutes or five hours, making acceptance clear to the student is essential.[7]

CONGRUENCE

Genuineness, the quality which Rogers first called congruence, emphasizes that there must be harmony between what a counsellor says and does and what she really is. She must be herself. This is sometimes misinterpreted as meaning that the counsellor must at all times say what she really thinks and feels, but a more realistic way of explaining this quality is to suggest that of all the thoughts and feelings which a counsellor experiences during the relationship, the ones expressed, either verbally or non-verbally, should be real. Sometimes students make perceptive comments about what they sense a counsellor is thinking or feeling, and when their comments are accurate the counsellor should be sufficiently genuine to acknowledge this, in a brief but honest way, without shifting the focus of the relationship from the student and whilst being aware of the use the student may be making of his perception. For example if a student suggests that I seem bored with what he is saying and I am bored, it is not helpful or genuine to deny it even though I know that to admit it will be hurtful; what does seem helpful is for us both to acknowledge the feeling and look at the way this affects the student and the feelings with which he responds to it and to me. This is not an easy process for student or counsellor and it is tempting to evade the pain of the issue by resorting to the defence of social convention and denying the boredom, but this is not counselling, and each time I do it I am aware that we move a step back in the relationship, not normally irretrievably so, but sufficiently for me to acknowledge the discrepancy.

Truax and Carkhuff[6] have also produced a scale which attempts to characterize differing degrees of counsellor genuineness or self-congruence beginning at a low level in which the counsellor defends and denies feelings or presents a façade, and increasing to a high level of self-congruence in which the counsellor is freely and deeply herself. They suggest that a high level of self-congruence does not mean that the counsellor must overtly express her feelings, but rather that she does not deny them, so that whether she is reflecting, clarifying, interpreting or in other ways working as a counsellor, she is being herself in the moment rather than presenting a professional façade.

Rogers and Truax[8] have suggested that the order in which these three therapeutic conditions occur is of special significance because of their interlocking nature. The element which is most basic to a counselling relationship is that of genuineness, and once this authenticity and reality of the counsellor as a person is established, communication of the non-possessive warmth and respect for the person of the student evolves as the second effective ingredient. When the relationship is characterized by warmth and genuineness, the actual work of counselling is facilitated by the empathic understanding of the meaning, significance and content of the student's experiences and feelings.

In 1965, the year that saw the introduction of university courses in school counselling, Elizabeth Irvine of the Tavistock Institute of Human Relations wrote of the casework approach:

> The caseworker is dealing with people who are not as a rule psychiatrically ill, but who are having difficulty in dealing with certain stress situations. . . . It is in trying to find the solution to problems of this sort that a consistent dynamic theory of human development and interaction proves indispensable, and psycho-

analysis is slowly but surely establishing itself as the professional discipline that has the most to contribute.[9]

Whilst I would not disagree that both Freud's science of psychoanalysis and Jung's art of analytical psychology offer some valuable conceptual tools which aid our understanding of human development, I question the validity of the claim that the discipline of psychoanalysis provides the most useful theoretical basis for the development of counselling in education, particularly at the school level. I acknowledge the importance of psychoanalysis as a process and as a theoretical system, but of all the counselling theories, as a practical approach to the stress situations which many of us encounter during our lives, it probably has much to offer to the smallest number of people. Analysis itself can be a valuable relationship through which a small number of people come to a greater understanding of their lives, but it is a lengthy, expensive process, in short, a luxury. Analytical psychotherapy offers similar advantages and suffers from the same limitations of availability. Brief psychotherapy, which is closely related to personal counselling, offers less depth and time, and consequently greater availability, but when we come to apply analytical thinking to casework, I wonder if we have not diluted both the theory and the therapy to such an extent as to make it inappropriate as a means of help for the wide variety of people and problems to which it is being applied. Perhaps the kind of diagnostic understanding which is the focus of the approach is often a way of looking at life which many ordinary people have difficulty in using in a meaningful way. It seems a rather esoteric idiom, which does not translate readily to the 'nitty gritty' of the everyday life of the majority of people and perhaps it was not originally intended that it should.

What seems to be needed by many students is a counselling relationship in which they can feel secure, yet free to express themselves as far as their verbal abilities will allow, together with opportunities for practical learning, both within the counselling relationship and in their everyday lives. This perhaps involves a more eclectic knowledge on the part of the counsellor and a more varied repertoire of approaches, although she will probably have her own preferences. Eclectic approaches tend not to be popular at the present time, but, as Gibran reminds us, 'Let us not be particular and sectional. The poet's mind and the scorpion's tail rise in glory from the same earth.'

The use of the counselling relationship in directive and eclectic approaches

As we have seen, Rogers, the client-centred counsellor, stresses the importance of the counselling relationship as the source of the help provided by the counsellor. Williamson,[10] a proponent of the directive counselling approach, also stresses the importance of the human relationship in counselling.

Representatives of the eclectic approaches to counselling, who maintain that a counsellor should not limit herself to one method but should attempt to vary her approach in keeping with the needs of individual students, also stress the importance of the counselling relationship. Tyler, who recommends that each counsellor should attempt to develop her own synthesis of theoretical concepts, seems herself to offer a fusion of the directive and the client-centred concepts in her particular developmental approach, spiced with a dash of behaviour modification and a liberal covering of the concept of individual differences. This particular combination will probably have great appeal to counsellors in education in this country. She uses a musical analogy to describe the interaction between a counsellor and student in a counselling session, likening it to the trained musician who in listening to a new piece of music first picks out the main themes which form the essential structure. Unlike musical themes, counselling themes are not usually explicitly stated in the opening bars of the work, but are more often to be grasped after long periods of confusion. The same activities are required of both the musician and the counsellor: listening, thinking and responding. 'It is the hardest kind of work, but worth the effort.'[7]

Counselling skills

The real power of counselling emanates from the creation of a warm, sincere, dependable relationship, and the main counselling skill lies in making such a relationship with each individual, because it is this relationship which creates the psychological environment in which the student may shape or become aware of his own unique personality through his choices and decisions. Nevertheless, there are counselling skills or techniques which can be learned and used by counsellors to facilitate the helping relationship of counselling, such as the ability to listen, the value of silence, the picking up of non-verbal communication, and these also will be discussed in the later chapter on the training of counsellors.

9
Research and the counsellor

Someone has said that counselling is like kissing. It is an activity
that is so intrinsically interesting that few people take the time to
evaluate its consequences.[1]

Just as there once was a tendency to divide teachers into those who
taught subjects and those who taught children, there is a tendency
to dichotomize and talk of counsellors who are behaviourist, objective,
rational and research oriented as opposed to counsellors who are self-
theorists, concerned with feelings and attitudes or unconscious motivation, socially perceptive and more interested in developing close
and sensitive counselling relationships than in developing a research
project. These over-simplifications do not do justice to the approach
of the majority of teachers or counsellors, for there are few who fit
either extreme. Some counsellors are more skilled in research than
others and incline towards research activities, but the purpose of the
two descriptions is to remind counsellors that their work in education
needs the personal, socially perceptive approach [2] together with the
more objective collection of organized information about the educational or the counselling situation. Organized information helps us
to check assumptions and generalizations about people against the
individual facts, as well as to recognize and acknowledge the
exceptions.
   Some people feel that research is likely to diminish their effectiveness in the counselling relationship because in research they will be
concerned with objective, rather than subjective, material. One of
the control group of students who completed a questionnaire in a
research project of mine felt so strongly about this that she wrote,
'This form leaves you as anonymous as you were before. Your form is
soulless, impersonal and therefore unattractive. I wouldn't bring a
problem to the machine that produced this.'
   We need to show that counselling does to some extent achieve
the aims for which it has been established. We shall not be given

149

money from the educational purse for the development of counselling services unless we can provide organized information to answer the kinds of questions which those who control the allocation of finances are likely to ask. The nature of such questions will vary according to the particular needs that a counselling service was created to meet; it is necessary to know what you are aiming to do before you can evaluate whether or not you have succeeded, but they may include queries along these lines: Does counselling do any good? What is it good for? Can it be shown that students who receive counselling are any better off in their later lives than those who do not? In which kinds of situations does counselling help and in which does it seem ineffective? Can it be shown that counsellors who represent one clearly defined theoretical system get any better results than those who espouse another? Do group counselling and individual counselling show differing results? Do some skills and techniques seem to work better than others? Which criteria are most meaningful in expressing counselling effectiveness? [3]

Counsellors have not yet the credibility to make omnipotent or omniscient claims about the merits of one type of counselling service as opposed to another, or about the superiority of one theoretical approach over another. We have very little evidence to support any such claims because the introduction of counselling is so recent and it seems unwise for counsellors to be too pedantic about who is and who is not a counsellor, and what is and what is not counselling. We should be moving towards some answers to these questions, and counsellors will have their own personal points of view, but they 'cannot afford to indulge in the process of sowing dragon's teeth, for not only are there more constructive operations, but it is likely that these teeth will eventually destroy the counsellors'.[4]

Counsellors should consider it part of their job to describe their activities and over a period of several years to carry out, or help others to carry out, some kind of evaluation and description of their work. Large-scale research must be left to those who have the resources and staff, such as university institutes of education. The research study carried out on school counselling by Alan Thompson [5] at Keele University is not the kind of project that a school or college counsellor could realistically undertake, but work on a more modest scale could be very valuable.

A counsellor may be the person in a school who collects and interprets information on aspects of education other than counselling. As a school counsellor I had a special interest in developing an orientation programme for the change from junior to secondary school and I tried to find out about the attitudes of junior school children towards the move to secondary school by devising a short open-ended sentence completion questionnaire which I administered on visits to the junior schools. The idea was that if we could find out the difficulties that boys and girls anticipated and the things they looked forward to, we could use this information in the orientation programme. Of added value would have been a follow-up questionnaire to be administered to the same children towards the end of the first term of their first year to show their actual attitudes to the experience.

The distinction between evaluation and research is that in evaluation we decide the value of an activity, whilst in research we are providing the information and the criteria upon which to make evaluations.[6]

Evaluation of counselling effectiveness

Counselling, being a counsellor's main activity, is the area about which she asks most questions, whether informally, to herself, or in the form of specific studies.

Four main ways in which evaluations of counselling effectiveness have been carried out are:

1. follow up studies of student attitude by means of questionnaires or interviews;
2. the opinion of the counsellor about changes which took place and [her] estimate of the progress made;
3. internal studies based upon a close examination of the verbal exchanges, interview by interview, by using transcripts or tape recordings;
4. methods based upon objective measures of behaviour changes, such as the use of a personality test before and after counselling.[7]

The first method, using the criterion of student opinion, is subject to the usual unreliabilities and biases of reporting because it is social convention to respond politely and positively when asked whether or not an experience which was intended to help did, in fact, do so. Nevertheless, no one other than the student knows how he feels and what he thinks about the counselling he received.[8] Perhaps an important task for researchers is to discover what forms of treatment are most appropriate for people in different situations, and information from those who have received counselling will help.

The second method, using the criterion of counsellor judgment or opinion, is subject to similar disadvantages. The counsellor has

151

personal needs invested in the counselling relationship, which may distort her perception of the change or growth which takes place.

The third method uses an internal criterion, the verbal responses of the student, interview by interview, on the assumption that if growth is taking place in, for example, the student's self-acceptance, there will be a decrease in defensive and negative self-descriptions and an increase in positive ones. The disadvantages of this method are the tendency for the criteria of effectiveness to become the goals of the counselling (which may not be in the best interests of the student) and the lack of information on the permanence of the changes.

The fourth method, the objective measure of personality change such as a personality test, has the limitation that it is difficult to show which changes may be attributed to counselling and which to other experiences in the student's life.

Evaluation of group guidance also raises questions. For example, the effectiveness of vocational guidance may be assessed from answers to questions such as 'Do pupils have a greater knowledge of vocational information as a result of guidance, do they actively seek information and do they make more realistic vocational choices?' To assess the effectiveness of educational guidance we might ask, 'Is the achievement of pupils who have received educational guidance any higher than it was beforehand?' 'Is there any improvement in their habits of study?' 'Do their teachers observe any change in attitude to work?'

Follow-up study

Another way of collecting and organizing information is the follow-up study, a popular method in America. 'The follow-up study has probably become the single most used and misused research tool in the secondary school—often resulting in sloppily designed, executed and interpreted follow-up studies.'[6] Two basic methods are used for follow-up studies, the questionnaire and the interview, and a study by Rothney and Jackson which investigated the comparative effectiveness of these two ways of collecting information suggests that the interview technique was preferable because it resulted in more complete answers, a greater number of responses showing evidence of adjustment and problems. Both the questionnaire and the interview showed that the student had problems which he indicated in one follow-up procedure, but not in the other. Questions requiring factual responses were answered more often than open-ended questions or those needing evaluation. Fewer responses were made on each succeeding page of the questionnaire, indicating that its length influences the number of items completed.[6]

Although this study suggests that the interview is a preferred technique, a counsellor will find that time and financial considerations make the use of a questionnaire much more feasible, particularly in view of the lack of research carried out in schools and the apathy representative of the attitudes of many educators towards research methods and findings.

The purpose of follow-up studies is usually to obtain information about the life of the former pupil or student and their opinions of the educational and vocational value of their educational experiences. The results may be used to evaluate a school guidance programme, or to demonstrate the need to have one, to evaluate the curriculum and to discover the need for changes in the content of certain courses, to determine why pupils leave school at the earliest opportunity or why students discontinue their education, and as a means of finding out about former students who need help, and of offering assistance. A number of young people feel that once they have left school or college they are no longer of interest to the staff, and although they are often right, some staff are really pleased to see those who pay a return visit. If the follow-up study is to be used to provide a service for former students in this way, the study made during the student's first year after leaving school or college is probably the most useful because it is during this early period that adjustment problems are likely to arise. The information from such studies can be useful in work with school leavers because it is based on the actual views of young people who have recently experienced the problems. The study which is to be used for evaluation should be conducted two or three years after the student has left, when he is in a better position to evaluate his school or college experiences, in the light of his subsequent experience, than is the young person who has recently left school.

It might be possible for several schools or colleges in an area to combine to produce a questionnaire, returned copies of which would be sent to the appropriate school for processing, prior to a comparison of responses which could provide useful indications of the ways in which the different schools were preparing their respective pupils for the transitional process into work or higher and further education.

It may be necessary to send out second copies of the questionnaire to those people who do not respond to the first one, and in some cases third copies. The main problem involved when the response is less than 100 per cent of the sample (as it often is) is that the information received may be biased and atypical of the total sample. Questionnaires should be accompanied by a covering letter explaining to the person the purposes of the study, who is carrying it out and why he is being asked to take part, emphasizing the importance of his response and assuring confidentiality. A letter in which the salutation addresses the person by name rather than calling him, for example, 'former pupil', is likely to result in a higher response rate. The shorter questionnaire is generally to be preferred, since a long one discourages people, and the questions should be adequately spaced so as to be clearly readable. Stamped, self-addressed envelopes should be included, and the instructions for completing the questionnaire should be quite explicit.

INTERPRETATION OF INFORMATION

The interpretation of the information obtained in follow-up studies and indeed in all research studies is obviously important both for the use that the school or college can make of it and also as a means of providing assistance, should they desire it, for those who have taken part in the study. There are three possible areas in the interpretation of data in which errors may occur: inadequate sampling, misunderstanding of causation and over-generalization in evaluating behaviour.[6]

An adequately large response is important to avoid an atypical representation, but there are other characteristics which may bias the sample and make it unrepresentative, such as the tendency of those who did well in school to respond more than those who did not and the likelihood that girls will respond more often than boys. The sending out of second and third copies of the questionnaire and, where possible, personal contact can be a safeguard against inadequate sampling.

It is unwise to assume a cause and effect relationship between specific items of information unless this is clearly indicated beyond any reasonable doubt. If a boy or girl who did well in a particular subject in school fails in that same subject at the end of the first year of a degree course, we cannot justifiably conclude that the student has been badly taught at university unless we have much more information on the presence or absence in that student's life of the many other factors which affect academic performance. We may in such a case legitimately draw attention to the relationship without ascribing a cause.

An error which is as tempting to the unwary as the misunderstanding of causation is over-generalization in the evaluation of behaviour. A recent survey (not a follow-up study) of prospective women students requiring college accommodation asked questions about preference for a single sex hall or a mixed hall. The information obtained was used to support two opposing views. Those who favoured the retention of a single sex hall made the point that 10 per cent of the respondents had said that they preferred such accommodation, whilst those who supported the idea that all accommodation should be for men and women said that *only* 10 per cent of the respondents had preferred a single sex hall. Does the 10 per cent preference for a single sex hall justify saying that the hall should remain a hall for women only? The most likely answer seems 'Perhaps'. It would be advisable to investigate other variables before reaching conclusions.

Counsellors should at least draw tentative, carefully worded conclusions as a result of the data that they obtain from follow-up studies in preference to merely presenting the information on paper and leaving people to draw their own conclusions, because generally counsellors are less likely, because of their training, to make false interpretations.[6]

Opinions and attitudes

Opinions and attitudes can be measured in various ways, including the opinion survey, scaled statement questionnaire, sociograms, sentence-completion and open-ended statements, essays and direct observation scales. The counsellor who has the co-operation of a competent educational psychologist skilled in their interpretation may sometimes wish to use projective techniques such as the Thematic Apperception Test, or the Rorschach. It is possible to use tested attitude studies which were designed for other investigations such as that given in Coleman's *The Adolescent Society*[9] or the sentence completion technique used in Friedenberg's *The Vanishing Adolescent*.[10]

A student says that '. . . some schools ought to be made to realize that there are more than two universities (Oxbridge) in Britain', and another feels that 'the main problem in this place is tedium, life gets very boring', while a third suggests that it would be better if there were 'more opportunity to see the counsellor immediately, where practicable'. Each student is expressing an opinion or an attitude, derived from his own experience, an amalgam of his feeling and perception. The recognition and identification of attitudes as components of personality which affect such educationally significant aspects of life as morale, identity and cognitive learning is an area which has had little attention, perhaps because it is like opening

155

Pandora's box. Peel points out the part that attitudes play in learning when he says,

> School teachers are more prone to neglect the role of attitudes in learning than they are to fail to recognise individual differences in ability and attainment. Many able teachers, masters of their subject matter and sensitive to the intellectual differences of their pupils, overlook the function of attitudes in connection with failure by the child, harsh treatment and thoughtless rebuff and later apathy in the pupil. ... Much of the trouble in the case of backward children who are not innately dull, and delinquent children, is capable of explanation in terms of attitude psychology. Such pupils do not want to learn and refuse to face up to the school situation.[11]

We may obtain an indication of pupils' attitudes by asking them directly, by using some kind of opinion survey or by using a scaled statement questionnaire. The reliability of such instruments is questionable because attitudes cannot be measured directly, they can only be inferred from responses. The fact that you are focusing on a particular attitude by asking questions about it may affect the attitude itself, and there are sometimes inconsistencies between people's expressed attitudes and their actual behaviour. Nevertheless, attitude assessments do have a utilitarian value for some counsellors and teachers who, having decided which attitudes they might most profitably measure, are faced with the problems of finding out how the attitudes developed, whether or not they should be influenced and, if they should, ways in which this might be done, for it is easier to measure attitudes than to change them.

Studies of counselling

'The central question to be asked in counseling and psychotherapy is "What are the essential characteristics or behaviors of the therapist or counselor that lead to constructive behavioral change in the client?" This question admits that not everything a therapist or counselor does in the therapeutic relationship is effective or even relevant for constructive change in the client.'[2]

Several types of studies which are feasible for a counsellor with moderate research skills and limited time and resources have been mentioned. It seems appropriate to illustrate these by using a few examples from the research literature. The examples are chosen for their descriptive value only; they will not be evaluated.

1. FOLLOW-UP STUDY TOGETHER WITH COUNSELLOR OPINION (N=39)
Reporting on the first year of a counselling service in a college of
education, Wilson evaluated the effectiveness of his counselling by
a follow-up study plus counsellor opinion.[12] He used five criteria of
effectiveness:

(A) A willingness on the student's part to understand his (her)
personal problem.
(B) The student's motivation for change.
(C) The actual positive change (evaluated according to each
student's condition and potential).
(D) The benefit which the student felt from the experience of
counselling.
(E) Improvement in performance of college work.

Each student was asked to evaluate counselling effectiveness by
assigning to each of the five criteria a score on a points basis in which
three points were given if he felt significant change had occurred;
two points if he felt that some change had occurred; one point if
little change had occurred, and no points were assigned if the student
felt that there was no change. There was provision for the student to
assign minus points (−) if he felt that he was more disturbed and
confused as a result of the counselling he had received. Wilson
also assigned points to the students he had counselled using the same
system, and notes 'it is significant that in most cases the ratings which
the student gave and that of the counsellor (who also checked his
rating of (C) and (E) with the student's tutor) did not differ
significantly'.[12]
Of the forty-six students who had more than one interview with
the counsellor, seven could not be assessed, and after converting the
points into percentages, Wilson used the following table to indicate
the effectiveness of the counselling received by the remaining
thirty-nine. (*No.* refers to the number of students in each category.)

Category	Points (percentaged)	Quality of progress	No.
A	76%	Excellent progress	5
B	51–75%	Significant progress	12
C	31–50%	Some progress	5
D	11–30%	Little significant progress	13
E	10% minus	No progress	4
		TOTAL	39

Wilson does not state whether he obtained the scores from the students by interview or by questionnaire.

2. FOLLOW-UP STUDY USING STUDENT OPINION (N=135)

In the follow-up study consisting of a questionnaire conducted after two years of counselling in a university (which is not yet completely analysed) three items were used in an attempt to evaluate the effectiveness of the counselling received. Unlike Wilson's study, the students I saw did not all consult with personal problems, some came for help with financial, accommodation or study problems.

One item consisted of the question, 'Are you satisfied with the guidance and counselling you received?' Yes, No, More or Less.

The responses were: Yes   58.5%
                    No   10.4%
                    More or less 29.6%

A second item consisted of the question, 'If you received help directly from the Student Counselling Service with which of the following would you agree?'

Helped me to see the problem and its outcomes more clearly	15.6%
Helped me to understand my feelings and to deal with them	10.4%
Helped me to choose some course of action	39.3%
Confused me and made me begin to doubt my judgment	0.0%
Was not particularly helpful	11.9%
Nil response	27.4%

Some students responded to more than one item. It is interesting that the response rate of 11.9 per cent to the view 'Was not particularly helpful' is close to the 10 per cent of Wilson's category (E), 'No progress' recorded.

The third item attempted to assess the effectiveness of the counselling using statements from Truax and Carkhuff's questionnaire to measure the level at which the counsellor is offering the three central therapeutic conditions of accurate empathy, non-possessive warmth and genuineness, and these were the criteria of effectiveness. I can present the overall percentage response of students to each item, but not specific information such as sex of student, type of problem which brought him to counselling etc. There was a nil response rate of about 33 per cent on all these items and many of the students commented that they did not think they could respond to the items because of their brief contact with the counsellor—only one session to discuss a practical problem.

	True	*False*	*Don't know*
A The counsellor seems to hold things back rather than tell me what she really thinks	20%	60.7%	12.6%
B The counsellor understands exactly how I see things	28.1%	30.4%	34.1%
C The counsellor understands my words but does not know how I feel	23.7%	48.9%	19.3%
D The counsellor often mis-understands what I am trying to say	8.9%	71.1%	12.6%
E The counsellor seems to like me no matter what I say	37.8%	17.0%	38.5%
F The counsellor nearly always seems concerned about me	74.8%	3.7%	13.3%
G Sometimes the counsellor will argue with me just to prove she is right	3.7%	63.0%	25.2%
H I feel I can trust the counsellor to be honest with me	74.8%	5.9%	10.4%
I Sometimes the counsellor seems to be putting up a professional front	17.8%	53.3%	21.5%
J The counsellor usually helps me to know my feelings by putting them into words for me	36.3%	24.4%	30.4%
K The counsellor seems a very cold person	3.0%	84.4%	4.4%
L The counsellor really listens to everything I say	71.9%	5.9%	12.6%
M I often cannot understand what the counsellor is trying to tell me	0.7%	83.7%	7.4%
N I am afraid of the counsellor	0.0%	89.6%	2.2%

159

	True	False	Don't know
O The counsellor sometimes seems more interested in what she herself says than in what I say	4.4%	80.0%	8.1%
P The counsellor often leads me into talking about some of my deepest feelings	25.9%	40.0%	25.9%
Q The counsellor makes me work hard at knowing myself	20.0%	36.3%	33.3%
R When the counsellor sees me she seems to be just doing a job	20.7%	57.0%	14.1%
S I can learn a lot about myself by talking with the counsellor	28.9%	31.1%	30.4%
T I sometimes get the feeling that for the counsellor the most important thing is that I should really like her	5.2%	63.7%	23.0%
U The counsellor gives me so much advice I sometimes think she is trying to live my life for me	2.2%	79.3%	10.4%
V The counsellor is a very sincere person	70.4%	2.2%	19.3%
W Usually I can lie to the counsellor and she never knows the difference	4.4%	37.0%	49.6%
X The counsellor never says anything that makes her sound like a real person	2.2%	77.0%	13.3%
Y I have the feeling that the counsellor is wrapped up in what I tell her about myself	10.4%	40.7%	41.5%
Z When the counsellor is wrong she doesn't try to hide it	40.7%	3.0%	48.9%
AA The counsellor treats me like a person	85.9%	0.7%	5.9%

These two extracts illustrate the ways in which two counsellors have approached the problem of assessing different aspects of the effectiveness of their work.

Although it does not assess the effectiveness of counselling, the follow-up study on the role of the school counsellor made by A. J. Thompson at Keele University is an attempt to describe the activities carried out by school counsellors and to obtain the opinions of counsellors and their head teachers on these. Twenty-five trained school counsellors (twenty men and five women) took part in the study and kept full records of their work during the year 1968–9. These records, together with the questionnaires which were completed by the counsellors and their head teachers, should provide an interesting and useful account of the early development of counselling in British schools.[5]

The Counsellor, the quarterly journal of the National Association of Educational Counsellors, occasionally publishes brief research studies by practising counsellors. The new *British Journal of Guidance and Counselling* published by the Careers Research and Advisory Centre, Cambridge, aims to cover four main areas of need relevant to practitioners and research workers. (See Appendix 11.)

AMERICAN RESEARCH

The third and fourth methods of evaluating counselling, internal studies of interviews and external studies based on some kind of objective measure such as a personality test, are illustrated from American literature, which offers much research material of varying standard. In America the terms counsellor and psychotherapist are sometimes used synonymously and sometimes separately.

The use of internal studies of interviews using tape recordings (originally gramophone records) and the typed transcripts of these seems to be attributable to the work of Carl Rogers, the American psychologist who developed the client-centred approach to counselling. His work has been characterized from its beginnings in the late 1930s by an almost constant analysis of the content and process of the counselling relationship. It is this linking of practice, theory and research which has made this approach valuable for its flexibility, its responsiveness to changing circumstances and its wide application to people with a variety of difficulties. 'In the last few years, in particular, some of the most promising as well as practical ideas in the counselling field have emerged from extensions of this research work.'[13] In 1951 Rogers wrote of America, 'ten years ago there were no more than a handful of objective research studies which were in any way related to psychotherapy. During the past decade more than 40 such studies have been published by workers with a client-centred orientation. ... The basis for this development has been first and foremost the accumulation of complete electrically recorded case-material.'[14] By 1967 Truax and Carkhuff,[2] building on the work of Rogers, were able to assemble a sizeable collection of research findings on the value and the ineffectiveness of counselling and psychotherapy. Tyler comments that in 1952 she was fairly confident that she had included in her book *The work of the counsellor* all research summaries of any importance. In 1960 the amount of research had increased so much that she was less comfortable about the completeness of her summaries. By 1968, and the third edition, she realized that complete coverage was an unattainable ideal and concludes that the escalation of research activity between 1952 and 1968 is a 'blessing or curse of our times'.[8]

The use of the internal method of assessing counsellor effectiveness, is illustrated in Rogers's own publications.[14,15,16]

The fourth method, using objective measures, is illustrated by the small British study by Lawrence[19] quoted in Chapter 4.

An important piece of American research using personality change and mentioned by Tyler[8] is that made by Volsky in 1965. This carefully designed study found all differences in personality after counselling to be non-significant, except for one factor involving problem solving ability, which was significant, but it had deteriorated, not improved. Such findings no doubt led Volsky to say that we should analyse what we mean by the question 'Does counselling really work?' If we mean can it help changes in behaviour and habits so that we do something differently tomorrow from today, or can we facilitate decision-making and do these things in such a way as to enable the person to lead a life which is of more benefit to himself and to society, then Volsky suggests that the answer is 'unquestionably, yes'. If, however, we mean can we change the person's basic personality, so that we are aiming to change him rather than his behaviour, then

> This is a function of a shift in the personality and if we are talking about a shift that does not represent training, that is training a person to be more sociable, as opposed to personality change, there is no evidence in existence that indicates that we can bring about basic change in personality under any normal conditions. We can change personality by scrambling the brain, by cutting the vagus nerve, but there is no evidence that we can change personality by psychotherapy and if this is what we mean by 'Does counselling work?' then in my mind, it does not.[18]

Various kinds of follow-up research have produced almost no evidence that measurable personality change occurs as an outcome of counseling. What does happen is that limited problems are solved, workable decisions are made, the client moves forward with more assurance than before. If we take a long range view of individual development, each step forward is a significant factor in the growth of a person. Counselors must get their satisfaction not from making people over but from helping each person to become more truly himself.[8]

Other aspects of counselling which provide interesting areas for research and survey are illustrated by two studies, taken from the American literature.

Proxemics
The proxemics of the counselling situation is the manner in which individuals structure personal space and their immediate spatial surroundings. A study was made by Haase and Dimatta[19] of the seating arrangements of the counselling setting which were preferred by clients and those which were preferred by counsellors. Three different seating arrangements were used.

In the first of these the chairs were set at an angle to each other and away from the counsellor's desk.

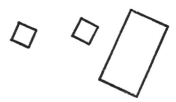

In the second the chairs were set facing each other, again away from the counsellor's desk.

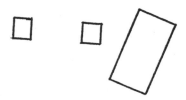

In the third arrangement the chairs were set facing each other across the corner of the desk.

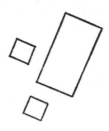

It was found in this study that most clients preferred the third arrangement with the chairs across the corner of the desk but that most counsellors preferred the first arrangement in which the chairs were angled, but away from the desk. The counsellors preferred the third arrangement the least. My own counselling situation offers none of these. I have three easy chairs and one hard-backed arm-chair surrounding a low round table.

Time-limited counselling

The second investigation, carried out in a college counselling centre, considered the effects of time-limited counselling, in an attempt to find an answer to the perennial problem of waiting lists. An arbitrary time limit for psychotherapy was set for a group of thirty-five students, and a study was designed in which the time-limited group was compared with short term and long term therapy groups. In this particular study by Muench,[20] the limited therapy was found to be as effective as short term therapy and more effective than long term therapy. It is suggested that the methodological effectiveness of the therapists and the degree of illness of the students were found not to account for changes during therapy.

Use of written records

The extent to which counsellors record information on students and counselling sessions varies considerably and is a matter of personal preference. Counsellors who have been trained in a casework approach prefer to write extensive case notes. My own records are brief and abbreviated. Because I do not regard general information as important, I do not obtain it; because my work is mainly oriented to the present and the future I do not use a case history. The information which seems relevant is the name, department and year of the student, source of reference, the dates of appointments and a note of any liaison I might have with staff, or outside agencies, together with a brief specific note on each interview. What should be stressed is that records must, like the contents of a counselling interview, remain confidential, and if such records are to be used by the counsellor for research purposes great care should be taken to preserve anonymity.

10
Counsellor education and training

The most significant resource a counselor brings to a helping relationship is himself.[1]

Counselling has been presented throughout this book as a helping relationship and although it may be stating the obvious to declare that a counsellor's most significant resource is herself, it is important to stress this particularly for the benefit of people who are interested in becoming counsellors. Skills and knowledge can be acquired and are helpful in the counselling situation, although when misused they can become a barrier. There is no particular 'personality' which serves as a model for the 'ideal counsellor', but there are personal characteristics which seem important. The counsellor is not an all-knowing, psychologically superhuman being, so emotionally stable as to be above the petty reactions of ordinary people; such a view is too divine and unrealistic, as is the idea that anyone whose heart is sympathetic can counsel effectively. Between the two extremes are the more realistic qualities characteristic of a counsellor in action.

Selection of counsellors

Rogers[2] has suggested that one of the first characteristics to be considered in the selection of counsellors is an individual's sensitivity to human relationships, which is shown in social situations.

SOCIAL SENSITIVITY

The person who is quite obtuse to the reactions of others, who does not realise that his remarks have caused another pleasure or distress, who does not sense the hostility or friendliness which exists between himself and others or between two of his acquaintances, is not likely to become a satisfactory counsellor. There is no doubt that this quality can be developed, but unless an individual has a considerable degree of this social sensitivity, it is doubtful that counseling is his most promising field of effort.[2]

Those whose job it is to select and train counsellors will devise and use ways in which this quality may be observed; the interview offered to applicants for most university courses will be inappropriate as a reliable means of selecting future counsellors, because it gives little opportunity for the demonstration and observation of this quality.

Although a capacity for social sensitivity is a good natural foundation on which to build counselling skills, there are other attitudes which are important.[2]

OBJECTIVITY

Objectivity, or controlled identification, is not a cold, impersonal detachment, but includes a genuinely receptive attitude and deep understanding which is not easily shocked and does not readily pass moral judgments. Although objectivity contains a capacity for sympathetic identification, it is not of the deeply sentimental kind in which the person becomes so wrapped up in the student's problems that as a counsellor she would be unable to help.

RESPECT FOR INDIVIDUAL

The person who is eager to reform students to fit her own value system is unlikely to have the capacity to respect the integrity of the student and to accept him as he is, so that he may then have room within the counselling relationship to grow and to resolve his difficulties within his own capacity and at his own developing level of adjustment.

AN UNDERSTANDING OF THE SELF

Some counsellors have difficulty in counselling for certain problems or working with certain kinds of people, and in such cases especially the counsellor needs a sound understanding of herself, through which she can recognize her own prejudices and the effects of her own emotions on the counselling relationship. It would therefore seem unprofitable to choose for training people who appear to have very rigid personality structures which may prevent them from becoming more self-aware.

PSYCHOLOGICAL KNOWLEDGE

'... a full knowledge of psychiatric and psychological information, with a brilliant intellect capable of applying this knowledge, is of itself, no guarantee of therapeutic skill.'[2] A basic knowledge of human behaviour together with its psychological, social and physical

167

determinants is an important foundation for the work of the counsellor, and, given the limited time available for training, it is perhaps desirable that a prospective counsellor should have some familiarity with this field.

Venables [3] suggests that selection of future counsellors should be closely related to a job analysis, which in the case of counsellors would include the ability to accept people and to listen to them, a sensitivity to non-verbal and other cues; the ability to tolerate differences of opinion or values, and being relatively free from prejudice. She would also include intelligence testing, an attitude scale or a personality inventory, individual interviews and two kinds of discussion group—one a task oriented group led by a selector and the other a leaderless group, both with a selector to act as recorder.

Nelson-Jones [4] suggests that the attributes of an effective counsellor are to be found on a selection-training continuum, which he describes as follows:

ATTRIBUTES OF AN EFFECTIVE COUNSELLOR

Selection————————————————————————Training

Suitable personality	*General conditions*	*Specific skills*
Relatively anxiety-free	Accurate empathy	Assessment and
Initially high on	Respect (non-	diagnosis
general conditions	possessive warmth)	Techniques of preferred
(see next column)	Congruence or	methods of
	openness to	treatment:
	experience	*a* psychotherapy
	Relevance	*b* group therapy
		c behaviour therapy
		d systematic training
		methods
		e role-play techniques
		f occupational
		counselling
		Knowledge of
		psychology and
		related areas
		Ability to assess
		research evidence
		Experience

He offers three main considerations for selection: academic, including subject level and quality of previous academic work; practical, covering employment possibilities, interest in further and higher education and in the financial support available; and thirdly, personal considerations such as emotional stability, any previous success in a helping role, the potential to offer the skills previously mentioned. These personal considerations are assessed from application forms and references, observer ratings of performance in a relatively unstructured group situation and independent ratings from a pair of interviewers. The IPAT Anxiety Scale is used and candidates are asked to reply as counsellors to statements taken from counselling transcripts.[4]

One piece of American research indicates that the personal characteristics relevant to success in counselling are different for men and women. Many of the women who were rated poorly as counsellors had excellent records as high school teachers and as graduates. Apparently those qualities which made them successful in these areas handicapped their effectiveness in the face-to-face counselling role.[5]

Training

> Most training programs parallel closely most books on psychotherapy: the interest and attention is upon the patient, his psychodynamics and his unconscious, pre-conscious and conscious thoughts and feelings. Such a program would well equip a student for being a patient. It is not at all clear how it would prepare him for being a therapist. Too often, after such training, the beginning therapist still wonders what kind of things to say, how to say them, what voice qualities to use— in short: *how to relate when he encounters the real person, not the textbook client or patient.*[6]

This comment points to the greatest difficulty in all professional training, that of co-ordinating learning and experience; theory and practice, intellect and emotion. This has been a problem in teacher training since prospective teachers ceased to be apprentices and were instead trained in colleges. The experience of teaching practice has a high emotional content which is related to parental relationships and to ways in which the student coped with previous experiences. There is evidence that the age range that a teacher chooses to teach has psychological significance as well as being related to his G.C.E. O and A level results. Students given an unstructured recall situation remember more incidents from the period of their lives corresponding to the age level they choose to teach. Generally junior school teachers have a higher personal need for nurturance and secondary school teachers a higher personal need for achievement.[7]

The counsellor in training is sometimes caught in the paradox of the contradiction between the way she is taught to behave as a counsellor and the way in which the supervisor behaves towards her. The didactic approach emphasizes the transmission of knowledge in a traditional teacher/student relationship and offers the counsellor the opportunity to form certain ideas about the things which happen in counselling, and the ways in which counselling is related to other aspects of education. This is important, but the approach does not offer conditions under which a counsellor is encouraged to work towards the depth of self-exploration and personal involvement which help her to become a genuine person in the counselling relationship.

The experiential approach sets out to elicit changes in behaviour and attitudes through a counselling experience, in the belief that the counsellor in training will 'grow' as a person, as a result. This offers opportunity for self-exploration but its limitations seem to lie in the tendency of counsellors to isolate counselling from other educational activities and sometimes from ordinary life itself, almost in an attempt to imbue it with some magical, esoteric qualities.

In general the training courses for counsellors which are offered in universities and colleges tend, because of the formal certification requirements, to have a large didactic element. Counsellors who have come into the work through their own experience of psychotherapy or psychoanalysis, as a means of help for their own needs, have had an experiential training which is not specifically related to the educational setting. These two approaches need not be mutually exclusive in counsellor training and they are often not so in practice. Counsellors in training need those conditions which research suggests are essential for psychotherapeutic personality growth, empathy, warmth and genuineness. The difficulty lies in finding people who are academically qualified to be accepted by the institution as lecturers, and who also are able to use counselling skills in the training of counsellors.

In 1965 Paul Halmos[8] gave the word 'counsellor' a very wide connotation and commented on the training of such people. He said that the social work field,

> comprises a miscellaneous assortment of training levels and counselling expertise. Some social workers have received a systematic training in social casework. Others, perhaps as many as half, engage in social casework from time to time, or even most of the time, without being especially trained and qualified to do so.

(The training of social workers has been extended since then.)

... doctors are untrained and, therefore, unqualified to render assistance through intimate personal consultation about moral or social problems. Those who select young men and women to be trained as doctors, neither know what personal qualities make for good counselling nor would they think these qualities to be decisively important in the selection of future workers ... in medicine.[8]

Modern psychiatrists [said Halmos] are medically qualified people having done three years postgraduate training in psychological medicine, leading to a Diploma in Psychological Medicine or some equivalent qualification. It is not a required part of their training that they systematically master a skill of counselling or a technique of psychotherapy ... but the majority freely engage in all forms of counselling and psycho-therapeutic procedures for which they have not received any systematic training, and for which they may not be very well suited on personality grounds.[8]

In 1971, the Royal College of Psychiatrists issued a memorandum, published in the *British Journal of Psychiatry*,[19] which offered guidelines for the training of general psychiatrists in psychotherapy during their initial three-year period of general psychiatric training. The educational objectives of these proposals were stated in general terms as the education of 'psychotherapeutically informed psychiatrists' who can use their psychological understanding and skills in the assessment and treatment of patients, and can undertake limited forms of psychotherapy.

Psychoanalysts may be either lay or medically trained and a number are formally qualified in psychiatry as well. Halmos suggests that we should not underestimate the psychoanalysts' importance, for in spite of their comparatively small number, their influence on clinical thinking and on general counselling practice is high. The authority of this small group is enhanced by stringent admission for training requirements and the intensive personal analysis which is required.

The Association of Psychotherapists is described as a group of people working as psychotherapists with a variety of qualifications, one being a training analysis of an 'eclectic and unspecified kind'. Halmos also suggests that psychologists are eclectic workers who may be used as diagnosticians, assessors, research personnel, psychotherapists or counsellors, who 'treat' or counsel 'using techniques which are congenial to them, often eclectically adapting what they have read, heard of, or seen done in the clinical setting

171

around them'.[8] Those who have completed a full-time university course of training in counselling appear to have been exposed to a far greater experience of counselling than, for example, educational psychologists, who often have a very small counselling element in their training and pick up what they learn of counselling in visits to Child Guidance Clinics.

This cursory look at the training of some of those who claim to use counselling as an element of their work may show trained counsellors who work in schools or colleges that their training and experience give them something to offer which doctors, psychologists, psychiatrists and social workers do not necessarily have. Those who train counsellors have generally paid too little attention to the task of helping their students to develop a realistic occupational self-image. They have rightly been afraid that counsellors might undertake cases beyond their competencies, or tread on the professional toes of psychologists or social workers, and have leaned over backwards to point out the dangers. This has often contributed to the beginning counsellor's overtentativeness and insecurity when faced with the verbal claims of other professions.

Counsellor education

The education of counsellors encompasses a much wider endeavour than training itself, for although it provides a professional training in counselling, it also includes the continuing education of the person of the counsellor in a variety of areas which have something to offer to those concerned with the study of people—areas such as literature, religion, anthropology, philosophy and sociology, in addition to the obvious discipline of psychology. My interest in a wider education for counsellors arises in part from my disaffection with the definition and approach of psychology as a study of behaviour—and in particular of laboratory behaviour—and the tremendous limitations which this places on our potential understanding of people as human beings and not merely as overgrown rats. Jung defined psychology as 'the empirical science of the soul', which points to the tremendously interesting paradox that is man. Freud is reported to have said[8] that he only wanted to feel assured that the therapy did not destroy the science. I want to feel assured that the reverse does not happen. One of the problems which we all face at some time, but which the student age group in particular finds pressing, is the problem of the meaning of life. The refinement of this issue can occupy a person throughout his whole life, but the counsellor who has not contemplated it to some extent for herself will be unlikely to understand student preoccupations with this question.

Pasteur, the scientist, suggested something of this mystery:

> I see everywhere in the world the inevitable expression of the concept of infinity. . . . The idea of God is nothing more than one form of the idea of infinity. So long as the mystery of the infinite weighs on the human mind, so long will temples be raised to the cult of the infinite, whether it be called Bramah, Allah, Jehovah or Jesus.
>
> The Greeks understood the mysterious power of the hidden side of things. They bequeathed to us one of the most beautiful words in our language—the word 'enthusiasm'—*en theos*—a god within. The grandeur of human actions is measured by the inspiration from which they spring. Happy is he who bears a god within, and who obeys it. The ideals of art, of science, are lighted by reflections from the infinite.[9]

It is an essential part of the education of a counsellor to have the opportunity to question, to discover, rediscover or strengthen her 'god within', for this will have an important bearing on her subsequent work. We each have our preference, which may be religious, humanist, psychological, philosophical, or have other derivations. Previous experience is important, but I question the argument that prospective counsellors must have a degree in psychology. Personalities aside, a degree in English may be equally as valuable to a counsellor as a degree in psychology because of the quality of experiencing and knowledge of people which is often involved in the study of that subject. My historical perspective, which developed when I was a student and later a teacher of history, has offered something very valuable to me as a counsellor.

There are several ways of training people to become counsellors, from the counsellor education provided by the one-year, full-time university courses, to personal psychoanalysis together with a course of lectures on various aspects of depth psychology which now form the required training of a psychotherapist, as recently laid down by the Association of Psychotherapists and the Society for Psychotherapy.[10] There are also part-time courses offered by other colleges, the Tavistock Institute for Human Relations and the Extra-Mural Department of London University. Many trained social workers consider themselves to be trained as counsellors, and although I am not convinced that the idea of such a transfer of learning is entirely valid, the notion that counselling and casework are synonymous is prevalent. It would be beneficial to train social workers, counsellors and even teachers side by side in the same institutions, in over-lapping courses, for I believe that these groups can learn from each other about working with people.

All methods of training offer in varying depth a practical, an academic and a personal element. I would emphasize the practical and personal aspects particularly because my experience as a counsellor has shown that these are crucial to the whole endeavour. Nelson-Jones [4] bases the course to train student counsellors, at the University of Aston, on several beliefs.

> First, that it is possible for skilled counsellors to provide learning experiences which will help many of their clients live more happily and effectively. Second, that both the psychotherapeutic and behaviourist approaches to counselling have much to offer and that the dichotomy between these approaches is some-what artificial. Third, that counsellor training to be effective must be functional. This means that the skills of successful counsellors should be taken into account in selection and training. Fourth, that counsellor trainees should participate in the formulation and evaluation of their training. Fifth, that the training programme should be regarded as a tentative hypothesis open to modification.

This particular course is a good example of counsellor training. The course content contains much that is of psychological, personal and practical value: the academic curriculum includes basic psychology, counselling theory, student problems, behavioural counselling, statistics, occupational counselling, human assessment, group interaction, counselling research, findings and methods, social contents, role of the counsellor and marital counselling. The practical training programme covers interview training—including empathy training, observation training and diagnostic training—test interpretation, observation of counselling, supervised counselling, quasi-group experience, field visits, case discussions, behavioural counselling, group counselling and occupational counselling.[4] It is a full programme and a valuable one; it seems to cater well for questions about the 'how' of counselling, but little for the more difficult questions about the 'why' of counselling and of life. This course sets out to offer a professional training in counselling, and succeeds. My view is that such training, though comprehensive, is not enough to equip a counsellor to do this very demanding work.

The Diploma in School Counselling offered at the University College of Swansea [11] illustrates courses for school counsellors, though not all the other courses follow exactly the same pattern. The

Swansea course consists of practical placements of two periods of a fortnight each in industry, former approved schools or remand homes, a careers advisory service, a school psychological service or a social service department of a local authority. Day visits to clinics and other institutions are arranged in conjunction with lectures by visitors from these specialist agencies. Students also spend one day a week in the same secondary school throughout the year doing a phased programme of practical work which includes individual and group counselling; parental contact and counselling; testing; case conferences and other relevant activities. The lecture programme of the course is related to the practical work programme. The theoretical aspect of the course consists of psychological studies covering developmental psychology, the principles of psychological measurement, social psychology and statistics. The section on the principles and practice of guidance and counselling includes the use of the interview; tests in relation to counselling; home, school and counsellor relationships; communication problems; group methods of counselling; the school care conference and welfare team, plus a detailed study of appropriate techniques for the counsellor, including the use of role playing, simulation and construct theory. Other areas covered are vocational and educational guidance; liaison with outside agencies; juvenile delinquency and the school as a socializing agency. The focus of counselling as a relationship is provided in this course by a term's lecture course on the casework relationship. An unstructured group situation is used to increase the perceptual and personal sensitivity of students.

Another section on sociological aspects consists of the study of social background; mobility and change in society; the influence of the family and other groups; the transition from school to work and the impact of mass communications. It also includes work on group dynamics; the basic needs of adolescents; the importance of group membership; the structure of groups; the elaboration of behaviour in groups; the forces of social control and the principles of group work and leadership. A final section looks at the education system and school organization under the headings of the changing status and role of the teacher; comprehensive education, the school as a social system; curriculum development, contemporary issues; further education and special educational treatment. Again this is a course which offers a combination of practical, personal and academic studies.

The part-time courses for the training of counsellors such as those offered by the Tavistock Institute for Human Relations and the Extra-Mural Department of London University seem to offer

175

a diluted form of the full-time courses in a lecture-discussion followed by group work format. The limitations of a part-time course seem to be in the areas of practical and personal learning, since if the course is to be recognized by the award of a certificate or a diploma the academic requirements must be met. There is a need for part-time as well as full-time courses; my concern is that these courses should not be so restricted by the academic requirements of educational institutions as to become inappropriate for the education of counsellors. A suggestion put to a meeting of the Standing Conference for the Advancement of Counselling (see Appendix 5) that we should work toward the establishment of an Institute of Counselling offers some hope that in the future we can combine a course with an appropriate qualification, which meets the needs of counsellors, without the compromise of having to meet the needs of college academic boards of study, whose members often have little notion of the type of course which is most relevant to the education and training of counsellors.

> Though counsellor training courses are a relatively recent innovation in England, the four I observed are all one year, full time, residential courses with rather selective controls on admission and allow much opportunity for small group instruction and interaction which thus far seems to be assuring a level and consistency of training that surpasses that of many practising counsellors in the United States. . . .
>
> As the demand for trained counsellors increases in England and the training programmes proliferate, the maintenance of established standards will obviously become more difficult, but I think no less important. . . . I would suggest . . . that appointment of counsellors should be restricted to those who are fully trained through programmes similar to those now existing. In other words, it might be well to try to increase the competence of all teachers for their role in pastoral care and to help them to recognise what lies within their competence and that which should be referred to those more highly trained in counselling techniques.[12]

Counselling skills

It seems important to look at some of the skills which a trained counsellor might employ in her work, several of which are used to develop the counselling relationship while others are used to facilitate understanding.

RAPPORT

Developing rapport is the first step in counselling and is the counsellor's attempt to communicate her acceptance of and interest in, the student. It may begin with expressions of normal courtesy, but although some counsellors like to build rapport through social conversation at the beginning of a session, others prefer a more straightforward, 'What would you like to talk about?' or just an attempt to communicate non-verbally through facial and bodily expression and eye contact that they have time to wait until the student is ready to talk. The mode of greeting and the start of a counselling session depend very much on the preference and style of the individual counsellor and the behaviour of the student coming for counselling.

The proxemics of the counselling situation, in which consideration is given to the use of space and the seating arrangements, can be important, too, but these are dependent on counsellor preference and the physical conditions available. I have counselled walking round a sports field because there was no room in which to sit. Other counsellors work in cupboards and cloakrooms, particularly in the school situation. A more appropriate situation is the provision of a warm, sound-proofed room with comfortable chairs for both counsellor and student.

The crucial establishment of rapport in counselling is created by such means as a warm, friendly approach, a smile, when it is appropriate, a genuine interest, expressed by careful listening and attention, by often meeting the eyes of the student, not in an embarrassing stare, but to maintain contact, in an atmosphere which is relaxed, unhurried and accepting. Someone once said that the counsellor must be spontaneous whilst weighing every word, and the creation of rapport has this ambivalent quality about it, in the sense that the professional counselling relationship is initially an artificial one which the counsellor tries to make as natural as possible.

REFLECTION OF FEELING

Accurate reflection of feeling is a skilled attempt by the counsellor to convey empathy, to understand and appreciate the intricacies and depth of the essential attitudes, rather than the content, expressed by the student; to mirror these and to synthesize the experience of them in simple and fresh expressions to help the student to understand himself and to communicate to him that he is being understood. It is not an interpretation in that it neither adds to, nor subtracts from, the meaning intended by the student. The depth of reflection should be on the level of meaning expressed by the student, though it will often go beyond the level of the verbal content to reach the meaning.

There are three main difficulties which face the counsellor when she attempts to reflect feeling. The first is her sensitive selection of an appropriate, essential, dynamic feeling for reflection, rather than choosing to reflect merely the verbal communication, which is mere repetition, or to reflect a peripheral feeling.

The second difficulty is that of avoiding stereotypical responses or using the same phrases repeatedly, either out of habit or from tiredness. An example is to preface every reflection with 'You feel . . .' I remember a small boy getting very cross with me in a school counselling situation because I said 'You feel . . .' and 'You seem to feel . . .' several times. It is often difficult to find fresh and varied approaches, but stock phrases can be very irritating or threatening.

A third difficulty is in the timing of the reflection, which is important, for if it comes too late, it may lose its value or cause confusion and if too early, it may fail to capture the essence of what the student is really trying to convey.

It may be helpful to illustrate one or two of the more common errors which counsellors in training and beginning counsellors make as they try to facilitate counselling relationships through their verbal responses. Sometimes the person confuses the counselling situation with other roles such as teaching; sometimes her own personality needs, or needs for authority and control of the situation influence the verbal responses.

If we imagine a situation in which a student sits tentatively on the edge of the chair and, whilst looking anywhere in the room except at the counsellor, says, in a rather hesitant and distracted way,

STUDENT I really don't know what to do . . . I've been to my tutor and told him I'm leaving my course but I really have no idea of what I want to do. . . . I just want to leave this place because it's so depressing. . . . I'm just not interested in my subject. . . . Everybody else is so happy here. . . . They've all settled down. . . . (*Student removes coat*) I feel warm.

These are several responses that a counsellor may make at this point to reflect the feeling expressed by this student. Some of the more inappropriate ones will be illustrated first.

Inappropriate responses

COUNSELLOR You want to leave this place because it's so depressing.

Everyone else is so happy here, they've all settled down, and you feel warm.
[Parrot-like repetition.]
COUNSELLOR You feel warm.
[Repetition involving reflection of safe, physical feeling rather than responding to the emotional content.]
COUNSELLOR You feel everyone else is happy.
[Slight approach to emotional feeling but out of focus—it is the student and his feelings about himself which are most important. His implication is that he is unhappy. The counsellor has not grasped this one firmly but is angling towards it.]
COUNSELLOR You feel emotionally disturbed.
[Interpretation rather than reflection of feeling. The vocabulary is inappropriate it has added something which the student did not express. The timing is ill advised, it is much too early in the relationship to make this kind of threatening statement.]

If the counsellor is to comment at all here, an interested 'Mm hmm' which signifies 'Tell me more' may be more relevant. The feeling behind this student's behaviour and remarks seems to be one of confusion. The counsellor might make a mental note of the college being depressing to the student, and other students appearing to be happy, before saying quite warmly, but in a fairly normal tone,

COUNSELLOR This seems to be a confusing time for you.

The counsellor would be expressing several things through her words and behaviour. One is that she understands and accepts that at this particular time the student feels confused and makes no judgment on this. She also conveys that she has concentrated on the student's feeling of confusion rather than the practical situation of his leaving his course, because feelings are important in counselling and she respects them. She has not concentrated on the apparent happiness of other people because this particular student is the focus of the relationship. The counsellor's statement is tentative rather than categorical—'this seems to be . . .' implying that the student has the choice of rejecting her remark and its implications if he so wishes and is able to do so. Although this seems to be a confusing time for the student, the counsellor's inference is that there are other times when the student is not confused. The hope is that through this the counsellor and student together may be able to look at some of the deeper motivations behind the student's present confusion.

REFLECTION OF CONTENT
There is a place for the reflection of content in counselling as an aid to

understanding. It is likely to come towards the end of a counselling session as part of the summarization, but it can also be used earlier to clarify what appears to be an important cognitive aspect. It may be necessary later in the counselling session with the student quoted above, to establish whether or not he had actually withdrawn from the college, but if the counsellor picks up such practical points right at the beginning of the session by a comment such as,

COUNSELLOR You've told your tutor that you're leaving your course. [This leads the student in a specific direction away from the area of feeling.]

EMPATHY

'Skill without empathy might fail while empathy without a vestige of conscious and deliberately applied skill might succeed.'[8]

Empathy is closely linked to reflection of feeling since it implies an active appreciation of another person's feeling experience. Whilst empathy is the sense of putting oneself in the student's shoes, of understanding his thinking and feeling his emotions, reflection of feeling is one of the ways of communicating the empathic understanding.

If we take the same student, behaving in the same way.

STUDENT I really don't know what to do, I've been to my tutor and told him I'm leaving my course but I really have no idea of what I want to do. I just want to leave this place because it's so depressing . . . I'm just not interested in my subject. . . . Everybody else is so happy here. . . . They've all settled down. . . . (*Student removes coat*) I feel warm.

Inappropriate responses

COUNSELLOR Yes, it's very warm today, but wasn't it cold yesterday? [The counsellor does not understand the difference between conversation and counselling.]

COUNSELLOR Oh, I know just how you feel, that happened to me when I first went to college. [This has been called the empathic trap. The counsellor forgets that it is the student who is the focus of the counselling relationship.]

COUNSELLOR Oh, lots of people have that problem, don't worry about it, you'll soon settle down. [Inappropriate reassurance. The counsellor is trying to make the student 'strong' by denying him his feeling.]

UNDERSTANDING

Understanding in counselling has been distinguished in two ways. Diagnostic understanding is concerned with intellectual descriptions of a student's behaviour and may use test information or counsellor observation. 'Its effectiveness is seen in the counselor's ability to describe, interpret and predict the student's behaviour.'[13]

Therapeutic understanding is concerned with the feeling aspect of the counsellor's reaction to the student and his self-perception, rather than with any knowledge or information that the counsellor may have about him. It involves seeing the student as he sees himself.

Effective counselling is a combination of both diagnostic and therapeutic understanding, but there is often imbalance in this duality, which leads beginning counsellors to emphasize one aspect at the expense of the other. For example, the counsellor who is preoccupied with information gathering might respond as follows:

STUDENT I really don't know what to do, I've been to my tutor—
COUNSELLOR What is the name of your tutor?
STUDENT Dr Smith. I've told him I'm leaving my course—
COUNSELLOR You've actually withdrawn from the college then, from which date?
STUDENT Er-well, I think it was Tuesday.
COUNSELLOR Tuesday, let's see that was the 25th.
STUDENT It might have been Monday, I don't remember.
COUNSELLOR Hm. You don't know whether it was the 24th or 25th?
STUDENT No, but I really have no idea of what I want to do.
COUNSELLOR What did your tutor say about your leaving?
STUDENT Well-er he said I should come to talk to you.
COUNSELLOR So you were referred here by your tutor?
STUDENT Yes, but I just want to leave this place because it's so depressing and I'm just not interested in my subject.
COUNSELLOR What is your subject? etc.

INTERNAL FRAME OF REFERENCE

The concept of the internal frame of reference is a useful way of helping a counsellor to understand the student from his own point of view, to think with him, rather than for him, or about him. Rogers[14] offers a description of the attitude of the counsellor who is trying to assume the student's internal frame of reference.

To be of assistance to you I will put aside myself—the self of ordinary interaction—and enter into your world of perception as completely as I am able. I will become, in a sense, another self for you—an *alter ego* of your own attitudes and feelings

181

—a safe opportunity for you to discern yourself more truly and deeply, and to choose more significantly.

Taking our student as an example, the counsellor working from an external frame of reference might think 'This student is going to leave his course. I must find out what is wrong and try to help him to stay at college.' The counsellor working from an internal frame of reference might think 'This student is confused, I must try to understand how he sees the problem and what he feels about it. Then I must help him to clarify his own thoughts and feeling so that he can make a decision based on what we discover about these two areas of his life and what choices are available to him.'

STRUCTURING

Structuring is a means of making the counselling relationship more secure by preventing the student from developing misconceptions about the counselling process. It is likely to be a continuous process covering the areas of responsibility, advice-giving, quick or inevitable solutions, etc. If too much structuring is done in the first session this may lead to the student becoming too dependent on the counsellor, or alternatively so defensive that he fears to return for further counselling. Structuring is a gradual, continuous process, and should be done in such a way that it does not conflict with the attitudes of acceptance, understanding and sincerity which are characteristic of the counselling relationship.

Structuring involves the setting of a time limit for the counselling session, by a comment such as 'Let's see what we can achieve in the forty-five minutes that we have.' Perhaps, too, at the end of the first session giving the opportunity for one, two or three further sessions depending upon the situation. 'There are great advantages in setting a time limit. Dr Johnson's aphorism "Nothing so concentrates the mind as knowing that you will be executed a week next Tuesday" is apposite. If the client knows that his time is up at twelve o'clock, at ten to twelve the counsellor is likely to hear . . . "But of course, the thing that's really bothering me is . . ." '[3]

Structuring may be used to define the limits of roles, particularly in a dual-role situation like that of the teacher/counsellor in a school. It may be helpful and indeed necessary for a teacher/counsellor to explain to a child that when she is wearing her teacher's hat she has certain evaluations and assessments to make, whereas when she is working as a counsellor, the child is at liberty to talk freely without being evaluated or judged. This is a difficult distinction for some children to accept.

The same student example is used to illustrate some structuring responses on the part of the counsellor.

Inappropriate structuring responses

COUNSELLOR You should attend lectures and take notes, and ask about things you don't understand in seminars.
[This is not counselling, it is advising.]
COUNSELLOR Well, do you want to leave college or don't you?
[Counsellor is rather rudely pressing for a quick decision.]
COUNSELLOR Don't you think you should get a degree so that you'll have a better chance of getting a good job later on?
[The counsellor has loaded the question and assumed the responsibility.]

A more appropriate response indicating some structure might be

COUNSELLOR This seems to be a confusing time for you, perhaps you will talk a little more about it in the forty-five minutes that we have, and possibly later on we can look together at what you might decide to do.

I would not recommend this kind of structuring so early in the interview with this particular student, because in his confused state he is unlikely to grasp what the counsellor is saying. However, I use it as an example of the sort of structured response which might sometimes be made, in which the counsellor sets the time limit of forty-five minutes and gives an indication that further counselling may be available. In saying 'Perhaps you'll talk a little more about it' the counsellor suggests that the responsibility belongs to the student, 'Possibly later on we could look together' implying a shared task —'at what you might decide to do'—again implying that the decision is one for the student to make.

SILENCE
Although silence itself is not a counselling skill, the use of silence in a counselling relationship is a skilful procedure, for silence may be a form of negative and rejecting or positive and accepting communication. In social settings silence is often regarded and used in a negative way—sending someone to Coventry being an outstanding example—and it can be greatly feared. A few years ago the popular singers Simon and Garfunkel had a record album called Silence, on which they sang 'Silence like cancer may grow'. Because of this social attitude towards silence as being like a malignant vacuum which must be filled the therapeutic use of silence is a skill which has to be learned.

Prolonged silences early in a counselling relationship may be interpreted by some students, and children in particular, as rejection, or used by them as a hostile resistance, particularly if they are still wary of the counselling situation and unsure of how the counsellor sees them. Later in the relationship silence is usually a more natural outcome at the end of a stage in the counselling process, or as a contemplative silence as a preliminary to some important work. Silence, too, may be an indication that the student is feeling some particularly painful emotion which it is difficult for him to express, or it may follow the expression of such emotion, and act as a respite.

The counsellor needs to be alert to the feelings behind a silence so that she may assess when to support a student through a silence by a brief verbal intervention and when to let the student assume responsibility for moving the relationship forward.

NON-VERBAL COMMUNICATION

Although the counselling interaction is conducted mainly at a verbal level, there is also much non-verbal communication. The student who sits on the edge of the chair, or wraps his coat firmly around him and peers over the top of his collar; the one who moistens his lips or blinks frequently, or another who shuffles his feet or bites his nails are all communicating non-verbally. The counsellor, too, conveys meanings in a non-verbal way and should be as sensitive to her own non-verbal communication as she is to that of the student. Sometimes the verbal message and the non-verbal communication contradict each other, as when the counsellor assures the student warmly that she is ready to listen and then proceeds to look through some notes, or glance repeatedly at the clock.

'The reality of the other person is not in what he reveals to you, but in what he cannot reveal to you.

Therefore if you would understand him, listen not to what he says but rather to what he does not say.'[15]

Sometimes students come for counselling determined not to reveal something about themselves, and they are often disappointed if they do not reveal it. Whilst the counsellor listens attentively to what is said and watches carefully for non-verbal communication, she simultaneously listens with what has been called her third ear, for the things which are left unsaid, or are avoided. Listening to what people do not say is one of the hardest skills for the trainee counsellor to learn, but what is left unsaid can be crucial.

These are just a few of the skills which may be used to facilitate the counselling relationship and to help a student to understand himself and his feelings, to reach a decision, to solve a problem, or to live through a crisis in his life.

Some ways of teaching counselling skills

Whilst the theoretical aspects of counselling theory and skills can be communicated by means of lectures, seminars and reading, the practical application of these skills is a much more difficult aspect of counsellor training to implement effectively. Pentony[16] suggests some of the ways in which counsellors-in-training may observe and practise counselling skills and divides these methods into two over-lapping groups, demonstration and practice.

DEMONSTRATION OF COUNSELLING SKILLS

The counselling interview can be demonstrated in several ways.

1. Conducting a counselling session before an audience either as an actual interview with a client or with someone role-playing the client. The easiest of the methods to arrange, particularly as a role-playing situation, it can be extremely effective if the counsellor conducting the demonstration can carry the person who is role-playing deeply into the role by her attitude and responses. On the other hand it can deteriorate into a stiff dramatic exercise with little authenticity and conviction.

2. Conducting a counselling session with trainee counsellors observing from one-way vision screens.

3. Using close-circuit television to demonstrate a counselling session.

Methods two and three are very similar and the extent of their use depends largely on the resources available. It is particularly useful for trainee counsellors to watch a sequence of counselling sessions with the same student to note the development of the relationship and the way in which the interaction progresses.

4. Using films, video-tapes or sound tape recordings of counselling sessions which have been conducted by others or recorded in previous years.

There are several demonstration films, made by well-known exponents of particular approaches to counselling. These are mainly American but they are now available in this country through the University of Keele Film Service. Sound tapes are

185

also very useful for teaching purposes and can be stopped at required points for discussion and then replayed as required.

5. Using multiple counselling in which the trainee-counsellor sits in as an assistant counsellor and works with the counsellor and the client in a triadic relationship.

The trainee counsellor is introduced to the student as an assistant who is gaining practical experience and who may be of help, but this would not be done without the student's agreement. The trainee counsellor takes little part in the early interviews, but usually becomes more active in later sessions. It would be difficult for a counsellor and a trainee counsellor of differing theoretical orientations to work harmoniously in a multiple counselling relationship. This method does have the advantage of offering a model, of providing the trainee counsellor with the opportunity of taking part in a counselling session, and then having helpful discussion with the counsellor afterwards. The counsellor, too, is encouraged by this method to make her own aims and assumptions explicit.

6. Personal analysis, psychotherapy or long-term counselling for the trainee counsellor.

This method is a basic requirement of psychoanalytic training, and it is essential that facilities for psychotherapy or long-term counselling should be available to all trainee counsellors. The disadvantage of this method, if it is used exclusively from the others, is that it usually offers only one theoretical approach and one model, so that the trainee counsellor has little or no choice. A counsellor's choice of theoretical orientation is a complex and personal one, and some alternatives should be available whenever this method is used.

PRACTICE OF COUNSELLING SKILLS

Some ways of enabling trainee counsellors to practise the counselling skills of which they have heard and read and, it is to be hoped, seen demonstrated, are:[16]

1. The trainee counsellor conducts counselling sessions with the supervisor observing from behind one-way vision screens or on closed-circuit television.

Because both the trainee counsellor and the supervisor are relying on memory (unless the session is video-taped or recorded on sound tape) the follow-up discussion will tend to be general in nature rather than concentrating on more detailed aspects of the interaction. However, it is a useful introductory method.

2. The trainee counsellor conducts a counselling session, as in (1) above, but the supervisor is able to transmit instructions to her during the session, by means of a microphone and a receiver which fits in the trainee counsellor's ear, rather like a hearing aid, so that the client does not hear what is said.

The advantage of this method is that the supervisor can give the trainee counsellor immediate feedback on what is happening in the session, so that she can do something to change the situation and see the consequences of that change.

3. The trainee counsellor records her interviews on a tape recorder and plays them back later for discussion with the supervisor (see Appendix 8).

This is a salutary experience for any counsellor because she is brought face to face, or rather ear to voice, with her own behaviour and responses in a counselling session, which are then available for detailed analysis. The errors and shortcomings are usually fairly obvious and the job of the supervisor is to help the trainee counsellor to look at them in more detail rather than merely to draw attention to them.

4. The trainee counsellor plays tape recordings of interviews conducted by experienced counsellors, stopping the tape at the end of each statement by the client and making her own response before she goes on to play the response of the experienced counsellor.

This method, like (1), is a useful introductory exercise, but again there may be some difficulty in co-ordinating the responses of people of differing theoretical orientations. This is, however, a useful way of helping trainee counsellors to develop responses, appropriate to a particular theoretical orientation.

Pentony [16] describes centres in Antwerp and Amsterdam which have set up 'language laboratory' situations in which the trainee counsellor can listen to a client statement, make her own response and then hear a model response of the required kind, for example, reflection of feeling.

During my training I was given practice in these methods with the exception of (2). It was a demanding, yet vital and living experience, but one of the more unfortunate results is that I now find the typical British case-discussion method of learning unhelpful, unimaginative and discrepant. Because of my training I know that often what people describe in a case discussion group does not correspond to the reality of the situation. Case discussion groups have a value, but they are not an efficient method of teaching counselling skills.

In addition to the practice of counselling skills, there is need for some feedback for the trainee counsellor as to the effectiveness and helpfulness of what she is doing. One way of doing this is to have a rating scale oriented towards whatever theoretical approach is being taught. The trainee counsellor can be evaluated on such a scale by supervisors and fellow students but such evaluations should be presented when there is time for follow-up discussion.

REVIEW OF COUNSELLING INTERVIEW

Date   Name of trainee counsellor
Circle the number which you feel best expresses the behaviour of the counsellor or the student being counselled.

Key: 1 Very good; 2 Good; 3 Average; 4 Fair; 5 Poor.

Degree of initial acceptance reflected through voice, facial expression and bodily movement	1	2	3	4	5
Skill in reflecting student's feelings and picking up student's lead	1	2	3	4	5
Degree of empathy expressed verbally and non-verbally	1	2	3	4	5
Lack of authoritarian, controlling tendencies by counsellor	1	2	3	4	5
Lack of moral judgments and persuasive methods shown by counsellor	1	2	3	4	5
Degree to which counsellor reflected acceptance of the student and any hostile and negative feelings	1	2	3	4	5
Extent to which student was given time to think and freedom to express his feelings when he chose	1	2	3	4	5
Extent to which student expressed feelings, rather than content or conversation	1	2	3	4	5
Extent to which student seeemed to achieve any significant self understanding	1	2	3	4	5
Extent to which counsellor was able to share mutuality of experience and adopt the student's internal frame of reference	1	2	3	4	5

What would you regard as the strengths of this counselling session?

Which skills do you consider the counsellor needs help in improving?

What do you feel you have learned from listening to and observing this counselling session?

A SUMMARY OF COUNSELLOR EDUCATION, SUGGESTING COMMENTS ON THREE ASPECTS [17]

1. Counsellor role

Counsellor role includes 'assisting the individual using referral sources; aiding in the development of decision-making processes; presenting relevant information and using ethical practices.'

2. Counsellor as a person

Counsellor characteristics include 'belief in the individual; commitment to individual human values; alertness to the world; openmindedness; understanding of the self and a professional commitment to the role of the counselor.'

3. Counsellor competencies

Professional studies, areas of preparation include

a. Background in social and biological sciences.

b. Practical experience, laboratory work (learning about counselling skills in training), practicum (working as a counsellor in an appropriate setting for say one day a week), internship (working in the counselling field on a longer basis whilst still studying).

c. Principles and practice of guidance.

d. Counselling theory and techniques.

e. Organization and administration of a guidance programme.

f. Knowledge of tests and measurement.

g. Knowledge of statistics and research methods.

h. Knowledge of individual analysis.

i. Knowledge of occupational information.

j. Knowledge of group work.

Perhaps the point on which to conclude a consideration of the counsellor's contribution to helping processes is the point at which all effective helping begins, that is, with an integrated and growing person, one who is personally productive and creative, one whose life is dominated by personal meaning and fulfilment. Without such persons in the helping role there is no hope in the world or for the world.[18]

11
Groups in guidance and counselling

The vitality and magnitude of the application of group efforts promise an eventual professional stature for groups in counselling and therapy that may provide equal acceptance with any individual one-to-one concept.[1]

Group guidance

Guidance is concerned with presenting information in a way which will enable each individual student to find some personal meaning in what he has read, seen or heard. It is not sufficient to present information to students, and to assume that they have all heard and understood the same thing, for each one reads personal meanings into what may be considered 'objective' facts. If we exclude group counselling, then group guidance becomes a set of activities used with a group of students to help each in his individual learning. It is mainly a cognitive process with little attention given to feelings or emotions and is concerned with helping people to discuss the meaning of various kinds of information. The focus is on ideas, explanations, and verbal expression as an aid to a personal understanding of information or to the completion of a set task.

The following purposes particularly emphasize group guidance in the secondary school setting.[2]

1. To assist in the identification of common problems.

2. To provide information useful in the solution of adjustment problems.

3. To provide opportunities for group thinking in regard to various problems and experiences.

4. To provide opportunities for experiences that promote self understanding.

5. To lay the foundations for individual counselling.

There are certain problems which are common to adolescents as part of the developmental processes of this age group, there are also certain kinds of educational, vocational and social information which can be of help to young people as they grow up. These may be presented in a group situation and discussed with the realization that their difficulties are not peculiar to them as individuals, as they often think, but are shared by fellow students.

CHOICE AND DECISION-MAKING

There are essentially two types of information needed for intelligent decision-making: information regarding oneself as a person with assets and liabilities, talents and limitations; and information regarding the particular situation about which a decision is to be made, or to which the self is related. When a person has this information he needs some way of dealing with it.

There are various models of choice or decision-making used by people in making vocational or other choices, which vary according to the individual concerned and his circumstances.[3]

Trait and factor model

The trait and factor model is based on the idea that any individual possesses a variety of traits and any occupation demands certain requirements of those who enter it. The individual can match his traits with the occupational or educational requirements and determine which job or course he is best fitted for. This model is often used in vocational guidance in our schools and its main disadvantage is that it is too static and does not take into account the changing and developing nature of either the student or the environment to which he must relate.

Economic model

An individual using the economic model chooses an occupation or a college which will maximize his gain and minimize his loss; for example, going to college might be a means of achieving greater status and mobility. The gains achieved are not necessarily economic or financial but may consist of anything which is of value to the person concerned.

Social structure model

The individual using a social structure model of choice is restricted in the decisions he can make because his knowledge of the various opportunities available is limited by family, social and economic circumstances. This is particularly so of disadvantaged students for whom narrowness of cultural or social class horizons places restrictions on their educational or vocational selection and often leads to

192

the equally narrow perspective of immediate gratification as the basis for choice.

Information processing model
A person may be forced into using the information processing model of choice when the facts necessary for him to make a decision are so overwhelming that he is pressured into a premature decision. Some students choose a particular college or job because their friends have done so, or because they are vaguely aware that a college has a particular reputation. This type of choice supports the individual's rationalization and reduces his anxiety.

Need reduction model
The need reduction model is a comprehensive one which subsumes certain elements of the other models. It assumes that an individual has a self-concept and that he implements this picture of himself in his choice of course or occupation, by gravitating towards a career, or a course of study which he sees as compatible with his needs and interests. This may be a result of unconscious motivation, or a relatively rational conscious choice. The advantage is that this provides for change in the person's behaviour, environment and expectations, and interaction between the individual and his environment. It suggests that making decisions about important areas of one's life is a complex and on-going process forming part of a developmental sequence extending from childhood through adulthood and not an isolated event at a particular point in time.

SOME WAYS OF PRESENTING INFORMATION IN GROUP GUIDANCE
It is no good giving information to students who see no need for it, so motivation should precede instruction in group guidance. The presentation of information is only part of the process and must be followed by some feedback to ensure that it reached each student accurately.

Large groups or assemblies
Whilst large groups offer an economical way of disseminating information, large group audiences tend to be passive listeners, or merely passive. We need to supplement this type of presentation by work in smaller groups and with individuals in which there is more opportunity for interaction and feedback.

Tutorial groups
Unless tutors in school have one period each day with their students

193

the tutorial group is not an effective way of providing information on which to base choices, or of providing help in other areas. Tutors also need training in group work, and the support of a carefully planned, effectively led guidance programme.

Orientation groups

Orientation usually takes the form of large group information giving, plus smaller orientation groups which continue throughout the year and are aimed at helping the students to develop independence. This applies at all levels of education, not just at the school level. American studies [3] indicated that three out of four college students had difficulties with the transition from the orderly, fairly directive secondary school to the non-directive environment of college. Some of the reasons given for these difficulties were unrealistic expectations of college social and educational life; an inability to organize their time; going to college without a strong desire to attend; and financial difficulties. Closed circuit television can be a useful medium for orientation purposes.

Discussion groups

Guidance groups are concerned with affective discussion about the impact of information and also about problems arising from some personal adjustment and difficulties. Affective discussion groups can be useful in this area, as they form a bridge between the purely intellectual discussion group and the counselling group with its emphasis on empathy. They need planning and structuring, and some of the techniques for initiating affective discussion are role-playing, case-studies, role-models, literature and audio-visual media.[3]

Anne Jones offers a useful description of their use in a secondary school in *School Counselling in Practice*.[4]

Although the two concepts of group guidance and group counselling overlap to some extent in the area of affective discussion, group guidance tends to be more cognitively oriented and is usually used in an attempt to personalize information, whereas group counselling is used in an attempt to meet emotional needs and is often closer to group therapy than it is to group guidance.

Group counselling

Group counselling is not simply individual counselling applied to groups, nor is it merely an economical use of counsellor time. Many of the features of group counselling are quite unique and it would be wrong to think of it as 'individual' counselling in the mass. Because of the differences in the two processes, a counsellor trained in the skills of individual counselling might find herself in difficulty if she attempted group counselling without having some training in group interaction. It is essential that a counsellor wishing to work with individuals and groups should have a thorough theoretical and practical grounding in individual counselling theory and practice together with some experience of the principles and practices of group dynamics.

The term multiple counselling is sometimes used to describe counselling carried out in groups. This seems a misleading term since it is not clear whether it is the counsellors or the students who are 'multiple'. It is used in this book to denote a situation in which there are two counsellors working either with one student, as in the chapter on training, or with a group. The term group counselling is used here to describe a situation in which there is one counsellor working with a group of students.

Group counselling is a relatively new way of working to help people, and although it has a unique contribution to make to our range of helping skills, it is not the complete answer for all psychological ills or needs.

Carkhuff has written quite strongly that

> Group processes are the preferred mode of working with difficulties in interpersonal functioning.
>
> We can do anything in group treatment that we can do in individual treatment—and more. Since groups are inherently interpersonal, they offer the helpee the means not only to relate to the helper and himself with the helper's guidance but also to relate to other members of the group and to the group as a whole. Group processes offer the prospect for the greatest amount of learning for the greatest number of people at one time.[5]

I find Carkhuff's unqualified approval as inappropriate and potentially damaging as attempting to gather peaches with a combine harvester. Certainly group counselling is sometimes successful with students who have not responded well to individual counselling, and there are several combinations of group and individual counselling in use. The two extremes are to use either group counselling or individual counselling only as a main technique. Some counsellors feel that it is unwise to make the two methods available to the same students at the same time because students may not bring out their deepest problems in the group, reserving them for the individual counselling sessions, which could inhibit the work of the group. Other counsellors feel that individual counselling offered concurrently with group counselling gives the opportunity for a student to discuss more deeply and extensively personal problem areas which they have been unable to bring out in the group, either because of their own inability or because of a lack of opportunity and a need to share the time of the group with other members.

Group counselling overlaps with group guidance in its partial cognitive and factual content and with group therapy in its emphasis on feelings and emotion, and it has some similarities to the individual counselling situation, with the addition of the interaction of other members of the group and the sharing of the counsellor. The effectiveness of group counselling may be partly attributable to the fact that, theoretically, it makes available the services of a number of potential helpers in the form of other group members, one or several of whom may be able to offer more help to a particular person at a particular point than is the counsellor herself.

Group counselling is a particularly useful way of helping adolescents for whom peer group values are important. The interaction which takes place in a counselling group offers the student a means of gaining insight and understanding into his own problems through listening to other students discussing their difficulties. Ideas and values which a student has previously found unacceptable may become more understandable and sometimes more acceptable. The counselling group not only helps the individual student to change, but also often encourages both his desire and his ability to help others through his relationships in an accepting and meaningful social situation, for any group is more than the sum of its members: it is also the sum of its interactions.

SOME PRACTICAL CONSIDERATIONS IN GROUP COUNSELLING

The physical arrangements which are desirable for a counselling group are similar to those which pertain to the individual counselling situation namely, a warm, sound-proofed room with fairly comfortable chairs. It is difficult, though not impossible, to conduct a counselling group in the average classroom, and even more difficult to conduct it in a cupboard. It is helpful if the same room can be used each time the group meets, because of the effect of a changed environment on the functioning of the group if their meeting place is not a familiar setting.

The time factor in the group counselling situation is related to the purpose of the group. If it is intended that most of the 'work' of the individual members is to take place in the actual group counselling session, it is necessary for the group to meet more often than it would if the counsellor and the group members feel that the students need time between meetings to absorb and test some of the experiences learned. It is usual for the counselling groups used in education to meet once, or perhaps twice a week. If the group meets too often, for example more than three times a week, there is the possibility that the frequency of sessions will restrict the group members' external social contacts and limit their opportunities for social reality testing outside the group. The length of each group meeting will be related to the age of the people involved, and the frequency with which the group meets, but sixty to ninety minutes is probably a reasonable time span for college students, thirty to sixty minutes for secondary school pupils and no more than thirty minutes for junior school children.

The composition of a counselling group is another practical consideration which is related to the purpose of the group. Sometimes it is felt that a homogeneous group consisting of students of the same age or sex, or students who seem to have similar problems is the most helpful, whilst other counsellors find that the wider talents of a heterogeneous group make for a better counselling situation. It is necessary to look carefully at the desired outcomes for the group, and to try to ensure that the purposes of the counsellor and those of the students are the same. It is important to recognize that groups can be homogeneous only in certain limited respects. A group chosen for homogeneity in sex or age is likely to be heterogeneous in other factors such as socio-economic background, maturity, motivation and, of course, temperament. It has been suggested that it is unwise to include in a counselling or therapy group people who are excessively aggressive or hostile because they are likely to destroy the atmosphere of acceptance in the group; people who are psychologically sophisticated or those who are not sufficiently in contact with reality have also been seen as undesirable group members, but it is difficult for the school or college counsellor to exclude students on these grounds unless they know them personally. A preliminary interview can help, though this may be more appropriate as screening for therapy groups than as a means of choosing members for a counselling group in an educational setting.

The size of a counselling group, like that of any guidance group, is related to the methodology used. A directive counsellor or one who prefers task oriented discussion may choose to work with a larger group than a counsellor who is aiming to encourage group interaction. A group of six to eight students is probably the best size for maximum group interaction.

THE ROLE OF THE COUNSELLOR IN GROUP COUNSELLING

There are two basic assumptions upon which a counsellor may choose to build her role. One is that it is the task of the counsellor to work with the group to encourage the students to be more self-sufficient and self-directed, so that the counsellor herself may then become another group member and the interaction of the group itself will provide any help which members need. An alternative assumption is that the counsellor works towards the development of the students' self-sufficiency, but because she considers that the group members are not always able to help each other she does not abdicate her special helping role.

Glantz and Hayes offer six phases which they believe are involved in group counselling, and offer a basis from which to consider the work of a counselling group:

1. rapport.
2. acceptance.
3. listening and observing.
4. promoting group and individual understanding.
5. problem solving skill development.
6. closing evaluation and procedures.

Whilst the counsellor's acceptance of all the group members and their problems is assumed in the nature of the role of the counsellor, as is the acceptance of the student in individual counselling, the creation of rapport and acceptance within and amongst the group members themselves, and between them and the counsellor, is a unique experience which differs from the one-to-one counselling relationship in its patterns of development.

Rapport involves the gradual building of an association of mutual respect and trust and it can be introduced by initial discussion of issues of choice, such as the time and length of meetings, the purpose of the group, whether the group should be 'open', so that members may leave when they wish or new members may be brought into the group as it proceeds, or whether it should be 'closed', retaining its initial membership for a specified period of time. Questions directed at the counsellor can be referred to the group for discussion and decision by means of a counsellor response such as 'What does the group feel about this?' If multiple counselling is being done, the role and function of the co-counsellor may be discussed. The structuring of the group by the counsellor in the early stages may also help in the growth of rapport. Structuring should be brief and should focus attention on the particular goals of the group, which may be self

198

appraisal, to encourage the free expression of feelings by group members to each other and to the counsellor, and the avoidance of purely intellectual discussion. The limits of the group may be expressed, for example, in terms of the permitting of verbal but not physical expression of hostile feelings. The emphasis of the observance by all group members and the counsellor of confidentiality about the proceedings of the group is also a part of structuring which can help to bring about trust.

Initial resistance is a natural phenomenon of groups and the creation of an accepting climate is a gradual process which the counsellor tries to encourage by her own acceptance of each student's feelings and his expression of them. From the counsellor the students learn to accept and help one another. Listening and observing actively and intensely are two of the essential skills of the counsellor, and a group situation gives an added complexity to the use of these in order to promote both group and individual understanding. 'The counselor's task is more complicated in group counseling. He not only has to understand the speaker's feelings and help him become aware of them, but he must also observe how the speaker's comments influence the group members. The counselor must not only be aware of the discussion, he must be perceptive of the interplay of relationships among the members.'[6] The counselling group can make little significant progress in developing the skills for solving problems until the initial stages of rapport, acceptance, understanding and insight have been established. It may be that the process of group counselling itself will uncover more problems than it actually solves, but if it is effective it also helps to bring about the attitudes and draws out the resources which will enable students to work at these problems themselves once they have been brought to conscious awareness. Alternatively it may lead them to seek individual counselling help for these.

SOME OUTCOMES OF GROUP COUNSELLING

As a result of research carried out into group counselling among pupils in a secondary school Ohlsen[7] reports that, with varying degrees of depth, each client discovered:

1. that expressing his own real feelings about people, things and ideas helped him to understand himself;

2. that at least one adult could accept him and that this adult, the counsellor, wanted to understand him;

3. that his peers had problems too;

4. that, in spite of his faults, which they wanted to help him to correct, his peers could accept him;

5. that he was capable of understanding, accepting and helping others;

6. that he could trust others.

Group counselling in education is not group instruction nor is it group therapy, but it is an experience which uses peer group support and identification in the social setting of the group to encourage students to accept and to learn more about themselves and at the same time to learn to accept and help others. 'Group counseling is characterised by experience not by words, by *being* something not by talking about it. If one can experience a sense of reality about one's self in the presence of others then a step forward has been taken in the realisation of emotional maturity and security.'[8]

12
Looking to the future

The only way to thwart the will of clients (pupils) is through 'counselling'. The open door college devotes much time and attention to this activity. In the college which Clark investigated, 80 per cent of the staff considered that counselling was as important or more important than instruction. The counsellor persuades the student to accept a type of education (and a type of career after its conclusion) which he was not at first disposed to accept. This process of thwarting the client's will is more picturesquely referred to as 'cooling him out'. The spread of counselling in our schools is one of the most potentially sinister features of the contemporary educational scene. It can become a device for restoring a teacher despotism which other forces have eroded. As more children of limited ability stay on in English schools beyond the statutory leaving age, we can expect to see an army of counsellors employed to cool them out.[1]

This represents the view of a British educational sociologist, on the possible future of counselling in our educational system and in our schools in particular. He is basing his view on Burton Clark's concept of the 'cooling out' system in some American secondary schools, and community colleges (which are perhaps most readily seen as sharing some of the features of both a sixth form college and a college of further education). I do not dispute Clark's findings, but I do question the assumption which Musgrove draws from them to project a role for counsellors in our schools which I find quite unacceptable, although I would acknowledge that counsellors can have a harmful as well as a helping potential. Certainly it is part of the counsellor's work to help students to try to recognize the reality of their own situation. For example, I would not delude an immigrant school leaver into thinking that the fact that he is an immigrant is irrelevant when he comes to look for a job. In many cases it is highly relevant and makes a big difference to his job opportunities. This may be reality for him and he can accept it or not, as he chooses, but it is not the only role for the counsellor. In addition to being *for* reality, the counsellor is also *for* change and her acknowledgment of reality does not carry with it a need or a desire to maintain the status quo, but often a responsibility to challenge it. There is much in our reality which we cannot change, but I also think that many of us do not use the freedom we have to bring about change, partly because it is often uncomfortable, threatening and inconvenient.

Although it is taken from a mental hospital setting, not education, and refers to psychiatric treatment, not counselling, the exchange between a young girl and her psychiatrist in Hannah Green's book *I never promised you a rose garden*[2] is appropriate here. The girl bitterly accuses her psychiatrist after an unpleasant incident in the ward, 'What good is your reality, when justice fails and dishonesty is glossed over and the ones who keep faith suffer. ... What good is your reality then?'

The response is '... I never promised you a rose garden, I never promised you perfect justice ... and I never promised you peace or happiness. My help is so that you can be free to fight for all of these things. The only reality I offer is challenge and being well is being free to accept it or not at whatever level you are capable. I never promise lies and the rose garden world of perfection is a lie ... and a bore too.'

Any relationship in education, or outside it, can be potentially sinister, it can also be potentially enabling and enhancing and it is this latter view of counselling which I see as its main strength and function. As for Musgrove's 'army of counsellors', I wish his pessimism could become my optimism.

Although I do not share the view that counselling will become a device for restoring despotism, the attitudes represented by this view do raise questions about the difficult area of ethics for counsellors.

Ethics

At some time in the not too distant future counsellors must undertake the complicated and time-consuming task of devising a code of ethical practices. It is likely that this will be done, as it was in America, by the professional associations concerned with counselling (see Appendices 3, 4 and 5). At the moment, the only statements on the subject of ethics are those made by individual counsellors in their writings, in their presentation of conference papers or in their annual reports to their various institutions.

A code of ethics may be expected to cover such matters as inter-professional relations, general responsibilities, competence, confidentiality, student welfare. As an example, the code of the Committee on ethics of the American Personnel and Guidance Association covers the following topics: professional attributes, general principles common to the work of all members, the counselling relationship, psychological testing, research and publication, counselling and private practice, personnel administration and preparation and training of counsellors and personnel workers.

The discussion, agreement and publication of a set of ethical standards for counsellors in education is one of the important tasks which face this new group of workers if they are to establish themselves as a profession.

In-service training

When the question of ethical standards for counsellors in education is considered, it is likely to include some discussion of the provision of in-service training and support for practising counsellors. The problem is particularly crucial for counsellors in education because often they are working in a school or a college as a department of one, which means that although they may have colleagues and friends amongst the teaching staff, professionally speaking they are isolated and the confidential nature of their work accentuates this.

The various counselling associations offer in-service training courses, or annual conferences, and the institutions which train counsellors also share in this work. These courses provide an opportunity to meet other counsellors, and to hear of fresh approaches, and new ideas. There is also an urgent need for regular 'problem-solving' groups, meeting weekly or fortnightly in a convenient local centre, at which some case-discussion may take place, but which also provide an opportunity for group members to raise any personal or professional issues which concern them. Group counselling for counsellors is an aspect of the provision of counselling services which local authorities and colleges should be prepared to support financially, through the secondment of personnel and the allocation of time, if they really want their counsellors to work at a reasonable level of efficiency. It is a need which counsellors themselves must be prepared to press for, both as a means of support for themselves and therefore ultimately as a source of gain for the students they counsel.

Encounter groups

Encounter groups, variously called T-groups, interpersonal relations groups and human relations groups are not an accepted part of education at the present time, although they may well become more acceptable in the future as we more fully realize that satisfying inter-personal living is not ordinarily a concomitant of eleven, twelve or sixteen years of formal education. As an aspect of the training and in-service training of counsellors, particularly in the development and refinement of sensitivity both to oneself and to others, they have a valuable function. There are dangers in the excesses which sometimes accompany this kind of group experience and it needs careful planning, competent leaders with professional training, working in an atmosphere of confidentiality, and respect for each individual's right not to respond to group concern if he so chooses. The well-run encounter group can be an exhilarating, moving, sometimes painful experience in personal growth; it is neither life nor a viable substitute for it, but rather a help toward more effective living.

Models of counselling

Educational counselling is still in its infancy in Britain. But despite a few frustrating initial experiences, counsellor education programmes are now flourishing and experienced staff with specialised training in counselling and guidance are becoming more common in schools. . . . There seems to be, however, a distinct lack of attention to the question of which theoretical approaches to counselling are the most suitable for use in British education.[3]

SOME BASIC MODELS OF COUNSELLING BASED ON BLOCHER [4]

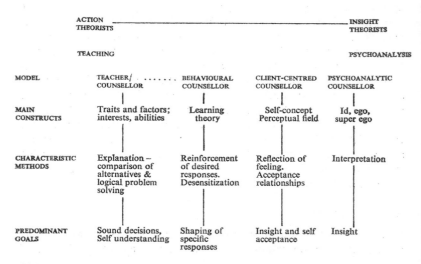

	ACTION THEORISTS			INSIGHT THEORISTS
	TEACHING			PSYCHOANALYSIS
MODEL	TEACHER/ COUNSELLOR	BEHAVIOURAL COUNSELLOR	CLIENT-CENTRED COUNSELLOR	PSYCHOANALYTIC COUNSELLOR
MAIN CONSTRUCTS	Traits and factors; interests, abilities	Learning theory	Self-concept Perceptual field	Id, ego, super ego
CHARACTERISTIC METHODS	Explanation – comparison of alternatives & logical problem solving	Reinforcement of desired responses. Desensitization	Reflection of feeling. Acceptance relationships	Interpretation
PREDOMINANT GOALS	Sound decisions, Self understanding	Shaping of specific responses	Insight and self acceptance	Insight

Woody goes on to distinguish between the insight theories as illustrated by psychoanalysis and client-centred counselling and the action theories of the behaviourists. He then makes a case for the adoption of the problem solving action model of counselling as a suitable basis for use in our educational settings and in our schools in particular.

Blocher [4] has compared the central characteristics of six models of counselling and an adaptation of his table opposite on a continuum gives a pattern of models, all of which may be of value to counsellors in education.

A further model of counselling which may well find acceptance in the future is that developed by Carkhuff [5] which offers a synthesis of insight and action models stressing not only the accepting aspect of the counselling relationship but also the active involvement of the counsellor in the helping process. He posits two principal phases of

	INWARD INSIGHT	AIMS
Stage 1	Development of counselling relationship characterized by empathic understanding, warmth, respect and concreteness.	To encourage communication and to help student to explore and understand himself and the relevant areas of concern.
		Leads to development of goals, followed by teaching of cognitive, emotional and social skills needed to achieve them.
	Transitional stage of relationship, counsellor moves from responding to initiating, acting as a model.	
Stage 2	Implementation of preferred action, vocational testing, counselling, environmental manipulation, behavioural techniques etc. Use of available appropriate resources.	Cognitive problem-solving approach leading to action to enable student to use his potential for growth. To begin to become what he can be.
	OUTWARD ACTION	

AN INSIGHT AND ACTION MODEL FOR COUNSELLING BASED ON CARKHUFF [5]

205

the helping process, the inward or self-exploratory phase and the outward or action-oriented phase (see table.) The aim of the helper during the first phase is to learn both the nature of the student's problems, and also how he sees himself and his world, while the aim during the second phase is to establish and put into operation a constructive way of resolving problems for the student.

Having effectively explored himself and having come to some highly functional understanding of himself, the helpee comes once again to address himself to the difficulties that brought him to counseling. The issue is, 'now what are we going to do about what we understand?' The answer is threefold: (1) 'We are going to consider the various courses of action available to you.' (2) 'We are going to consider the advantages and disadvantages, long-term as well as immediate of each.' (3) 'We are going to take steps to operationalise the best mode of action available.'[5]

Growth and acceptance of counselling

At a national conference of Guidance and Counselling in British schools held at Exeter University in 1968, Raymond Gawthorpe[6] presented a realistic, thoughtful paper on 'The School Counsellor from the Local Education Authority's Viewpoint' in which he looked at the hard facts which hamper the growth of counselling in this country. He also commented on the provision of pastoral care, saying, 'Comprehensive education, whether we like it or not, means large schools. Large schools have the danger of becoming impersonal schools, or we fear they may. A good deal of thought has been given to the "pastoral" care of the student and I have seen the housemaster, tutor group system working splendidly. The question is how does the counsellor fit into such an organisation?'

I believe the counsellor fits in as a specially skilled member of a guidance team. I think she also fits in as a 'people person', for the housemaster, tutor group system is too often merely an administrative expedient designed to make the running of large schools easier. If there is any time which is not taken up by the roles of teacher and administrator, the housemaster and tutor may, if they feel so inclined, and many of them do, concern themselves with pastoral care. The administrative demands come first because if they are not met it becomes difficult for the school to function. Children do not make a formal protest when they are neglected, but the tutor who neglects an administrative task is likely to be sharply reminded where his responsibilities lie. Is it asking too much to make provision in education for a small group of people, namely counsellors, whose specific job it is to put the needs of people first? As Gawthorpe pointed out, many counsellors in American High Schools are administrators; this defeats the whole purpose of counselling by reducing it to a routine relationship and a paper and pencil exercise, and I agree with him that this is not the way most of us see the job of a counsellor in our schools and colleges.

The provision of counselling services cannot be made cheaply; the uncertainty about the direction in which these services may develop requires a tentative commitment. Many local authorities are showing an interest in the provision of guidance as evidenced by their working party reports on the subject; they are tentative, but lack commitment. Other local authorities have not yet reached the stage of considering the provision of such services. Colleges and universities seem to be in a similar position, some, like Keele being wholly committed, others providing no professional counselling services.

Perhaps the impetus for counselling will come from the students themselves as it did in my own college. The National Union of Students had a comprehensive and carefully thought out item on counselling services at its Margate Conference in 1969 which said that:

Conference is seriously alarmed by the increasing drop out rate of students and particularly the estimate of 20,000 in universities alone by 1980. Many of these will be through causes other than lack of academic ability. Conference believes that much of the money wasted on these students could be saved by a policy of prevention, not simply tackling the problems as they occur. Conference further deplores the situation where such work is left solely in the hands of amateurs such as wardens and deans.

Conference therefore urges that counselling services should be set up in each institution on the following basis:

1. Staff working in these services should be fully trained.

2. The services should be seen as an integral part of the educational programme complementary to teaching.

3. Services should not merely tackle individual problems as they arise but should look constructively at ways in which they can
   (*a*) adapt institutions,
   (*b*) improve learning situations,

207

(c) help individuals to take proper advantage of opportunities available to them, so that the typical manifestations
of student problems do not occur.

4. Those involved in welfare of students must be entirely
separate from those who have disciplinary roles.

5. The strictest confidentiality should be maintained at all times
in connection with welfare services.

Conference therefore instructs the Executive:

1. to produce and circulate to all constituent organizations,
Vice-Chancellors and Principals a report based on the above
proposals including details of counselling services already
available in universities and colleges and the extent to which
they are successful;

2. to negotiate with the Department of Education and Science
to establish that all colleges should have a counselling
service on these lines and to ensure that the principle is
implemented.

This was not debated, but I hope that future conferences will find
time for this issue.

In September 1972, the annual Conference of the Union of Women
Teachers passed a proposal that 'this conference welcomes the assistance of counsellors in schools, provided that they are qualified and
experienced teachers, who have been properly trained for counselling'.

Finally, a brief summary of the difficulties which are likely to
restrict the development of counselling services in education in the
future.

Counselling should be implemented at the primary school level
in order to develop the capacity of educators to anticipate and
avert crisis. At the present time too often we cannot help but agree
with George Birdwood[7] that 'only education enjoys the dubious
privilege of having the power to make matters worse'.

On economic grounds, by default of educational administrators
and lack of a clear lead, supported by financial backing, from any
government we may expect to see counselling a non-starter certainly
at primary school level and in much of secondary education also.
The development of counselling services in higher education is very
dependent on a wider recognition and awareness of the nature of
student problems. Here again, there is a need for a preventive role,
whereas the tendency is to see counselling as a palliative for
crises.

Only if counsellors themselves will work towards the achievement of sufficient recognition for the counsellor to be in a position to affect policy and effect change will the task of counselling develop its twin aspects of prevention and remedy.

'Some of the most significant learnings have come from the resounding failures and the glowing successes of our attempts to adapt the principles and procedures of successful counselling to education.'[8]

References

Chapter 1

1 TIEDEMAN, DAVID V. 'Predicament problems and psychology: the case for paradox in life and counseling psychology'. *Journal of Counseling Psychology*, Vol. 14, No. 1, 1967.
2 HALL, R. K. and LAUWERYS, J. A. (EDS) *Yearbook of Education 1955* (Evans Bros., London, 1955).
3 RUSSELL, JOHN M. 'Reflections of an American Visitor'. *The Counsellor*, No. 9, December 1971.
4 BARON and TROPP 'Teachers in England and America' in Halsey, Floud and Anderson *Education Economy and Society* (Free Press, Glencoe, Ill., 1961).
5 BARNETT, B. and SMART, P. 'Some notes on the role of a school counsellor'. Paper presented to National Association of Educational Counsellors, 1968.
6 WRENN, C. G. 'The Counselor in a Changing World'. American Personnel and Guidance Association, Washington D.C., 1962.
7 PATTERSON, C. H. *Counselling and Guidance in Schools* (Harper & Row, 1962).
8 TYLER, L. E. *The Work of the Counselor* (Appleton Century Crofts, New York, 3rd ed., 1969).
9 URBICU and GROSS 'Counselor education: a profession on the move'. *Journal of Educational Research*, Vol. 64, No. 8, April 1971.
10 LYTTON, H. 'School counselling and counsellor education in the United States' (N.F.E.R., 1968).
11 HEGINBOTHAM, H. *The Youth Employment Service* (Methuen, London, 1951).
12 DAWS, PETER 'Who cares? A discussion of counselling and pastoral care in schools'. Council for Educational Advance, 1970.

References

Chapter 2

1 TYLER, L. E. *The Work of the Counselor*, 3rd ed. (Appleton Century Crofts, New York, 1969).
2 BRAMMER, L. M. and SHOSTROM, E. L. *Therapeutic Psychology* (Prentice Hall, Englewood Cliffs, N.J., 1960).
3 RIEFF, PHILIP *The triumph of the therapeutic; uses of faith after Freud* (Chatto & Windus, London, 1966).
4 REVANS, R. W. 'Involvement in School', *New Society*, Vol. 6, No. 152, 26 August 1965.
5 CENTRAL ADVISORY COUNCIL FOR EDUCATION *Children and their Primary Schools* (Plowden Report) (H.M.S.O., 1967).
6 CLARK, JOAN 'An unqualified success'. *The Counsellor*, No. 8, September 1971.
7 DAWS, P. in 'Who cares? A discussion of counselling and pastoral care in schools'. Council for Educational Advance, 1970.
8 WILSON, BRYAN 'Approach to delinquency'. *New Society*, 3rd February, 1966.
9 THOMAS, A. 'What shapes the child?' *New Society*, November, 1965.
10 HEMMING, JAMES *The Problems of Adolescent Girls* (Heinemann, London, 1960).
11 FREUD, ANNA *The Ego and the Mechanisms of defence* (Hogarth Press, 1937).
12 HAMBLETT, C. and DEVERSON, J. *Generation X* (Tandem Books, London, 1964).
13 N.A.M.H. Report of Working Party on Counselling in Schools, London, June 1970.

Chapter 3

1 HUGHES, P. M. *Guidance and counselling in schools. A response to change* (Pergamon Press, London, 1971).
2 SHERTZER, B. and STONE, S. C. *Fundamentals of Guidance* (Houghton Mifflin Company, Boston, 1966).
3 ROSENTHAL and JACOBSON *Pygmalion in the Classroom* (Holt, Rinehart & Winston, New York, 1968).
4 JACKSON, R. and JUNIPER, D. F. *A Manual of Educational Guidance* (Holt, Rinehart & Winston, London, 1971).
5 *Marked for life.* Published by Anarchist Group, University College London Union, London, 1972.
6 WALKER, A. *Pupils' school records* (Newnes for N.F.E.R., 1955).

7 CLARK, J. 'An unqualified success'. *The Counsellor*, No. 8, September 1971.
8 TYLER, L. E. 'Theoretical principles underlying the counseling process'. *Journal of Counseling Psychology*, No. 5, 1958.
9 JONES, A. *School Counselling in Practice* (Ward Lock, 1970).
10 SCHOOLS COUNCIL Working Paper No. 15, 'Counselling in Schools' (H.M.S.O., 1967).
11 RIDGWAY, L. 'A socio-educational system' in Pedley, F. M., *Education and Social Work* (Pergamon Press, London, 1967).
12 LAW, W. 'Counselling and the Social Work Professions'. *The Counsellor*, No. 3, June 1970.

Chapter 4

1 TOLBERT, E. L. *Introduction to Counselling* (McGraw-Hill, New York, 1959).
2 HOLDEN, A. *Teachers as Counsellors* (Constable, London, 1969).
3 N.A.M.H. Report of Working Party on Counselling in Schools, London, June, 1970.
4 WARTERS, J. *Techniques of Counseling* (McGraw-Hill Book Company, New York, 1964).
5 MOORE, B. M. *Guidance in comprehensive schools, a survey* (N.F.E.R., 1971).
6 MILLER, G. W. *Educational Opportunity and the Home* (Longmans, 1971).
7 HUGHES, P. M. *Guidance and Counselling in Schools, a response to change* (Pergamon Press, London, 1971).
8 TYLER, L. E. *The Work of the Counselor* (Appleton Century Crofts, New York, 3rd ed., 1969).
9 TAYLOR, H. J. *School Counselling* (Macmillan, London, 1971).
10 MCINTYRE REPORT *Time and facilities for careers work in secondary schools*. Published for National Association of Careers and Guidance Teachers by Cornmarket Careers Centre, London, 1970.
11 RUSSELL, J. M. 'Reflections of an American Visitor'. *The Counsellor*, No. 9, December 1971.
12 NATIONAL ASSOC. OF COUNSELLORS IN EDUCATION *The Work of the School Counsellor*, 1973.
13 DAWSON, A. 'The Education Welfare Officer' in Craft, M., Raynor, J. and Cohen, L. *Linking Home and School* (Longmans, London, 1967).
14 HEMMING, J. *Pupil guidance in secondary schools* (Berkshire County Council, 1965).
15 MOORE, G. D. and FULLER, J. A. School counselling: a survey of

References

the roles of the counsellors who qualified at Reading in 1966 after one year's experience in schools.
16 KAGAN, J. and MOSS, H. *Birth to Maturity* (John Wiley, New York, 1962).
17 LAWRENCE, D. 'The effects of counselling on retarded readers'. *Educational Research*, Vol. 13, No. 2, 1971.
18 SISTERSON, D. 'Educational guidance at a junior school'. *The Counsellor*, No. 12, September 1972.

Chapter 5

1 RYLE, A. *Student Casualties* (Allen Lane, The Penguin Press, London, 1969).
2 HAMBLIN, D. H. 'The work of the school counsellor, a reaction'. *The Counsellor*, No. 7, June 1971.
3 MILNER, P. 'Counselling with students, its scope and essence' in *Student Counselling: Scope and Training*. Proceedings of the third conference on Student Counselling convened by the Department of Higher Education, Institute of Education, University of London, 1972.
4 MILNER, P. 'Sex education in a university' in *Sex education in perspective* (National Marriage Guidance Council, London, 1972).
5 MILLER, G. W. 'Planning courses for student counsellors: a role for psychology'. *Bulletin*, British Psychological Society 23 (1970).
6 MILNER, P. 'A counselling service for students'. *N.M.G.C. Journal*, November 1970.
7 VOLSKY, T. 'Counselling Research—Outcomes and Implications' in *The World of Guidance Educational and Vocational. Counselling and Guidance of the Student in Higher Education*. Third International Round Table of Educational Counselling and Vocational Guidance, 1971.
8 FREDERICK, J. *Student Counselling: Scope and Training*. Proceedings of the Third Conference on Student Counselling convened by the Department of Higher Education, University of London, 1972, final discussion section.
9 NEWSOME, A. 'The need for counselling in higher education' in *The World of Guidance, educational and vocational. Counselling and Guidance of the Student in Higher Education*. Proceedings of the Third International Round Table of Educational Counselling and Vocational Guidance 1968 IRTECVG (now IRTAC), London, 1971.
10 ARBUCKLE, D. S. *Counseling: philosophy, theory and practice* (Allyn and Bacon, Boston, 1965).

Chapter 6

1 GIBRAN, KAHLIL *Sand and Foam* (Heinemann, London, 1927).
2 FREUD, S. G. *An autobiographical study* (Hogarth Press, London, 1936).
3 BARCLAY, J. R. *Foundations of Counseling Strategies* (John Wiley, New York, 1971).
4 —— *Counseling and Philosophy: a theoretical exposition* (Houghton Mifflin, Boston, 1968).
5 POPKIN, R. H. and STROLL, A. *Philosophy made simple* (W. H. Allen, London, 1969).
6 HUGHES, P. *Guidance and Counselling in Schools, a response to change* (Pergamon Press, London, 1971).
7 TYLER, L. E. *The Work of the Counselor* (Appleton Century Crofts, New York, 3rd ed., 1969).
8 WEINBERG, CARL *Education and Social Problems* (Free Press, New York, 1971).
9 TAYLOR, W. 'Family, School and Society' in Craft, M., Raynor, J., Cohen, L. *Linking Home and School* (Longmans, London, 1967).
10 WEINBERG, CARL *Social Foundations of Educational Guidance.* (Free Press, New York, 1969).
11 LEIGHTON, A. H. *My Name is Legion* (Basic Books, New York, 1959), quoted in Weinberg, C. (10) above.
12 COLEMAN, JAMES S. *The Adolescent Society* (Free Press, New York, 1961).
13 WRENN, GILBERT C. 'The culturally encapsulated counselor' *in* Mosher, R. J., Carle, R. F. & Kehas, C. D. *Guidance: An Examination* (Harcourt, Brace, New York, 1965).
14 WRENN, GILBERT C. 'Where counsellors must be wise'. *The Counsellor.* Journal of the National Association of Educational Counsellors, No. 7, June 1971.
15 CICOUREL and KITSUSE, JOHN *The Educational Decision-makers* (Bobbs-Merrill, Indianapolis, 1963).
16 DOUGLAS, J. W. B. and ROWNTREE, G. *Maternity in Great Britain* (Oxford University Press, London, 1948).
17 DOUGLAS, J. W. B. and BLOOMFIELD, J. M. *Children Under Five* (Allen & Unwin, London, 1958).
18 DOUGLAS, J. W. B. *The Home and the School* (Panther Edition, 1967. First published by MacGibbon & Kee, London, 1964).
19 DOUGLAS, J. W. B., ROSS, J. M. and SIMPSON, H. R. *All our Future* (Peter Davies, London, 1969).
20 CENTRAL ADVISORY COUNCIL FOR EDUCATION *Children and their Primary Schools* (Plowden Report) (H.M.S.O., 1967).

References

21 —— *Half our Future* (Newsom Report) (H.M.S.O., 1963).
22 FRIEDENBERG, EDGAR *The Vanishing Adolescent* (Dell, New York, 1959).

Chapter 7

1 STEFFLRE, B. and MATHENY, K. *The Function of Counseling Theory* (Houghton Mifflin, Boston, 1968).
2 CARKHUFF, ROBERT R. *Helping & human relations*, Vols. I & II (Holt, Rinehart & Winston, New York, 1969).
3 BRAMMER, L. M. and SHOSTROM, E. L. *Therapeutic Psychology: fundamentals of counseling and psychotherapy* (Prentice-Hall, New York, 1960).
4 BARCLAY, J. R. *Foundations of Counseling Strategies* (John Wiley, New York, 1971).
5 LONDON, P. *The Modes and Morals of Psychotherapy* (Holt, Rinehart & Winston, New York, 1964).
6 TYLER, LEONA *The Work of the Counselor* (Appleton Century Crofts, New York, 3rd ed., 1969).
7 PATTERSON, C. H. 'What is counselling psychology?' *Journal of Counselling Psychology*, Vol. 16, No. 1, 1969.
8 BROWN, J. A. C. *Freud and the post-Freudians* (Penguin Books, 1964).
9 ROGERS, CARL *Counseling and Psychotherapy: newer concepts in practice* (Houghton Mifflin, Boston, 1942).
10 —— *Client-centred therapy* (Houghton Mifflin, Boston, 1951).
11 —— *et al.* (eds.) *The therapeutic relationship and its impact: a study of psychotherapy with schizophrenics* (University of Wisconsin Press, Madison, Wisconsin, 1967).
12 ROGERS, CARL R. and STEVENS, B. *Person to person: the problem of being human* (Real People Press, California, 1967).
13 ROGERS, CARL R. *Encounter Groups* (Allen Lane, The Penguin Press, London, 1971).
14 KRUMBOLTZ, J. D. 'Behavioural counseling: rationale and research'. *American Personnel & Guidance Journal*, No. 44, 1965.
15 MICHAEL, J. and MYERSON, L. 'A behavioural approach to counseling and guidance' in *Guidance: An Examination* (Harcourt, Brace, New York, 1965).
16 AUTHOR UNKNOWN.
17 EYSENCK, HANS 'Effects of psychotherapy'. *International Journal of Psychiatry*, Vol. 1, January 1965.
18 MAYER, J. E. and TIMMS, N. *The client speaks: working class*

impressions of casework (Routledge & Kegan Paul, London, 1970).

19 BLOCHER, D. H. *Developmental Counseling* (Ronald Press, New York, 1966).
20 GLASSER, W. 'Reality therapy'. *The Counsellor*, No. 10, March 1972.
21 SCHMIDT, L. D. and KAULT, J. 'The rational-emotive counselling of Albert Ellis'. *The Counsellor*, No. 6, March 1971.
22 DOLLARD, J. and MILLER, N. E. *Personality and Psychotherapy: An analysis in terms of learning, thinking and culture* (McGraw-Hill, New York, 1950).
23 BRONFENBRENNER, U. 'Toward an integrated theory of personality' in Blaue, R. R. & Ramsey, G. V. (eds.), *Perception: an approach to personality* (Ronald Press, New York, 1951).

Chapter 8

1 ROGERS, C. R. *Client-centred therapy*. (Houghton Mifflin, Boston, 1951).
2 BIESTEK, FELIX *The Casework Relationship* (Allen & Unwin, London, 1961).
3 MORAN, MARGARET *Pastoral Counselling for the Deviant Girl* (Geoffrey Chapman, London, 1968).
4 ROGERS, C. R. 'The characteristics of a helping relationship' in McGowan, J. F. & Schmidt, L. D. *Counseling readings in theory and practice* (Holt, Rinehart & Winston, New York, 1962).
5 WILSON, J. 'A student counselling service in a college of education'. *The Counsellor*, No. 4, September 1970.
6 TRUAX, C. B. and CARKHUFF, R. R. *Toward effective counseling and psychotherapy: training and practice* (Aldine Publishing Company, Chicago, 1967).
7 TYLER, L. E. *The Work of the Counsellor* (Appleton Century Crofts, New York, 3rd ed., 1969).
8 ROGERS, C. R., GENDLIN, E. T., KEISLER, D. and TRUAX, C. B. (eds.) *The therapeutic relationship and its impact: a study of psychotherapy with schizophrenics* (University of Wisconsin Press, Madison, Wisconsin, 1967).
9 IRVINE, E. 'Renaissance in British Casework'. *Social Work* (Tavistock Press reprint, July 1965).
10 WILLIAMSON, E. G. 'Characteristics of the Counseling Relationship' in Kennedy, E. G. (ed), *Current status and future trends in Student Personnel* (Kansas State College, Pittsburgh, Kansas, 1961).

References

Chapter 9

1 BLOCHER, D. *Developmental Counseling* (Ronald Press Company, New York, 1966).
2 TRUAX, C. and CARKHUFF, R. R. *Toward effective counseling and psychotherapy: training and practice* (Aldine Publishing Company, Chicago, 1967).
3 MILNER, P. 'Counselling with students, its scope and essence' in *Student Counselling: Scope and Training* (Department of Higher Education, Institute of Education, University of London, 1972).
4 HAMBLIN, D. H. 'The Work of the School Counsellor, a reaction'. *The Counsellor*, No. 7, June 1971.
5 THOMPSON, A. J. M. 'Effect and effectiveness of Counselling in English Schools', S.S.R.C. Report 1970.
6 CRAMER, S. *et al. Research and the School Counselor* (Houghton Mifflin, Boston, 1970).
7 BRAMMER, L. M. and SHOSTROM, E. L. *Therapeutic Psychology* (Prentice-Hall, Englewood Cliffs, N.J., 1960).
8 TYLER, L. E. *The Work of the Counselor* (Appleton Century Crofts, New York, 3rd ed., 1969).
9 COLEMAN, JAMES S. *The Adolescent Society* (Free Press, New York, 1961).
10 FRIENDENBERG, E. Z. *The Vanishing Adolescent* (Dell Publishing Company, New York, 1959).
11 PEEL, E. A. *The Psychological Basis of Education* (Oliver & Boyd, London, 1956).
12 WILSON, J. R. 'Report of the first year of a counselling service in a college of education'. *The Counsellor*, No. 4, September 1970.
13 HUGHES, P. M. *Guidance and Counselling in Schools* (Pergamon Press, London, 1971).
14 ROGERS, C. R. *Client-centred therapy* (Houghton Mifflin, Boston, 1951).
15 —— *Counseling and psychotherapy: newer concepts in practice* (Houghton Mifflin, Boston, 1942).
16 —— *On Becoming a Person* (Houghton Mifflin, Boston, 1961).
17 LAWRENCE, D. 'The effects of counselling in retarded readers'. *Educational Research*, Vol. 13, No. 2, 1971.
18 VOLSKY, T. 'Counselling Research—Outcomes and Implications' in *The World of Guidance, Educational and Vocational. Counselling and Guidance of the Student in Higher Education.* Third International Round Table of Educational Counselling and Vocational Guidance, 1971.

19 HAASE and DIMATTA 'Proxemics—manner in which individuals structure personal space and their immediate spatial surroundings'. *Journal of Counseling Psychology*, Vol. 7, No. 4, 1960.

20 MUENCH, G. A. 'An investigation of the efficacy of time-limited psychotherapy'. *Journal of Counseling Psychology*, Vol. 12, No. 3, 1965.

Chapter 10

1 APPELL, M. L. 'Self understanding for the guidance counselor'. *American Personnel and Guidance Journal*, No. 42, October 1963.

2 ROGERS, C. R. *Counseling and psychotherapy: newer concepts in practice* (Houghton Mifflin, Boston, 1942).

3 VENABLES, E. *Counselling* (National Marriage Guidance Council, London, 1971).

4 NELSON-JONES, R. 'Student Counsellor Training' in *Student Counselling: Scope and Training*. Proceedings of the Third Conference on Student Counselling, Department of Higher Education, Institute of Education, University of London, 1972.

5 MCCLAIN '16 PF scores and success in counseling'. *Journal of Counseling Psychology*, Vol. 15, No. 6, 1968.

6 TRUAX, C. B. and CARKHUFF, R. R. *Toward effective counseling and psychotherapy: training and practice* (Aldine Publishing Company, Chicago, 1967).

7 O'NEIL, A. M. 'Childhood memories and grade level selected for teaching'. *Journal of Counseling Psychology*, Vol. 16, No. 2, 1969.

8 HALMOS, P. *The Faith of the Counsellors* (Constable, London, 1965).

9 DUBOS, R. J. *Louis Pasteur* (Boston, 1950).

10 *Psychotherapy: definition and training* (Association of Psychotherapists, London, 1971).

11 Diploma in School Counselling. Department of Education, University College, Swansea.

12 RUSSELL, J. M. 'Reflections of an American Visitor'. *The Counsellor*, No. 9, December 1971.

13 BRAMMER, L. M. and SHOSTROM, E. L. *Therapeutic psychology: fundamentals of counseling and psychotherapy* (Prentice-Hall, Englewood Cliffs, N.J., 1960).

14 ROGERS, C. R. *Client-centred therapy* (Houghton Mifflin, Boston, 1951).

15 GIBRAN, K. *Sand and Foam* (Heinemann, London, 1927).

References

16 PENTONY, P. 'Some aids in the training of counsellors'. *The Counsellor*, No. 9, December 1971.
17 URBICU and GROSS 'Counselor education: a profession on the move'. *Journal of Educational Research*, Vol. 64, No. 8, April 1971.
18 CARKHUFF, R. R. *Helping and human relations; a primer for lay and professional helpers*, Vol. 1 (Holt, Rinehart & Winston, New York, 1969).
19 *The British Journal of Psychiatry*, Vol. 119, No. 552, November 1971.

Chapter 11

1 GLANTZ, E. C. and HAYES, R. W. *Groups in Guidance* (Allyn & Bacon, Boston, 1967).
2 KRITCH, D. E. and MCCREADY, W. H. *Improving guidance programs in Secondary Schools* (California State Department of Education, Sacramento, 1950).
3 CRAMER, S. H. and HERR, E. L. *Guidance of the college bound* (Appleton Century Crofts, New York, 1968).
4 JONES, A. *School Counselling in Practice* (Ward Lock, London, 1971).
5 CARKHUFF, R. R. *Helping and human relations: a primer for lay and professional helpers*, Vol. II (Holt, Rinehart & Winston, New York, 1969).
6 SHERTZER, B. and STONE, S. *Fundamentals of Guidance* (Houghton Mifflin, Boston, 1966).
7 OHLSEN, M. M. 'Counseling within a group setting' in Muro, J. J. & Freeman, S. L. *Readings in Group Counseling* (International Textbook Company, Pennsylvania, 1968).
8 WRENN, G. C. 'The evolution of group counseling in the United States'. Paper given at A.P.G.A. Conference, Las Vegas, Nevada, April 1969.

Chapter 12

1 MUSGROVE, F. and TAYLOR, P. *Society and the Teacher's Role* (Routledge & Kegan Paul, London, 1969).
2 GREEN, H. *I never promised you a rose garden* (Holt, Rinehart & Winston, New York, 1964; Pan Books, London, 1972).
3 WOODY, R. H. 'British behavioural counselling'. *Educational Research*, Vol. 10, No. 3, 1968.

4 BLOCHER, D. *Developmental Counseling* (Ronald Press Company, New York, 1966).
5 CARKHUFF, R. R. *Helping and human relations: a primer for lay and professional helpers*, Vol. II (Holt, Rinehart & Winston, New York, 1969).
6 GAWTHORPE, R. 'The school counsellor from the local authority's viewpoint' in Lytton, H. & Craft, M., *Guidance and Counselling in British Schools* (Edward Arnold, London, 1970).
7 BIRDWOOD, G. 'The don'ts of drug education'. *Drugs & Society*, No. 4, Vol. 1, January 1972.
8 ROGERS, C. R. *Client-centred therapy* (Houghton Mifflin, Boston, 1951).

Appendices

Appendix 1

Some ways of using an orientation programme for entry to secondary school

A. PRE-ENTRY

1. Discussion between the counsellor and staff of secondary school first year forms and teachers in the junior schools to determine needs which an orientation programme might meet, e.g. knowledge of curriculum and methods of teaching to bridge the gap of method between secondary and junior school was considered important. The facilities offered by the local district Teachers' Centre were useful in co-ordinating the work of primary and secondary schools.

2. Regular visits, both ways, of staff and children. It was helpful to take a representative group of first year children (not just the clean and intelligent ones) back to their primary schools to talk to the children who would be coming to us. Their view of the school is often more relevant than that of a teacher or counsellor.

Junior class teachers' comments can be most helpful but we should not overlook the value of enabling a child to make a fresh start as far as possible, without prejudice from his past.

3. An evening meeting of parents and children to introduce them to the school, to give them general information and enable them to meet the head, deputy head, house or year head and some of the staff teaching the first year.

4. A school prospectus, although expensive to produce and possibly needing annual revision because of staffing changes, can be helpful to some parents and children.

5. A one-day visit of new pupils before the beginning of term to see the school and meet some of the staff and each other. They were shown round by the sixth formers and it gave them an opportunity to get the feel of the school, before being overwhelmed by the other 1500 pupils on the first day of term.

This can be a useful occasion on which to start the cumulative record card and to tell the children the procedure on their first day at school.

B. ENTRY

1. It seemed helpful to the children if the first day could be a 'welcoming day'; for example, it is not a suitable occasion for the administration of tests, if these are to produce meaningful results, but the children do like to feel that they have done some 'work', so it seemed advisable to keep them occupied.

This is a time of excitement and stress for most children. There are many new experiences to attract their senses, so that some of them will fail to understand even the clearest of instructions, they may not understand their timetable, they will lose their way repeatedly and this may continue for a week or longer. They can often solve their own problems if they have the courage to ask someone where the language lab. is, etc., and other children and staff who are prepared to be helpful during this time can reduce the stress.

C. POST-ENTRY

My own part in the orientation programme continued throughout the first year because I met each of the nine first-year forms for a single period each week. Most of the work that I did with these groups could be done by tutors or form teachers, since it was guidance, not counselling, although individual counselling did arise from these weekly sessions.

Work for the first year included the following items:

Autumn Term

1 Your school. Its past: covered history of the school, how it was formed, why it was formed, how they came to be there—catchment areas.

Its present: covered the organization of the school, house system, how it works, why it exists, names and locations of houses, house masters, house rooms, departments of the school, heads of department, what they do; people in the school, each form meeting the headmaster, the deputy headmaster, the senior mistress of the school for one lesson at least.

Its future: covered opportunities of school including clubs and societies, educational opportunities. I talked to all the groups, including the remedial classes, about G.C.E. 'O' and 'A' levels and about further education in colleges and universities. Personal opportunities to work, to play, to waste time etc. Code of behaviour of school was discussed.

2 My feelings on my first day at school—this marked the beginning of the emphasis on themselves, their feelings and personality which was continued throughout the first year. They were not at a mature enough stage of development to be able to do any deep self-analysis, but some were beginning to have the ability to stand back from themselves and to recognize their feelings.

3 Following from (2) we had an optional piece of writing called 'A week in my life', in which the children wrote a diary for about a week, filling in entries at roughly two hourly intervals. The entry indicated what they were doing at that particular time and also what their feelings were. This encouraged some of them to examine their feelings under different circumstances.

4 We concluded the term with a sociometry questionnaire; a creativity test and a twenty-item test on the history and organization of the school and the people in it. I did not take this last test very seriously, but some of the children found it quite threatening, nevertheless, partly because it was labelled a 'test'. I think questionnaire might have been a better word.

5 Interspersed with these activities we had a general discussion lesson about once a month in which the children could talk about any problems or discuss subjects of their choice.

Spring Term

1 The children wrote a paragraph or two on 'The kind of person I think I am'; then on 'The kind of person other people think I am' and completed this with 'The kind of person I should like to be'. This was another exercise in very simple self-analysis, which can be useful for picking out the children with a very poor self-concept, who perhaps would benefit from some individual help.

2 People: similarities and differences between people, covering physical, environmental, personality, belief, dress etc. The children provided the information as a list of similarities and differences which we then discussed, mentioning their importance or insignificance to different people. The children then wrote on 'What is a person?'

3 Group talks on any subject chosen by the group. They divided themselves into groups and organized the content and presentation, each person aiming to speak for about one minute. Comments and questions from other groups followed each talk, the aim being constructive criticism, and this was followed by a brief written comment on each group talk.

4 Once a month we had the general discussion lesson.

Summer Term

1 Vocational guidance introduced in a general form. We began by linking up with the work done on similarities and differences in people last term and related this to basic job requirements. This was done very simply by choosing any job, e.g. postman, deciding what the job involved and then considering the sort of person who might find that job suitable. We defined work and occupations or jobs, the children writing their own ideas, I contributed a dictionary definition of work, my own definition and a poet's definition and we talked about these.

The children brought 'situations vacant' columns from the local newspapers and sometimes the national ones and from these they found jobs suitable for several people described to them, e.g., 'Young man aged 18, "A" level Maths and Physics, interested in electronics, wants to work in this area,' or, 'school leaver, girl aged 15, artistic, interested in working with people'.

We also listed the things the children considered important when choosing a job and discussed them.

2 The story of my life. This was optional, written in three parts: birth to five years; five years to entry to secondary school; and the first year at secondary school. Part one included date and place of birth, if known, position in family, earliest childhood memory, first impressions of primary school, memory of first teacher. It ended with any illnesses remembered, or accidents. Part two included hobbies, interests, holidays, travel abroad, illnesses, memorable times either sad or happy, and memories of primary school. Part three covered the period of time spent in the secondary school using similar headings.

3 Incomplete sentences test: A list of incomplete sentences which the children completed in their own words.

4 The children wrote letters to the children in their former junior school who would be joining us in September, telling them something of our school.

5 Some of the children visited their former primary school to talk to the children and to answer their questions. They practised this in class before they went.

6 We had our usual discussion lessons as before.

7 Preparation for entry to second year and house system.

This programme of guidance was carried out with first year children for two years. Had it been continued I should have made changes, having asked the children for suggestions at the end of their first year, and perhaps at the end of each term. Some children either did not wish or were unable to take part in some of the activities and this was accepted.

Some schools are now developing guidance programmes for all years throughout the school.

Appendix 2

One form of personality assessment on school records

To simplify a comprehensive assessment, a check list of personality traits is provided, but entries should be made only where behaviour indicates a clearly individual characteristic, and should be shown by a tick in the appropriate box.

In addition to the check list, it is helpful to provide space for the tutor to make a descriptive or interpretative comment if he so wishes. Such comments are most valuable if they are based on objective observation, but subjective comments have their place if it is clearly indicated that they are expressions of opinion.

The check list itself is divided into three sections covering attitudes to work, social attitudes and attitude to self. A general description of each characteristic follows based on the meaning of these words in describing personality.

SECTION A. ATTITUDE TO WORK (activities, school work, hobbies, games, etc.)

accurate — work is precise, exact and usually correct

apathetic — unable to show interest in any school activity

consistent — approach to work is almost invariably the same, whether it be good or poor

critical — analyses ideas and relationships, usually discovered by someone else

enquiring — likes to find out things for himself, interested enough to question facts

erratic — work produced is of variable standard, sometimes good or bad, but noticeably so

hardworking — puts a lot of effort into his work, which is not necessarily apparent from the results

indifferent — seeming to care little about success or failure in work

initiative — makes little or no original contribution yet shows sufficient imagination to see the value of other people's ideas and to use them

interested — shows interest in work without necessarily having much ability

lazy — consistently unable or unwilling to recognize the need to make any more than minimum use of abilities

logical — work consistently shows his capacity to reason logically though not necessarily conventionally

meticulous — work shows careful attention to detail of content and often an obsessional concern for presentation

original — makes distinctly original and significant contribution, approaches work with active imagination so that he contributes something that is his own

persistent — perseveres in spite of real difficulties, not easily discouraged, determined even when wrong

SECTION B. SOCIAL ATTITUDE (attitude to other people)

aggressive — generally hostile to people who frustrate him and sometimes so when unprovoked, often quarrelsome

co-operative — eager to help, sometimes undiscriminatingly, enjoys being one of a team or helping others

courteous — showing thought for others in behaviour and/or speech

destructive — so critical of the ideas, relationships or property of others that he seeks to destroy these

dominant — anxious to make others follow him, often dictatorial

law-abiding — will keep the rules even when unsupervised

leader — has the ability to make others follow him, for good or ill, often has original ideas

rebellious — defiant of authority often anti-social

self-centred — pre-occupied with own ideas, opinions, wishes or personality.

sociable — enjoys the company of others and often seeks social activity, usually popular

submissive — conventional, leans on others, seems to lack ideas and initiative

uncooperative — shows antagonism to the ideas and wishes of others, highly engrossed in self

unselfish — showing consideration for others above regard for personal satisfaction

SECTION C. ATTITUDE TO SELF (temperament or relations with himself)

alert — very interested in world and people, active, reacts quickly to environment

cheerful — smiling, amenable to discipline and life in general

231

Appendix 2

diffident — inclined to hide feelings, occasionally bursts into action or expresses feeling, mainly to individuals

excitable — easily moved to strong emotional expression

imaginative — uses images and ideas derived from experience to form a new image of something which has not been experienced

impulsive — acts suddenly, seemingly without foresight and sometimes without prudence

independent — unwilling to be under an obligation to others, preferring own judgment

moody — fickle, changeable in mood, tending towards depression or sullenness

reserved — avoids groups of people and strangers, but friendly towards a few acquaintances

self-assured — confident, may become reckless or cocksure, often unwilling to accept advice because he is sure of his own abilities

self-controlled — normally in command of emotions and behaviour

self-satisfied — sees no reason for any effort to change behaviour or work habits, because he finds himself entirely satisfactory

sense of humour — able to join with others in laughing at himself

slovenly — uncaring about appearance or work

spiritless — gives up on encountering any difficulty

undisciplined — has difficulty in exercising self-control

Appendix 3

National Association of Counsellors in Education
(formerly the National Association of Educational Counsellors)

In 1966 several mature students converged on a hotel in Stratford-upon-Avon, and after some hours of negotiation and compromise between the 'Keele group' and the 'Reading group', the National Association of Educational Counsellors was created.

The association was formed by students from the first courses in counselling at Keele and Reading Universities at a crucial time in their professional and personal lives. They were at the end of a demanding course which had deliberately challenged their existing attitudes to people and to children in particular, and had questioned accepted values of education, producing in most cases some illusion of change in those values and attitudes, the reality of which had still to be tested in the work situation. Perhaps because they were pioneers, these newly trained counsellors were conscious of the need to have a group to which they could relate, one which would provide some mutual reassurance and would help to facilitate communication between colleagues in similar work who were often geographically as well as personally isolated.

Although this need was felt and expressed at the first meetings, because the association is a national one, attendance at meetings invariably involves quite a long journey for many people, and this is a deterrent. Two alternatives have been used in an attempt to overcome the difficulty of travelling; one is the formation of regional branches, and the other the introduction of weekend gatherings. The first of these, held at Malvern in March 1970, produced a very encouraging response, and others have been held in Coventry.

Meetings have included talks and films on group counselling in Britain and America, vocational guidance, the establishment of new courses for training counsellors, the use of video tapes in counsellor training and in telling teachers about counselling, a course on group counselling and another on ROSLA. A short course on group counselling (in conjunction with the Careers Research and Advisory Centre) was held in 1973. Information about these meetings may be obtained from W. G. Law, Hon. Sec. N.A.C.E., 33 Chesilton Crescent, Church Crookham, Hants.

N.A.C.E. aims to establish a professional code of ethics and to organize the profession of counselling in education by furthering the study of counselling through the dissemination of ideas and research findings and by establishing and maintaining contact with other professional bodies in sympathy with the aims and objects of N.A.C.E.

The Counsellor is the quarterly journal of N.A.C.E. and is sent to all members of the Association free of charge. Subscription only to the journal costs £1.00 per year. It contains articles covering a wide range of guidance and counselling activities. There is also a Library Service available to members which provides photocopies of articles in current issues of the *Journal of Counseling Psychology*, the *Personnel and Guidance Journal*, and *The School Counselor*. Further information and application forms for membership from the Membership Secretary, T. J. King, Compton, 120 Straight Road, Old Windsor, Berks.

N.A.C.E. has published a paper on 'The work of the school counsellor'. Enquiries about this should be addressed to the Hon. Sec.

Although the Association was originally started to further the interests of school counsellors, membership now reaches beyond the schools into higher and further education, although the Association for Student Counselling was formed as an independent body having links with N.A.C.E. in an attempt to serve the special interests of those working in counselling in tertiary education.

Appendix 4

Association for Student Counselling

This association was created in 1970 with the following aims in mind:

(a) to provide a professional organization for anyone concerned with the counselling of students and young people;

(b) to further the education and training of counsellors;

(c) to further the study of counselling through research and the dissemination of knowledge;

(d) to promote the acceptance of counselling in tertiary education;

(e) to establish and maintain contact with other professional bodies in sympathy with the aims and objectives of the association.

Membership of A.S.C. at the end of 1973 was approaching two hundred. There is an annual conference which is usually held in May, and a twice yearly newsletter. Further information about the association is available from the Chairman, Patricia Milner, Student Counselling Service, University College, London, Gower Street, London WC1E 6BT.

Appendix 5

Standing Conference for the Advancement of Counselling

The Standing Conference for the Advancement of Counselling was formed in 1971 with the aim of providing:

a body to which all kinds of counsellors and all kinds of counselling institutions could belong;

a forum for multi-disciplinary discussion;

a clearing house for information and a platform for the expression of views.

This is an umbrella organization which, since its formation, has set up several working parties to report on various aspects of counselling. Further information about the work of S.C.A.C. may be obtained from the Secretary, Mrs Joan Burnett, 26 Bedford Square, London, WC1B 3HU.

Appendix 6

International Round Table for the Advancement of Counselling

The International Round Table for the Advancement of Counselling, formerly known as the International Round Table for Educational Counselling and Vocational Guidance, holds international conferences and seminars on various aspects of counselling every two years. Topics have included Counselling and Guidance of the Student in Higher Education, and the Social Implications of Counselling.

The Sixth International Round Table will be held in Cambridge, England in 1974 and the topic will be Counselling, the Community and Society.

The Chairman of I.R.T.A.C. is Mr Hans Hoxter, Centre for Studies in Counselling, North-East London Polytechnic, Livingstone House, Livingstone Road, London E.15. The Secretary is Dr D.A.L. Hope, Brunel University, Kingston Lane, Uxbridge, Middlesex.

Appendix 7

Educational Redeployment Service

In May 1969 a grant was made available to Dr Nicolas Malleson, Director, University of London Research Unit for Student Problems, by the Leverhulme Trust Fund for the purpose of setting up a pilot organization which, for the following three years, would look into the whole field of the problems of the student drop-out to see where and how best the needs could be met.

The scheme is concerned with students who drop out from graduate courses at university, polytechnic or college of further education and those leaving colleges of education. The section of the population chosen for initial investigation consisted of Inner London Education Authority grant aided students who were notified, if they failed their courses, that it was open to them to consult the Educational Redeployment Service. Those who register are interviewed and given all possible advice and help with the object of finding the alternative education or the employment with training most suited to their capabilities. Additionally the service seeks to establish itself as a central enquiry service to which any student drop-out can write for information and by reason of its knowledge and its contacts will be able to direct him to those people best placed to help him. The cases dealt with by the service provided the basic material for research. It is hoped by these various means to change the climate of opinion where the drop-out is concerned, so that there is no persisting stigma attached to him by reason of his initial failure to graduate.

The initial grant expired in 1972, but the Educational Redeployment Service continues under its director, Mrs Mary Blake, financed by the D.E.S.

The registered office of the Educational Redeployment Service is 20 Gower Street, London WC1.

Appendix 8

Edited extracts from a trainee counsellor's tape-recorded initial interview with a final-year student at an American University

COUNSELLOR What would you like to talk about?

STUDENT Well I think that I would like to talk about something which has always bothered me and that is where am I going? I am a senior, and in Political Science and I think I belong in my major and I graduate in eight months and I just don't know where I am going to go. I think I want to go to a graduate school and stay, like within a university centre, but I really don't know what I want to study, so what do you do about that, you know?

(Pause)

I have got some old catalogues and looked up programmes but it really is a hang-up. It really bothers me. I don't know how many places or how many people to talk to about it, or what questions to ask myself to find out what you really want to do. Sometimes I wonder if it really isn't a matter of lack of information about things and maybe that is why I was wanting to get catalogues.

COUNSELLOR Mm hmm. [Indicating 'I am with you so far, carry on.']

STUDENT I just don't know. . . .

(Pause) [Silence communicating 'take your time, and go on when you are ready'.]

STUDENT It isn't as bad now but when I was a sophomore it was very depressing because it involved an identity crisis and 'do you belong in Political Science? Can you really make it there? And is there really something that you can do better than you are doing this?' I don't know. I thought there was always one thing that everybody in the world was better at than everybody else, and I just wanted to find that thing—you know? *My* thing. I had a room-mate, freshman year, and she loved philosophy, she lived it, she ate it, she spoke about it. It was my life is going to be teaching philosophy, studying philosophy. And I envied her. I was *so* jealous. I really was. Like 'what is my life going to be? Could it really be like that?' And I guess maybe that is why in sophomore I got so involved in it, because I couldn't see Political Science as my major, as my life, like my room-mate could. Then I thought, well maybe she is just exceptional—that everybody in the world just isn't like that.

COUNSELLOR Uhm. So this is a problem that you have thought a lot about. . . . And it is a problem you have some information on, but although you've thought about it and although you have a certain amount of information you seem to feel that you don't really know where you are going?

[Reflection of content and feeling.]

STUDENT Mm hmm. That sounds good.

COUNSELLOR And the question you seem to be asking yourself now is 'I have been in this field for three years. I graduate very soon. What I am going to do next?' Although time is shorter now, you suggest that you feel better able to cope with the problem.

[Further reflection seeking clarification and expansion of student's self understanding.]

STUDENT I think so. I have become more comfortable within myself to go through some type of self-examination or self-questioning to try finding out, but I just don't know where to begin to ask the right type of self-questions and maybe that is why I sought out help. I thought about something like higher education administration, because that would mean I could stay in a university centre and be exposed to the intellectual level of the people and I would be working with people but I don't know enough about what it involves. I know it represents a master's programme. It would send me to another school which would eventually prepare me to work in a school but then I always wonder if I would be better off in the academic ground—you know, there is your history and your studying angle—like would you prefer that?

COUNSELLOR Uhm. [Student seems to be avoiding looking at herself as a person by talking about practicalities. Counsellor notes her need to do this.]

STUDENT . . . I even thought of an interdisciplinary study but where do you go from there? It is just like delaying making a decision. O.K. I will study a little more history and some sociology, which is very interesting to me too. But then what? Can you go to school for the rest of your life without saying 'Where is the goal? Where are you going? Is there ever going to be a straight line or are you ever going to make circles?' You know. Maybe that is how people live—making circles—I don't know. It just seems to me that it

could be so much easier if there was a goal and you could say
'O.K. I want to be a technician and I know what I have to do
to get there.' But I don't have that goal so I don't know what
I have to do to get there.

COUNSELLOR You feel that in order to get anywhere you must have a
goal first and you are having difficulty finding one for yourself?
[Counsellor generalizes the problem to include personal as well as
occupational goals, implying that the two go together. The student
picks up this inference and restates the vocational aspect.]

STUDENT Yes. A goal in terms of employment.

COUNSELLOR Mm hmm. [Non-committal.]

STUDENT . . . or something like that. There are other goals in life that
I have, you know, but in terms of that, yeah, that is probably the
best way to put it. (*Pause*) [Student seems to reject counsellor's
inference that life goals and employment goals are related. She
maintains vocational aspect of problem and returns to practicalities.]

I thought of like applying to a lot of areas and see what comes
up in terms of offers or money, or maybe the school will write
and tell me about something interesting, but I wonder whether
that isn't just rationalizing it in my own mind and giving me a
delaying tactic about making a decision, which I really don't
want to do. I would rather find the means to make that decision.
I guess no matter who it is and what they want, there always is
the practical end to 'O.K. Where *can* you go in terms of realities
and practicalities?' How much money do you have to work with
and how far is it and what is the transportation and the apartment
situation—so that . . . would always be more of a governing
factor in terms of which programme. And I wouldn't want that
to be the case because that is a *terrible* way to make a *decision*.

COUNSELLOR You seem to be saying that you would rather choose
something that you really want and like and think about these
material things afterwards, rather than think about the material
things and see where they lead which may not be exactly where you
want to go? [Reflection of ambivalence between practicalities and
personal feelings.]

STUDENT Which is like letting somebody else make your decisons and
I don't like somebody else making up my life and my decisions.
As it's going to affect me I am going to have to do it. But I just
can't seem to find the *means* to do it. You know? How many
people do you talk to? (*Pause*) [Silence—communicating this is a
question which you can answer.]
. . . I guess the only person is yourself but how do you do that?

(*Pause*) Some things—to a lot of people things are very obvious about your talents or your efforts or the things you like, but to you sometimes the most obvious to everybody else is like hidden or secret. Although it is right out in the open you just don't see it, you're just blind to it.
(*Pause*)

COUNSELLOR You think you are going to need more self-perception in order to make this decision?

STUDENT Maybe that. Yeah. How do you go about getting that? [Slight rejection but also communicating that 'if you want me to do this you must help me'.]

COUNSELLOR How do you look at yourself? (*Pause*) Try it. (*Pause*) Now.

STUDENT How do you look at? . . . you mean, how I would if I had to start right now?

COUNSELLOR Mm hmm. (*Pause*) [Silence: take your time.]

STUDENT That is a tough one! Ah . . . (*Pause*) Well, maybe I would start with what you do with your extra time outside of school? Maybe that would be an indication of what you like . . . well my first two years here I threw myself into student government a lot and I really like that. I don't know what it *shows* though. That I am interested in people maybe or that I like to be busy. I like to feel important. . . .

COUNSELLOR Mm hmm. [Tell me more.]

STUDENT I am depended upon, maybe that too. That I like helping people—it's a good feeling for me. I guess that is the same as wanting to feel important, needed. . . .
(*Pause*)

COUNSELLOR Mm hmm.

STUDENT . . . But I don't know what else, you know? How I perceive myself? Maybe what subjects I like best—that would show an area interest? I think last year I did a great deal with South East Asian history. . . . It was something completely new, and my instructor tried to give us a cultural view of it too. He used to say 'Shed your cultural skins. Try to imagine life in another place without being an American and totally Westernized.' . . . I really grooved with that. But I still don't know exactly what it says about me and my directions. I know I am a social science person. I am a people person and that is how I live.

COUNSELLOR Ah ha [Encouragement.]

STUDENT . . . but as far as other self-perceptions, I don't know.
(*Pause*) I think I am probably more sensible and stronger than I

usually give myself credit but I don't know what that means either. I don't know how else to approach it.

(*Pause*)

COUNSELLOR Well you have presented a few self-perceptions as you see them, now, can you think of a few areas—areas of work, areas of study—into which these self-perceptions might fit? [I accept that this was difficult for you, can you accept that the sort of person we are is relevant to the work we choose.]

STUDENT Oh. I can think of a few but it also represents a lot of different interests. For instance my helping people. If I ever wanted to go forward in counselling—counsellor education, or something like that. ... (*Pause*) ... I don't really think I could do that twenty-four hours a day and not bring my problems home and kill my family with them. You know? I seem to be all right in a dormitory. I don't get so involved that I go around moping, and I guess I surprised myself there. I was interested and cared but it wasn't so much that I ruined my own capabilities, but I don't think I can go on to counselling because I still think that a twenty-four hour a day job—or, not twenty-four hours, O.K. nine to five job, that's unrealistic. But it would be so intense or to such a point that that would happen.

COUNSELLOR Mm hmm. [You seem to be saying something important here.]

STUDENT ... and I don't know if I have the abilities to really be a full-time counsellor. That would be, you know, people helping and people dependent? Less than a counsellor I don't know of positions which would serve those same needs. ... Of all my policy courses I really like the ones in international relations the best ... like the one I have on American foreign policy and what my country has been doing all over the world for the past—well mostly in this century, since the end of the 1800s really ... concentrating on the post-war period. I just think about it and say 'Well it would be nice' and then I say 'I don't really want it that much.'

COUNSELLOR Uhm. [No it's not easy.]

STUDENT Then I can always go into an academic study and put myself into history because that grooves. I look at pictures of the Versailles Palace that my friends have and I think of Napoleon staying there—I get the chills, but I guess a lot of people do that without having to go into a master's programme in history. And then I say 'So O.K. What do you do with that? Teach? Can you teach? ... Do you want to teach? ... Can you write? Do you have the ability to go for your Ph.D.' I think I could go through

243

my Ph.D. because I think I have enough schmaltz to keep up with
it but I don't know if I would like to teach it. I don't *know*. And
would you be any good standing up in front of 200 people?
Would you shake in your boots? I probably would. But all of it
sounds interesting but nothing enough to say 'Yes, that is what
you want. That is for you, or that is what you want to attempt
to do.'

COUNSELLOR Ah ha.

STUDENT So that is an awful broad introspace but nothing enough to
say 'O.K. Do it for two years.'
[Silence probably communicating counsellor's uncertainty and
loss of contact with student.]
Then I considered taking off for two years—doing something like
the Peace Corps or maybe Vista, which is, you know, one of our
local things.

COUNSELLOR Ah ha.

STUDENT Or even working. Being a stewardess and travelling, and
that would sort of see how other people live, cultures, but I don't
know if I want to be out of it for that long. I get selfish and say
'Well maybe not'. I could use the money because my parents have
stopped supporting me, I pay most of my bills and once I get
out of college I pay all my bills. So that is a problem to deal with
too, the practicalities. And all these ideas fall around and I just
haven't grabbed on to any.

COUNSELLOR Mm hmm. [I am as confused as you seem to be.]
(*Long pause*)

STUDENT I was thinking of just applying to education schools and
getting their catalogues, because everybody has always said it is
a good thing to have a masters in education.

COUNSELLOR Uhm.

STUDENT I don't know what you do with it. My mother has always
said, 'Take an education course—it is always good.' I wouldn't
take it at undergraduate level but maybe looking into the school
of education, and I might find a programme which might be more
interesting, or something I might like but I don't know.

COUNSELLOR Uhm. You seem to be saying that one way out of this
confusion that you are experiencing might be to get more information. [Counsellor makes an attempt to regain contact with
student, but chooses the wrong theme.]

STUDENT Uhm. But then I wonder if that is really going to help me?
[Student recognizes counsellor's error.]

COUNSELLOR You feel it may confuse you still further? [Counsellor
acknowledge her mistake.]

STUDENT Right . Or just not go anywhere. Or just completely after all this work and after all this reading, which I really only have time for in the beginning, because I'll be hard at work, you know, after I *do* all this and I get *nowhere* and it's *November*, then I am further in the hole. [Student needs reassurance.]

COUNSELLOR Mm hmm. (*Pause*) I have the impression (*Pause*) that this confusion might be resolved if somebody were to say to you 'Right, think about this particular job.' You would then take hold of this idea, mull it around and either accept it or reject it. [Acknowledging student's need for reassurance, but not really supportive of feelings, busy trying to resolve the confusion by narrowing the field of exploration.]

STUDENT You mean like teaching? And completely think of all the angles, then throw it away? If I wanted to do higher education administration work that would put me in a school. I would go and talk to someone in the Education Department about it.

COUNSELLOR Yes, if you haven't sufficient information yourself. [Counsellor caught in the information trap and recognizes this.]

STUDENT Well, I don't think I would have come up with it except for the recent developments among some of my friends when they have graduated. They have all seemed to have gone into student personnel or higher education or talked about things like the new policy sciences programme . . . and I don't know that much about it but it seems like an outlet for a lot of these types of activities.

COUNSELLOR Uhm.

STUDENT I don't want student personnel because it seems to me that lately it is the thing when a lot of people who don't know what to do and perhaps they like people, and I don't like that attitude. It just doesn't jive.

COUNSELLOR Ah ha.

STUDENT And I guess my father always said that he thought I would be good at an administrative position.

COUNSELLOR Mm hmm. [Counsellor doesn't encourage student to develop any of these ideas, interview is almost over.]

STUDENT . . . or a personnel officer. He once told me I should work for a big firm as a personnel director or something but he is too materially orientated anyway and I don't want to work in big business. I just don't like it.

COUNSELLOR Mm hmm. (*Pause*) All right! What are you going to think about this week? [Urging and directing.]

STUDENT This week, maybe higher education, counsellor higher education, because maybe I will go and make an appointment with people to talk and see what they have to say about it.

COUNSELLOR O.K. Think about higher education and next week perhaps we can talk about what you have found out. What you have thought and how you feel about it. [Suggestion, advising, but the student has the opportunity not to accept the tentative offer of a further appointment expressed in 'perhaps we can talk about. . .'.]

STUDENT O.K.

Although the presenting problem here was one of occupational choice, there is personal confusion accompanying this. As the trainee counsellor I fell between the two stools in this session, but not irretrievably so. The relationship which developed in this initial session was sufficiently empathic to bridge the loss of contact.

Appendix 9

Edited extracts from a taped, simulated introductory group counselling session with a group of students in a College of Education

Counsellor structures the group by explaining its purpose, which is to provide the opportunity for the students to learn about themselves as individuals in relationships with others in the group. Two limits are set, the first concerns confidentiality, the second concerns behaviour —no physical violence.

COUNSELLOR This is group counselling session, and the objective is to try to enable you to learn a little more about yourselves, as people, about your feelings and about your attitudes, by noticing what is happening in this particular group. Not just by listening to what the people say but by trying to hear what they really mean, what is behind what they have said. You did decide that the topic you would like to talk about was relationships and, in fact, you will be making relationships in this particular group, so it seems a fairly good topic for a group of this kind. Anything that we say in this group is confidential to this group, it won't be talked about with anyone outside it. You are free to say anything at all that you like, you are free to say if one of us makes you angry, that you would like to punch them on the nose; you are not actually free to do that. In other words the limit is no physical violence; you may say whatever you wish; if you feel angry you may express it verbally, but not physically.
(*Pause*)

[Silence communicating that after the counsellor's introduction it is now open to the group to begin work. A student attempts to place responsibility for the group with the counsellor by trying to discover what her expectations are.]

247

TOM Are you looking for the feelings of the group as a whole or individually, . . . or what?

[Counsellor turns the question back to the group and the same student picks it up and this time tries to involve the other group members.]

COUNSELLOR Well what do you feel is likely to happen within a group?

TOM We will probably get feelings of individuals at group time, but probably we will all get into some sort of sub-group and I should imagine we will have separate groups within the group if we talk on this problem. I don't know how anyone else feels about it. (*Long pause*)

[Counsellor reinforced Tom's attempt to involve other group members by a direct question concerning their understanding of sub-groups in group process. After a further pause another student risks an answer.]

ELLEN He is meaning that we identify ourselves with other people in the group on the particular subject. (*Long pause*)

[Since the original question came from Tom, the counsellor does not respond.]

TOM Yes I think it is something like that. (*Pause*)

VICKY Do you think we identify ourselves with different people on different parts of the topic because it will split itself up into family relationships and also student relationships etc., and I expect will identify the different people in each category. (*Long pause*)

[Counsellor attempts to shift the attention of the group to their own present experience and gets some response from Wilda. The Counsellor briefly reflects the feeling expressed, and interprets the feeling, getting several responses.]

COUNSELLOR You have speculated what will happen, what is happening?

WILDA A good deal of apprehension on my part, on what I say and on how people will take it, and whether I want other people to even hear in the first place.

COUNSELLOR You are uncertain.

WILDA Yes.

248

COUNSELLOR There seems to be a feeling in the group that they share that uncertainty.

VICKY Does this mean, therefore, that we are frightened to start with of other students, people of the same age as us, because I know I am.

DOREEN I think you are afraid of revealing too much too quickly.

[This was the only verbal communication made by Doreen in the group session.]

CARL I think you are afraid of revealing anything at all. I mean you sit here and there is a feeling and you are afraid of breaking it, you want to build up on what you have got, which makes us more reticent. . . . It feels as though it might be dangerous.
(*Pause*)

[Stan picks up behaviour of group members in focusing on the person who is speaking.]

STAN One feels very conscious of the group, the whole attention of them turned on to you if you are saying something, every movement, that you become the actual focus of it and that people hang on every word until you say it.

[Counsellor extends the idea of focus to herself. This brings up the notion of the counsellor being the group leader, which she questions, leading Tom to acknowledge the counsellor's initial expectation that the group would assume some responsibility.]

COUNSELLOR I am conscious that you were talking to me; though you occasionally look at other people, you look a lot at me.

TOM Is this possibly because you are the group leader at the moment?

COUNSELLOR Am I the group leader?

TOM I should think at the moment . . . at the start of the session I think you were definitely the group leader and afterwards you expected us to take on the responsibility.

[Students then talk about relationships, but concentrate on those outside the group, with tutors, for example.]

VICKY Also the fact that we have never met you before this morning, whereas we have met each other, and this makes a difference. It is easier to speak to someone you don't know and somebody whom you are never going to see again than it is to people who are going to see for the next year, perhaps two years.

TOM This is what tends to make students in college put the barriers up with a view to talking about student relationships with lecturers which very often happens, where you know you are going to see the lecturer again, and you put the barriers up just because of this fact. You won't so openly give all your feelings towards this lecturer and this is one of the problems in college at the moment, I don't know if anyone else feels this way.

COUNSELLOR What you seem to be saying is it is easier to talk to a stranger than to talk to somebody you know you are going to have to meet again in certain kinds of relationships.

STAN I don't think you can really generalize on that point because it depends on who it is and how well you know them, if you get to know them fairly well and you can build up a fairly good relationship when you can chat to them on a wide variety of things. If it's just a sort of person you meet in a lecture and occasionally in passing then, you know, there is no chance of building up any sort of relationship. . . . Would you rather sit down and talk in a situation like this to a stranger or a friend.

TOM Yes this is true. Do you ever really go with the idea of being open with a tutor? For instance, I often feel I have a certain inferiority complex that the tutor is something just that little bit above me and in this respect I have a special relationship with that tutor.

STAN Is that feeling generated by you from inside or does the tutor give that impression that he is superior to you?

TOM Yes, sometimes, it just depends and varies from tutor to tutor but some do have this effect, the relationship depends very much on this. . . . I feel, actually, I can be more honest with people in this group, rather than, say, with a tutor, in certain respects, not in all respects.

ELLEN Is this because you think the people in the group go through the same sort of problems as you, because they are the same age?

TOM Yes I think this is it.

ELLEN We are likely to be experienced in the same sort of thing, as a rule.

TOM Yes, I think so. I believe that at one time or another students do feel the way I do, whether they do or not I don't know. It will be interesting to find out whether anybody does agree with me.

WILDA I think I agree with you but I think what you were saying about —or what Ellen was saying that we all have the same sort of experiences and the same sort of problems is occasionally getting a bit muddled up because you talk to somebody who you think maybe . . . going through, but the point is they are at the same stage as you so you don't really get any further, because you are all in the same complications, whereas if you talk to a tutor or maybe talk to somebody older there is a possibility that they have been through something and maybe they have got a more mature out-look on it. I don't know. . . .

VICKY It means that you can feel more relaxed with people of your own age, I think, sometimes but as Wilda said, you do go around in circles because you can't find a solution to the particular pro-blem.

[Counsellor brings focus back to what is happening in the group.]

COUNSELLOR Are we going around in circles now?

ELLEN Yes, to a certain extent I think we are.

STAN It's safe, isn't it?

CARL It's very easy to talk about, well . . . it's fairly objective to talk about relationships with lecturers because on the whole . . . we see them in lectures and we see them around and that's it, whereas with personal relationships that really matter to us . . . these are the ones we are with all the time in college and out of college, in our rooms and out of our rooms and these are the ones, the biggest problems perhaps, and yet the ones we are least able to talk about. The ones I'm least able to talk about. . . .

TOM I feel that a stranger who is definitely going to try to help you in a problem of particular matter . . . is better equipped . . . to help you cope with this problem rather than if you went to a tutor. I personally wouldn't like to tell any tutor in this college, except probably a very small minority, anything about my personal life at all, whereas I would feel more disposed to talk to a stranger who I would probably never see again, this is something that's basic in everybody's character and make up.

[Counsellor confronts Tom with the discrepancy between his intellectual statement about the ease of talking to strangers and his unwillingness to reveal much of himself to her. Tom heard but gave himself a breathing space. The counsellor need not have repeated her statement and should not have done so for maximum impact. Tom is supported by Wilda and regains his composure.]

COUNSELLOR You are not talking to this stranger about yourself as a person . . .

TOM Pardon?

COUNSELLOR You are not talking to this stranger about your personal feelings very much.

TOM No.

WILDA He is surrounded by six other people as well.

TOM Yes I think it has got to be a very personal basis and any group of this sort is very artificial in some respects I feel, in that all the

251

time somebody or members of the group have got barriers there still, they don't completely fall.

CARL Yes, fair enough, but any group in college has got barriers of sorts, hasn't it? I mean what is the barrier here that is really different to any group, people sitting down around coffee, so we haven't got coffee, but I mean apart from that. I mean we didn't select ourselves, but that is the only difference.

WILDA But it is quite a big difference, isn't it. The fact that we didn't select ourselves?

Because the people you do select you tend to gradually, well since you come to college you choose certain people.

(*Pause*)

CARL Do you?

WILDA Well the system allows you to choose certain people, you get thrown together, to a certain extent, but then you choose who you let your barriers down to, don't you?

CARL I don't know.

(*Pause*)

WILDA I mean eventually.

CARL Oh, you let your barriers down, I don't know whether I choose who I let them down to, I suppose I do, but then I mean how do you choose a person who you have never seen before?

WILDA Well, you gradually do see them, don't you, I mean there are acquaintances, you see each other about and there are some people who are more than acquaintances, to acquaintances you say hello, you say goodbye.

STAN I think you have a good point there, that we are not really friends, we are, in fact, acquaintances, none of us know each other very well, we have all seen each other about and some of us live in the same Hall, but we aren't really all within the same sort of group, any of us, whereas it is not like sitting down among a group of friends and just chatting, or we are not quite sitting among strangers and chatting.

[Counsellor again tries to relate what is said to the actual group and the dialogue which follows. This leads up to a quite spontaneous remark from Wilda, followed by some interaction more centred on the group itself.]

COUNSELLOR What is the purpose of a group like this?

VICKY You said at the beginning it was to help us to get to know ourselves and perhaps we are, within ourselves, thinking much more now, but we are certainly not saying very much more to other people about it.

WILDA Is it necessary that to get to know ourselves we have to let the group help us?

CARL It is a matter of letting it happen.

WILDA We can stop it then.

CARL Can you?

WILDA Yes, I think so.

COUNSELLOR Are you stopping it happening?

WILDA Yes.

COUNSELLOR Can you tell us about it?

WILDA Well I have just got the feeling uppermost in my mind that if I open my mouth too much I shall say something I really mean. (*Pause*) If I shut it I won't have to. . . . Maybe I'd get over it in the next minute or two but I would probably go away and think, my God, what do they know about me. Maybe it is not disastrous for other people to know, I don't know that, I just know I feel that way so maybe I am not going to say anything personally.

VICKY Because we have said we don't know each other very well and therefore we are not going to ruin any beautiful relationship by saying things that we would later regret, and yet we are still worried about what we are going to know about each other.

WILDA Ah, but do we want to form any beautiful relationship anyway?

VICKY No, I don't think we could try to, therefore, sort of theoretically there is no reason why we shouldn't be honest.

STAN We are all sitting here trying not to communicate. . . . No there is a definite mental block that I think each one of us is setting up, consciously or sub-consciously against say, . . . and the talk is really just sort of to break the silence between people saying something, anything about yourself or about anyone else, feelings come into it, so that we don't just sit around in a circle and look at each other.

(*Pause*)

COUNSELLOR Are we afraid of what we might see, or what other people might see?

TOM We are mainly afraid of what other people might see. I don't think we are probably afraid of the group itself, we are not particularly concerned with how members of the group would take it . . . when we say anything, but I have got a feeling that we are scared of communicating because of what other people might think, after this particular group session.

STAN Yes. One of the things you said at the beginning was that this is confidential, but you still get the idea that perhaps it isn't, that probably—er—is Carl probably going to run out afterwards. . . .

CARL Trust you to say that.

WILDA I don't know whether it is just what we think other people will think, but also because of what we think ourselves; and maybe if that's not very nice we are not giving anybody else the opportunity to think on it.

[Counsellor picks up Tom's feeling and the word trust and tries to relate it to the feelings of the group members. Carl, who had first used the word trust in a rather different way, responds.]

COUNSELLOR What you seem to be saying is that you are not sure yet whether you trust the group, but are you also saying you are not sure whether you trust yourself?

CARL I am sure that I trust the group, but I am not sure that I trust myself.

COUNSELLOR Would you tell us a bit about this feeling of trust that you have in the group?

CARL It is quite simple really, we are all the same, in the same boat, in the same situation as individuals and then why shouldn't we trust each other? . . .
The confidential part of it is the same for everybody, so unless somebody doesn't open their mouth we are all together.

[Counsellor makes quite a large and not entirely accurate leap at an interpretation here.]

COUNSELLOR So you trust the group so long as everybody keeps within their own little capsule, and doesn't reveal themselves.

CARL Well I trust the group anyway, whether they reveal themselves or not, whether I reveal myself or not. It is the difficulty of getting in and doing it, this is what I am finding difficult, actually the process, not whether I want to or not but the act of doing it, this is what is difficult.

COUNSELLOR Is the difficulty putting this trust to the test?

CARL No, it's not the trust that's the difficulty, it's more what exactly the process is and exactly how to do it.

[Counsellor again confronts the student, this time with his statements about trust and his actual behaviour. He wryly acknowledges this and there is quite a long reflective pause.]

COUNSELLOR I hear you saying that you trust the group, but I don't see you trusting the group.

CARL Mm.
(*Long silence*)

WILDA I wonder what sort of things . . . I know I personally would be
afraid of telling to them, but I must admit I wonder why we are
all so, I don't know . . . but I don't want to talk too much because
I might say something and we have all got something that we are
not going to tell each other, and is it because it's bad or——?

VICKY I have a feeling at the moment about a close personal relationship, that the more you talk about it the more it loses something
of what's there and if you talk about it too much you tend to
lose, perhaps the magic of that relationship, and therefore, I
don't even want to talk about it too much with very close friends,
so I am not likely to talk about it to the group; that's perhaps the
thing that means most to me at the moment, whereas I would be
much more prepared to talk about my relationship with the family,
or with ordinary friends in college, because they don't mean so
much, there is not so much to lose.

COUNSELLOR What about your relationship with the people in the
group?

VICKY Within the group or outside the group?

[Counsellor is really expressing her own feelings here and says so.]

COUNSELLOR Within the group . . . You see I feel quite a lot of
frustration building up. We began with a bit of fear, which I
think is giving way to a feeling of frustration, we are still in a sense
going around in circles. . . .

[Ellen tries to justify the group's behaviour.]

ELLEN But by revealing ourselves are we going to feel any better
afterwards? I mean I think I feel a lot better by saying nothing
and just listening to everybody else, so I am not going to gain
much from revealing myself to everyone, so you tend to keep
your thoughts to yourself, apart from very superficial ones. There
is very little you can say to people in a group like this. If we were
complete strangers I think you would get a lot more from us, or
if we were very close friends. As it is we are neither and I think this
casts quite a heavy shadow on it.

COUNSELLOR What are we trying to be?

ELLEN I am not really sure. I think if we talk about something slightly
less personal, like the family it would ease it, ease the tension.

COUNSELLOR Less threatening because the family is not here.

ELLEN Yes, I mean everybody has a family and a family relationship
whereas we all have different relationships which are personal
in the group.

COUNSELLOR You feel we have relationships in the group.

255

ELLEN Yes, we also have relationships out of the group which are individual to ourselves.

(*Pause*)

TOM I think that the group has formed its structures somewhat, mainly from what it has brought in outside and the relationships that we have in the college community. I think we have slightly different or deeper relationships with different people within this group—I think what I feel in the group is that we have got a sub-group there already and we probably made certain relationships with people before we have actually sat down in to this group and I think it's these that perhaps hold the . . . that put the barriers up and hold people back from being honest with this particular group.

(*Pause*)

[Counsellor indicates that the group has almost reached its time limit and asks group members to suggest what they feel has happened, by way of a summary to end the group session. Her own brief summary is a reflection of what the students have said.]

COUNSELLOR Well we're coming to the end of the first session of this particular group, what do you feel has happened?

VICKY I feel quite relaxed in the group now, whereas to begin with I didn't, if we have a long silence it doesn't matter.

STAN I think there is slowly being built up a feeling of confidence in the group, not that we are getting to know each other, or to know ourselves, but we are getting used to each other, maybe just sitting around, and when you go to say something you don't think quite so hard before you say it. It is still not really an easy atmosphere, a comfortable one, but I think it is a lot better than it was half an hour ago.

ELLEN I think I feel quite guilty as well now, for not, I suppose I feel guilty because I am not capable of being sort of outgunned and trusting people in the first place.

COUNSELLOR So something has happened while we've been sitting here. Some of you seem to feel that the group has changed and individuals in it feel differently towards it.

STAN I think this is something to do with the group identity rather than just an individual identity . . . that realizing that everyone else is in the same boat and all experiencing the same feelings and thoughts, or similar ones anyway.

In this particular session I put pressure on the group to examine and experience the here-and-now group situation and steered them toward the group objectives. Talk about relationships outside the group, with lecturers and family was usually met with a response which directed attention to the group itself. This was a difficult environment in which to conduct a group, the members were sitting on the floor in a television studio, with technicians around. Despite the unpromising situation the group interacted warmly and responsively and by the end of the session were quite enthusiastic about the whole experience and wanting to continue the group on a regular basis.

Appendix 10

Training courses for counsellors

Since the first training courses for School Counsellors were started in 1965, an increasing number of colleges and universities have started courses to train both school and student counsellors. By 1973 the following courses were available:

University of Aston, Birmingham: One-year full-time diploma course in Counselling in Educational Settings.

University of London Extra Mural Department: Two-year part-time course in Student Counselling.

South West London College: Four-term part-time certificate course in Counselling and Welfare; three-term part-time advanced course in Counselling and Welfare.

City of Birmingham College of Education: Full-time supplementary certificate in Health Education and School Counselling.

University of Bristol: One-year full-time or two-year part-time diploma in Education course with special study option in Counselling.

University of Exeter: One-year full-time diploma course in Guidance and Counselling.

University of Keele: One-year full-time diploma course in Counselling.

University of Manchester: One-year full-time diploma course in Educational Guidance.

University of Newcastle: Diploma course in Advanced Educational Studies (Counselling).

University of Reading: One-year full-time diploma course in Guidance and Counselling in Education.

University of Swansea: One-year full-time diploma course in School Counselling.

North East London Polytechnic (Barking): One-year full-time diploma course in School Counselling.

Edge Hill College of Education: One-year full-time diploma course in the Education of Children Under Social Handicap.

Edge Hill College of Education: One-year full-time diploma course in Counselling and Careers Guidance.

Middlesex Polytechnic (Hendon): Two-year part-time Diploma in Counselling.

University of Leicester: One-year part-time course in Pastoral Care and Guidance (no qualification awarded).

Tavistock Institute of Human Relations: One-year part-time course on Aspects of Counselling in Education (no qualification awarded).

The Association of Psychotherapists runs a part-time course in London.

Short courses include D.E.S./A.T.O. Courses, those run by some L.E.A. and those offered by the National Marriage Guidance Council, which provide a useful introduction to the work of the counsellor, but not a comprehensive training.

Appendix 11

Counselling journals

BRITISH JOURNAL OF GUIDANCE AND COUNSELLING, a new journal published by the Careers Research and Advisory Centre, Cambridge.

The growth of guidance and counselling
The last five years have seen an unprecedented growth of interest in guidance and counselling. Counsellors are appearing in secondary schools and in institutions of further and higher education to meet the personal needs of young people. Traditional educational and vocational guidance services are regarding counselling as being more and more central to their function. Outside education, youth counselling centres are appearing in areas where young people gather in large numbers. The occupational guidance units set up to help adults seeking a change of employment are finding a demand and need for counselling among their clients. Many social welfare services that have not hitherto undertaken counselling are recognizing that this is an important avenue through which they can help their clients. In a service-orientated society personal helping services of many other kinds may be expected to appear and develop on the basis of skill in counselling.

The aims of the new journal
The growth of guidance and counselling has produced a demand for a journal to which practitioners and research workers can turn with the confident certainty of finding relevant writing and reporting of high quality. The Careers Research and Advisory Centre has accordingly invited Dr Peter Daws (Keele), Dr Barrie Hopson (Leeds) and Douglas Hamblin (Swansea) to join Tony Watts of C.R.A.C. in editing *The British Journal of Guidance and Counselling*. Many other leading authorities have offered their support in an advisory role and as potential contributors. Keeping closely in mind the editors' understanding of the British scene and its needs at the

260

present time, the journal will cover four main areas of relevance to those needs:

(a) the techniques of counselling and the limits of their effectiveness;

(b) the identification of community needs for guidance and counselling;

(c) the training arrangements available to practitioners and their training requirements;

(d) the organizational and professional development of guidance and counselling services.

The journal will also contain abstracts of relevant papers appearing in other journals, research reports, notes of topical interest and book reviews. It will provide a comprehensive source from which practitioners and research workers can keep abreast of the latest thinking and research in the guidance and counselling field.

THE COUNSELLOR
The Counsellor, quarterly journal of the National Association of Counsellors in Education, is described in Appendix 3.

AMERICAN JOURNALS
Relevant American journals are: *Personnel and Guidance Journal*; *Journal of Counseling Psychology*; *The School Counselor*.

Index